PELICAN BOOKS

A166

GLASS THROUGH THE AGES

E. BARRINGTON HAYNES

GLASS
THROUGH THE AGES

BY

E. BARRINGTON HAYNES

PENGUIN BOOKS
HARMONDSWORTH · MIDDLESEX

FIRST PUBLISHED 1948

Made and Printed in Great Britain
for Penguin Books, Ltd., by Wyman & Sons, Ltd.,
London, Fakenham and Reading
Collogravure Plates printed by Harrison & Sons, Ltd.,
London, W.C.2

CONTENTS

PART I

The Glass of the Eastern World

PART 2

English Glasses of the 18th Century

PART I

THE GLASS OF THE EASTERN WORLD

INTRODUCTION

The chapters which follow are in no way intended to compete with the standard text-books on glass. Still less are they to be regarded as a comprehensive story of a product known to man for at least thirty-five centuries and one which (in some eyes at least) is as yet in its infancy.

It may be doubted whether any one author is qualified to write such an encyclopædic account, and in any case it would certainly neither appeal to the publishers of these admirable booklets nor to the many thousands who read them. What follows will indeed give nothing but a bird's-eye view of what may be called the table glassware of other lands, and a somewhat closer view of that of the British Isles, but it will serve to direct attention to more exhaustive works on particular phases of its history. It is designed to arouse interest rather than to give instruction; to show where knowledge can be found rather than to offer it; and to excite inquiry.

The phases of early glass-making about which we know something have always seemed to me to stand in undue isolation in our popular text-books. In these chapters an effort has been made to link these phases and it is hoped that some connected picture will disclose itself. It may prove to be distorted, since speculation has so often to replace knowledge, but with a glance at history and logical possibilities, even an imperfect picture will enable the less instructed reader to visualize the inception, the rise and decay, and the revival of a manufacture which has had as profound an influence on human convenience, happiness, and well-being as has any other discovery whatsoever, the printing press not excluded. What that thirty-five-century-old discovery may yet lead to can only be guessed at. Its convenience in daily life and its services to scientific knowledge have stretched far indeed, yet its industrial application on a really large scale has perhaps hardly begun.

If, never having known such a thing, you were suddenly to find yourself able to manufacture an infinitely tractable substance that could be either opaque or transparent at will, in a wide range of colours or without any colour at all, and one that was impervious to moisture and unaffected by any ordinary chemical, and if further you could do all this at insignificant expense and by employing the commonest raw materials, you might justly anticipate public enthusiasm and applause. And that is precisely what did happen when glass-blowing was discovered, and it had precisely that result on the Roman world which saw it happen.

If, on the other hand, you endeavour to picture a world without glass, without any glass or equivalent substitute at all, you will quickly be reduced to speculation as to what our civilization would now be. Could the more northerly latitudes, for instance, ever have developed much more than an Eskimo standard of living without window glass? The many who have recently been temporarily deprived of their windows will appreciate the point, and it is hardly too much to assert that the civilizations and cultures of the ancients existed in the Mediterranean and Near-Eastern areas simply because—lacking window glass—only in those warm climates was any noticeable civilization or culture possible.

And, further, consider where science would stand had there been no glass. Medicine, without the microscope and the test-tube, might still be fighting disease with herbal remedies, charms, and incantations, our years but two score and ten. Chemists would still be alchemists and astronomers remain astrologers.

Travel might still be limited to the pace of horse or sail. There would be no wireless and no electric light. Many of us would peer dimly through spectacles of horn and all of us grope forward in a permanent Dark Age. We would shave and our women would powder before a metal mirror. Diamonds would have to replace paste. There would be no cinemas, no cameras, and no illustrations to these essays. As it is, thanks to some unknown experimentalist and the glass he blew, progress seems illimitable.

Clearly enough, the place of drinking vessels in this wonderful development is relatively unimportant, but it is not therefore a humble one. That is because the bowl and the beaker could also be a vehicle for art, and possess a human value as well as a mechanical or useful one. So drinking glasses become collectable, are studied, valued, and preserved. In the same way, perhaps in lesser degree, the stained glass that has served to enrich so many ancient buildings possesses human value, whereas the oldest of plain window-glass arouses little interest. I count that a pity even though these pages will deal so exclusively with table glassware.

There are many other objects made of glass well worth study. We in England neglect them because they are seldom beautiful, because they lack the personal touch, or again because we have forgotten for what they were intended and are insufficiently interested to find out.

There are, for instance, certain jug-shaped objects with a long spout, an oversized handle and a wide top. They look like crude tea or coffee pots, adequately but not attentively made. These were designed to hold oil for filling the lamps so widely used in the days when, or the places where, gas had not begun to creep smokily through a cobweb of iron pipes. Nowadays they are made of metal, presumably for reasons of safety rather than of cleanliness. Then there are numbers of the lamps themselves, growing daily fewer through carelessness and neglect. There is a whole host of semi-scientific glass appliances, chemical apparatus, bottles and phials, and odd little things whose purpose is obscure or unknown—trivialities, some of them, but they had their place in bygone days.

Where you may pay pounds for a wine glass and find it matched in the next collection you chance to see, you will pay pence or shillings for these unpopular and unsought-for things, a good collection of which will tell posterity something fresh and not repeat the already known.

That is not to say that the study of drinking vessels is completed. It has very far to go yet and finality will never be reached. Very much has been written and much more has been copied. It is the hardest thing not to be over-influenced by what authoritative writers have unanimously laid down, and once a theory receives general acceptance it is almost impossible to eradicate it even when it has been utterly discredited.

The classic instance in glass is of course the popular belief that Waterford glass has a distinct bluish tinge. Waterford is a euphonious name and for all I know a lovely and romantic spot. Its glass certainly is lovely and has many qualities, but a bluish colour is not amongst them. That is romance indeed.

It will be fair then to ask every student to read what others may have written, to hold their views in mind, but to accept nothing as completely true—not even what he is about to read here—if it should conflict with his own experience and deductions. But he will not fail to recall that experience comes only from the constant handling of specimens, and deductions only from the inquisitive mind and eye. Glass-knowledge can be acquired from books to a considerable extent, but connoisseurship cannot, and an opinion based on academic learning alone is obviously untrustworthy and in extreme cases but the reflection of tradition. And that is why actual possession and active collecting is so valuable.

CHAPTER I

Beginnings

Most books on glass refer quickly to the picturesque story told by Pliny, writing in the 1st century A.D., how certain merchants encamped on the sands of the River Belus placed their cooking pots on some of the cakes of natron they were engaged in transporting. In the morning, they found that the sand and the soda had fused together, forming glass.

This story, purporting to explain the origin of glass, is probably one of those myths which are born to account for a fact, the fact in this instance being simply that Syrian glass-makers did make much use of the sand deposited by this particular river. A good judge, however, avows the possibility of some foundation for the tale, although nothing like the glass we know could have resulted. It may be that the earliest glass pastes fused at a lower temperature than some 1500 degrees centigrade, which is that now employed. Even so it may be guessed that the merchants would have found their dinner a trifle overcooked.

Strictly speaking, the earliest glass we know of is a product of Nature herself, who anticipated man by some thousands or millions of years by manufacturing obsidian, a greyish natural glass differing little in analysis from our own. Some considerable use of it has been made by the Mexicans, and visitors to the Yellowstone National Park in the United States can hardly escape being shown the Glass Mountain, one of the many marvels there, but less impressive than some others for looking much like any other tree- and herbage-clad mountain.

An axe or knife or arrowhead might logically be the starting point for any glass collection, but there will be a vast gap before any man-made specimen can be found. Still, we have since made amends, and when our first glass does come to light it is found, as might be expected, in that oldest and most favoured of civilizations, the Egyptian. Most favoured because so well protected from outside interference, with deserts on east and west, with sea and desert on the north, and with a narrow defensible boundary (wherever it might chance to be) on the south. To such fortunate geographical circumstances the Egyptians owed their comparative immunity and steady progress. It must be seldom that ribbon development has so lucky a result.

It must not be imagined that there have been no changes in conditions. It is believed that the Nile raises the level of the adjacent land by four and a half inches in a century, that is (neglecting other factors) by some thirteen feet during the period under review. It can therefore easily be understood that the Nile was formerly more widespread in its annual flood. The rainfall may have been heavier and Egypt's western boundaries more distant and more habitable. That would be in keeping with the encroaching tendency of the desert band which stretches from the Atlantic to the Persian Gulf. Elsewhere the Sahara and the Libyan deserts have encroached, slowly but remorselessly. Timbuktu, once Queen of the Sahara, is now Timbuktu the Mysterious. South-west of Cairo, Lake Moeris is gone and ancient water-courses are now always dry. Even the barriers of Niger and Nile may not always stand.

The important point to us is that Egypt was formerly much more wooded. The primary requisites for a glass-maker are silica, alkali, and fuel. There could be no shortage of silica, the natron lakes supplied soda with ample generosity, and acacia groves were there for fuel. So the people made glass.

At some date prior to 3000 B.C. they had learned how to make a vitreous glaze, opaque and highly coloured, and with it they covered the objects of stone they modelled or the sandy compositions they moulded. A few hundred years of practice endowed them with a high degree of skill and in due course it was found that if the glaze was made thick enough it needed no substance to support it, and it could be cut into small pieces and used at discretion for inlay or surfacing work. Still later, someone discovered that it could be laid thickly on a suitable core of the requisite shape and the core removed, to leave a small vase or bottle which would not collapse in use and which could be made to stand up. All this may have taken time, for as will be seen, Egyptian glass-makers (and perhaps others of her craftsmen) were of a conservative disposition.

Some of the books already referred to speak of certain wall paintings of the 12th Dynasty at Beni Hassan which are, or were, alleged to portray glass-blowers at work. The amended view is that they were ironworkers, and as no glass vessel, blown or otherwise, has been found of any earlier date than the 18th Dynasty, that is *circa* 1500 B.C., this view may easily be accepted. There can be no doubt as to these particular vessels because three of them carry the cartouche of Thotmes III.

But two things are worth noting. First, that not less than 1700 years had elapsed since the first specimens of glazed ware had been manufactured, and second, that these vases suddenly appear, fully fledged so to speak, without the trace of an ancestor. It cannot be excluded that earlier and cruder specimens may have been made, but none have been recognized.

The natural location of Egyptian glass-makers was in the Delta and the Fayum, in proximity to the natron deposits and fuel. But Akhenaton, who abandoned the monumental city of Thebes, *c.* 1450–1400 B.C., and founded Tel el Amarna, two hundred miles to the north, had the fancy to order that glass should be made near by and the actual site has been discovered, a by no means suitable spot for lack of —at least—fuel, but Egyptian monarchs had a way of disregarding the exigencies of time and place.

During the next fourteen hundred years or so our Egyptian glass-makers continued to demonstrate their lack of enterprise. There was first a decline, and then an apparent cessation from 1100–600 B.C., followed by a strong revival, sponsored perhaps by Alexandria with an eye on Mediterranean trade. This later period produced most of the specimens we have, similar to but less worthy than the glasses of 1500 B.C., and in worse condition.

One might have expected a so-long-fashionable style to have survived into the blown glass era, but it vanishes almost as suddenly as it came. Some reminiscent surface-enamelled blown forms are known from the Greek Islands, and some decadent hybrids from Syria, but the technique hitherto practised completely disappears.

It was simple enough, although with the available conveniences no small degree of skill must have been necessary to produce the really beautiful results which were so often obtained. On the end of a tapered metal rod a core of sand was modelled to the desired shape. This was dipped into the crucible of molten metal (for specimens with surface bubbles or blow-holes may be found) or where better results were required the metal may have been otherwise applied and all irregularities ironed out by 'marvering', that is, rolling on a flat surface. Some bottles have so smooth a surface that they look as though turned and polished.

When sufficiently coated and whilst still hot and therefore soft, threads or trails of coloured pastes might be superimposed, and these were not only rolled into the pasty substratum until flush, but the surface might also be dragged into a series of bands or zigzags to fulfil the fancy of, or the orders to, the workman. A feathery 'palmette' pattern (Pl. 1b) can be most effective, and obviously a discreet use of contrasting or graded colours could give a highly decorative result. When cool the rod was withdrawn and the sandy core extracted.

The possible variations of pattern are almost infinite. In practice certain types are a good deal more common than others. Possibly they best pleased the Egyptian eye, or possibly convention or superstition ruled, for such types are not necessarily the most attractive to a modern one. While decoration might be confined to neck or shoulders or might cover the whole of the vessel, a dark opaque blue was most commonly chosen for the body, and yellow and pale blue predominate in the decoration. A delightful green is sometimes found, a jasper red, and a white with or without black or deep violet decoration, evidently in imitation of the much-beloved native aragonite. Some greens and blues have survived in as perfect a state as when made, but the white inlay is rather subject to corrosion.

Although one calls these pastes opaque, it must be understood that their opacity depends to some extent on thickness. The blue, for instance, can be more or less translucent, and as time went on and firing methods may be assumed to have improved, this translucency is likely to be more marked.

In form there are three main types of vessel (Pl. 1). A cylindrical phial or *alabastron*, varying to a fat cigar-like shape, may be the earliest because the simplest. There is a pear-shaped *amphora* with a pointed base finishing sometimes with a little ball or button. Most of the *alabastra* have a pair of applied rudimentary handles or diminutive loops, or tiny pegs, though some, including the rare lotus-headed ones, are entirely without. *Amphoræ* are more likely to be adequately supplied. Both these types are somewhat or entirely unstable. The third type is a small ewer or jug (*œnochoe*) with a flat base on which it could rest, and this had a single handle one could safely use. The form will appear again in another sixteen hundred years or so.

A period of fifteen hundred years gives time for quite a small industry to turn out quite a lot of glass, and our museums hold considerable numbers of these small vases. Those in private hands are relatively few. But there is no evidence that olden Egypt made glass on any large scale, and it must have been regarded as a luxury trade. It is guesswork, but for every single Egyptian specimen we may well have fifty Roman pieces, and since these were made in a quarter of the time and since from their greater fragility and often trivial nature their chances of survival must have been vastly smaller, it is certain that Egypt never approached the output of the Roman world during the first four centuries after the discovery that glass could be blown. It cannot then be wondered at that on all the counts of antiquity, beauty, and rarity, the Egyptian paste vases rank highly in a collector's estimation.

It is supposed that cosmetics were carried in all these things. Indeed, an illustration in Nesbitt's *Catalogue of the Slade Collection* shows a lotus-headed *alabastron* with a spatula still inside it. Kohl, for darkening the eyelids and rendering the eye more lustrous, has been in immemorial use in the East, and no doubt then as now there was a wide choice of preparations an Egyptian beauty could command or have foisted upon her. Yet these vessels must have had their disadvantages. Their interior was far from smooth and the relics of the sand core can often be seen, which suggests a gritty hazard to a smooth Egyptian skin.

Concurrent with these vases, doubtless preceding and certainly post-dating them are beads of similar paste, occasionally reaching magnificent size. There are glass scarabs and there are little amulets of glass, both much commoner in other materials. There are also button-like objects, and bracelets, for an account of all of which recourse must be had to archæological literature. These are fascinating little fellows, small in cost, and more indicative of a nation's customs and beliefs than all its priceless artistic treasures.

* * *

At the foot of each chapter a note is given of the standard works in English which treat of the subject in question. Our own literature on Continental glass is very inadequate. A full if necessarily incomplete bibliography will be found in Thorpe's *History of English and Irish Glass* and elsewhere. When first mentioned the reference is given in full; subsequently the titles are curtailed.

FOR FURTHER READING

DILLON, E. *Glass*. 1907.

EISEN, G. A. *Glass*. 2 vols. New York. 1927.

HONEY, W. B. *Glass*. *Victoria and Albert Museum Handbook.* (Published since this book was written, and to be consistently referred to on every phase of the world's glass.)

CHAPTER II

The First Four Centuries

I. THE GLASS-MAKERS

ALREADY it has been suggested that the exploitation of the blow-pipe to fashion what we call 'blown glass' was one of man's most far-reaching achievements. Like so many truly great innovations, it was one of the simplest character, and one of which there is no record whatever.

It is established without much doubt as having taken place about half a century before the birth of Christ, by whom now matters little. An unusually enterprising Egyptian, less satisfied than his fellows with the unchanging products of 1500 years, may have been responsible, and there is certainly sure evidence that the sand-core process had already been supplemented by a press-moulding process (Pl. 2d). Rather more probably the discovery was a Syrian triumph of ingenuity over tiresome monotony, the incentive a high commercial reward. The profit motive has contributed far too much to human progress always to be anathematized as selfish or vicious.

It was not a discovery to arouse surprise. The surprise is rather that it did not come earlier, for it only needed somebody to think of replacing the original iron rod by a hollow one, so as to simplify manipulation and perhaps make the use of hotter furnaces more bearable. Then sooner or later somebody's lips were bound to stray to the free end and puff —and the discovery was there.

To avoid a break in the story it has been thought best to assume a knowledge on the reader's part of glass-blowing, the tools and the technique of which have never changed in essentials. The processes are fully explained in several accessible text-books.

Once the blow-pipe was in common use the manufacture of glass developed with a rapidity altogether surprising, and more progress was made in fifty years than had been made in fifteen hundred. All this glass of the first four centuries is generally termed Roman, but that only means that it was made in the Roman world, not necessarily at Rome or by Romans. Two styles or trends in manufacture soon showed themselves.

There were the Syrian and the Egyptian (Alexandrian) sides of the industry. Both sides made utility glass for household and commercial purposes, the Syrians because they wanted to and had their eye on the popular and middle-class markets, the Alexandrians because they could not afford to ignore such competition and the quick profits the demand offered. The Syrian trend was towards simplicity and lightness. It did not concern itself unduly with the character of the metal, i.e. the substance of the glass, and perhaps at first had not the necessary knowledge and experience. So its products come in a wide range of greens and yellowish tints which are difficult to gauge because the depth of every colour varied with the thickness of the glass. There was a strong naturalistic leaning in Syrian glass, bottles or vases being made to represent shells, bunches of grapes, dates, pomegranates, and cacti (Pl. 3b) complete with ribs or spines and rootlets. Others were moulded in the form of heads of various types, not always very decisive, and some (the Janus bottles) had two heads (Pl. 3c). As attractive as any are bottles or cups with elaborate moulded designs of classical (Pl. 2c) or sporting or gladiatorial import. Colour, especially blues and purples, was used, but at first there was no particular accent on it.

The Alexandrian glass-masters, however, had a tradition of colour and a power to control it which they exploited to the full. Apart from the household glass they had to make, all their instincts were towards the elaborate expensive articles in which ingenuities of technique and patient careful craftsmanship counted before all else. So we quickly find them making their millefiori bowls, and other colourful articles imitating marbled or streaked stone which are generally accepted as the 'murrhines' of antiquity. The best of these made notable prices, Pliny (A.D. 23–79) recording the sale of two cups for 6,000 sesterces, something between fifty and sixty pounds in our money. He also mentions a vase destroyed by Petronius to prevent its falling into Nero's hands; one modern writer values this vessel at £50,000 by adopting the earlier valuation and mistaking *sestertii* for *sestertia* and so magnifying the result a thousand times.

The Alexandrian shops also introduced the art of drawing upon glass with a graving tool, line-engraving in fact, and developed the use of tools until they could cut glass with grooves or facets, or carve it in relief, or—most intriguing of all—both carve and undercut at the same time so that a bold design would be attached to and yet stand out from the walls of the bowl and appear as a network around it. This is something no modern has succeeded in rivalling. Then there was the art of combining cutting, carving, and colour-control all in one specimen. The best-known example of this is of course the Portland Vase, where white opaque glass is laid upon a blue base and then cut, carved, and ground away to leave a cameo design in white upon the blue ground. Intricacies of shadow are attainable by controlling the degree to which the overlying white glass is removed. Wedgwood, and Webb and Son in England, and Gallé and others in France reintroduced the technique in the later years of the 19th century, but work of the Portland Vase quality is not a commercial proposition and its artistry has never again been attained.

Such is my reading of the individualities of the Syrian and Alexandrian schools, though a certain amount of overlap may be presumed. It is a classification by style, but there is also a classification by time, known to students as Roman I and Roman II. Roman I covers the first two centuries and includes glasses of the simpler techniques. Roman II covers the 3rd and 4th centuries and includes the more elaborate glasses, such for instance as have feet and angular handles, or superimposed decoration. It is really a division of convenience, with obvious and I think damaging limitations.

Other areas where glass has been found are Hebron and Tiberias in Palestine; Cyprus and Crete; and eastwards the Euphrates basin is not without its relics. We must infer from Strabo, who wrote early in the 1st century, that Rome had already established glasshouses of her own.

A good many glass-makers are known to us by their names or trademarks moulded on the bases of the vessels they blew. Of them all, Ennion and Artas, both of Sidon, and Frontinus in Picardy are perhaps the most famous. And that is virtually all we do know about them, but we can infer a considerable measure of competition from the very existence of their various names and marks, coupled with an occasional impressed slogan exhorting the user to remember the maker, a simple form of advertisement which glass collectors must regret was discontinued. We might also assume that such makers were the firmly established ones, but there is no real evidence.

For the simplicities of glass manufacture were such that a small company of peripatetic craftsmen could travel from site to site, set up a simple furnace, supply a local market, and move on again when business or welcome languished. It was easier to take the furnace to the market than to face the risks and difficulties of despatching the finished article. Equally it was easier to take the furnace to the fuel than vice versa.

Such a restlessness has always been a feature of the trade, a tradition followed by the workers themselves as late as the 19th century, although the glasshouses had perforce stabilized themselves. So we can visualize a gradual penetration by itinerant glass-makers wherever Roman culture, which is to say Roman arms, ruled, from Syria to Rome, from Rome to the Rhône valley, thence west and south to the Spanish littoral and North Africa, and northwards to the Seine and Amiens and to the Rhine and Cologne. And there is nothing to prevent our assuming (without present proof) that it reached Britain and such places as Colchester and Faversham.

2. THE GLASS THEY MADE

THE great majority of Roman glass is of the simplest kind. There were plates and dishes, bowls and beakers; there were bottles innumerable, square, squat, globular, and tapered, all to be regarded as household goods. At first blown and flattened beneath so that they would stand up, a foot-ring either tooled or applied came to be added, in order to improve stability and line. A 'double-blown' foot was also used, that is to say, a secondary inflation was formed at the base and then flattened out and pushed upwards in the centre so that the vessel rested on a double rim. Stemmed vessels are relatively scarce and belong to Roman II, and at least as far as the inexpensive pieces are concerned they are single-piece glasses blown and fashioned from one gathering only.

The minor variations of form are innumerable and impossible of survey here. A collector always looks for the specimen that is different, but I think it is the exception to find two identical pieces of Roman glass. Distinctions in terms are confusing, for a drinking bowl is but a cup, a bottle can appear to be a vase, and a beaker with a pointed base is more often than not a lamp.

Besides this table-ware there were very many *unguentaria* (Pl. 3 d, e), that is, toilet and scent bottles, for oil and scent took precedence of soap in Mediterranean lands when a hardier North disdained both. The tradition is not yet extinct. All these vessels could be, and were, deposited in the graves of deceased persons without too great a strain upon the family exchequer. Even the deceased himself might be deposited in a glass urn after cremation. For those too poor to provide or spare such things there were tiny conventional alternatives of the cheapest sort, and in spite of their complete unimportance they are not without charm. Most of this glass was of the Syrian school.

While at least one authority thinks that little, if any, glass was especially made to serve as grave goods, there are these tiny inconsiderables and also other vessels of greater consequence and size, but blown so thinly that it is difficult to believe they could have been intended for daily use. I have, for instance, a 9½-in. carafe understood to have been found in a crypt in Jerusalem. This holds no less than three pints (60 liquid oz.), but it weighs only 4½ oz., whereas the water bottle in my bedroom holds 24 oz. and weighs a pound. When filled it seems eminently desirable to raise this Syrian carafe with care, and to support the base with one hand lest either the neck come away from the body or the bottom fall out of the whole. Quite a number of beakers are equally fragile, some having a rough unaccommodating rim never smoothed by fire or tool (Pl. 2a).

Apart from this mass of cheap glass there are finer pieces obviously made for more wealthy people. There are graceful *amphoræ*, and some rather tall ewers of delightful line, plain or wrythen, both often furnished with handles or applied decoration in a different colour. Such pieces are scarce; while the demand for them was smaller, their size and quality meant a natural reluctance to consign them to the grave, so comparatively few have come down to us. They may be said to come between the cheap utility glass and the luxury items already referred to as the products of the Alexandrian side. It would seem from the early classical writers that this luxury glass was far more plentiful than the few relics of it which we now possess would indicate. We find it difficult to imagine anything finer than the Portland Vase, wrongly said by some to have been the property of the Emperor Alexander Severus, yet it is not unlikely that this was only one from stock, so to speak. It may be as fine a glass as ever was made; if so we are fortunate, but there is no telling. It is to be regretted that the artist did not sign his work and so ensure for himself a place in honour no less high than that of the Emperor he is supposed to have served.

One other type of glass of the 3rd century and after must be mentioned although little enough of it, and that but fragmentary, will be seen outside a museum. It comes almost entirely from Roman catacombs and is peculiarly but not invariably associated with contemporary Christian life. To the bases of the glasses in question a layer of gold leaf was applied, and this was etched with a needle to show conventional Christian scenes. Occasionally colour was employed in addition, and when the plate or vessel was complete a further disc of glass was laid over the gold and fused to it. It is chiefly to these bases, found cemented into the tombs, that we owe acquaintance with this special technique, one which many centuries later came into great popularity in Bohemia.

By the 3rd century A.D. the picture is one of a Roman world everywhere producing or using glass in a profusion not to be equalled until another fifteen centuries had passed. This glass ranges from real crudity through all grades of serviceability and beauty to artistic heights at which we still reasonably wonder. And it was not confined to table-ware and magnificent ornaments.

There was the slit-window glass, designed rather to keep out the weather than to let in light as is evident from excavations at Pompeii. The use of glass mosaics over the walls of Roman rooms and especially Roman bathrooms became most fashionable, and it was occasionally used for floors in place of the usual *tesseræ* pavements. There its disadvantages will quickly have been realized by careless bathers or carefree diners. In this as in many other respects Rome had a modern trend all her own.

In the year A.D. 200 Rome may well have seemed stable and strong enough, and withal rich and amusing enough. In the year A.D. 300 it may not have appeared very different, but a century of struggle to maintain an unknit Empire had sown the seeds of disaster. To glass students the great events of this 4th century are, first, the recognition of Christians in 313 and of Christianity as the religion of the Empire in 324, and second, the building of Byzantium (Constantinople) and the transfer to that city of the seat of government in the year 330.

In the year A.D. 400 there can have been little complacence. Alaric was invading Lombardy and in 410 was to sack Rome herself. It happened again in 455, and twenty years later the break-up of the Western Empire was complete.

But for the time being these momentous happenings made singularly little difference to the capacity of the world to make glass, although they may materially have affected its preservation. For one thing the industry had spread too far and was rooted too securely, particularly in the Seine-Rhine areas, to be seriously menaced. Here the aforesaid firm of Frontinus developed some notable individual styles, for instance chain-handled jugs and mould-made bottles of barrel form (Pl. 4c), on which latter it had the forethought to impress its mark in differing letterings. Its blown glass, at the Amiens end, has a peculiar bright greenish tint and a surface texture or sheen all its own. Indeed it is not too much to say that the greater cities of Gaul preserved the arts they owed to Rome when those same arts had been overwhelmed in Italy.

For another thing, Constantine had not migrated to his new capital without good reason. It was from the East that the wealth and resources of the Empire had been derived, and the Rome on the Tiber could not control them as could the New Rome on the Bosphorus. With Constantine went his glass-makers, too, and if the subsequent history of the Empire is chequered, at least it retained reputation and vigour enough to stand a sufficient bulwark between Europe and the Asiatic hordes, and to remain the centre of the world's culture for a thousand years.

The Syrian and Alexandrian glasshouses had but to switch their exports to Constantinople, so that for the remaining seventy years of the period under review (A.D. 330–400), there was no more alteration in the kind of glass manufactured than can be accounted for by natural development and elaboration. There may have been some drift of glass-makers yet further east, as formerly there had been a flood to the west, for no small amount of glass has been found in the Crimea.

But the change meant the eventual elimination of Egyptian competition, if only for reasons of propinquity, and a gradual orientalization of styles until what had been Roman glass developed into Byzantine. It is just at the end of our first four centuries that the hitherto plentiful supply of specimens begins to fail, and where speculation has to begin supplementing and replacing actual evidence.

FOR FURTHER READING

Works as listed for Chap. I.

THORPE, W. A. *English Glass.* 1935.

And for glass-making technique

McKEARIN, G. S. and H. *American Glass.* New York. 1941.

PELLATT, APSLEY *Curiosities of Glassmaking.* 1849.

POWELL, H. J. *Glassmaking in England.* 1923.

THORPE, W. A. *History of English and Irish Glass.* 2 vols. 1929.

CHAPTER III

The Second Four Centuries

1. THE WESTERN EMPIRE

WHEN history itself becomes confused it is not surprising that the story of a minor art should be obscured. A study of the times is needful to realize how anarchical conditions became in the 5th century and how chaotic daily life must have been; it is essential if any sort of comprehension of contemporary arts and crafts is even to be guessed at. The impact of history upon civilized progress is all-important.

The 4th century had been one of depression and depopulation, of tyranny and taxation, evils accentuated no doubt by luxury and waste in high places, but of which the root cause was the increasing strain of maintaining the Empire's boundaries. The pressure upon them had been slowly increasing since the beginning of the first century, and the more or less controlled admission of very many barbarians and their enlistment in camp and at court had become a dangerous if inescapable palliative. Its source was the northern Teutonic lands in the basins of the Oder, of the Spree, and of the Vistula, where the tribes were wholly pagan. This would have mattered less had they not also been predatory by instinct and destructive by nature, characteristics it would seem which twenty centuries have not wholly eradicated.

As long as Rome could firmly hold the barriers of the Rhine and the Danube, the expansionist fervour of these barbarians could only be directed eastwards, and some at least of the Goths did move to what is now South Russia, the Dniester-Dnieper area. It seems not improbable that others, as well as tribes disturbed by that early drive to the east, sought or gained admittance to the Empire, and to this result both the spread of Christianity and a real appreciation of Roman civilization may have contributed.

When, however, Roman power no longer sufficed to maintain the barriers, a westward and a southward surge of the northern barbarians followed inevitably. And when Attila and his all-devouring trans-Caspian Huns decided to press westwards they added to the confusion by driving both the West Goths and the East Goths within the Empire's gates, where they (the Goths) seem to have behaved with relative propriety and even friendliness. Indeed, since many of their blood had preceded them and had been assimilated, a stable Romano-Gothic state would doubtless have emerged eventually in spite of an Italian abhorrence for the unorthodox (Arian) Christianity now professed by the Goths.

It is also to the credit of all concerned, and the Visigoths in particular, that they turned with one accord upon the Hun and eliminated that danger in the Châlons area (A.D. 451). He at any rate was an inexcusable interloper to no man's fancy, and for his disappearance Western Europe had good reason to be thankful.

One gets the impression that the main migrations, being genuine migrations, were carried out with some measure of order. A certain amount of lip service at any rate was at first paid to the nominal supremacy of the Emperor, and no doubt a certain amount of real deference was felt for the traditional reputation of Rome and the value of her civilization. It is even possible that the migrants may themselves have desired something better, something more progressive, than their age-old savagery.

For it need not be supposed that any of the immigrant processions was either very numerous or, in the 5th century, totally pagan. The hazards of their journeying and their contacts with Christianity would in any case soon have abated their numbers and modified their paganism.

All these incursions of Franks, Burgundians, Vandals, Sueves, and Goths took place within the first fifty years or so of the 5th century. Their peregrinations are a matter of history, as those of lesser tribes and even more predatory bands are not. And so, collisions of these moving bodies were bound to occur, not only with the relics of Roman power but with each other and with their forerunners, always of course with unhappy results for those already settled in the vicinity.

Hence any fusion in Italy was delayed, and at just the wrong moment the Eastern Empire, Justinian ruling, found enough means and strength to destroy the kingdom of the Vandals in Africa (533) and, much less easily, the kingdom of the East Goths in Italy (533–555), but it had not the strength to hold either of them. He had ample excuse, because the African Vandals had not only turned pirate but had sacked Rome in 455 with every sort of persecution of its religion. Still, it was unfortunate for Italy because the northern vacuum was quickly filled by Lombards from the Brandenburg country, still plundering pagans, and at their hands much of Italy was subjected to massacre, destruction, and pillage.

Rome, Ravenna, and certain maritime cities, Venice and Pisa among them, found a measure of independence in self-reliance and remained under the ineffective jurisdiction of the Empire. It is said that Venice was founded by refugees fleeing from the barbarian invaders. It is quite possible that its lagoon and island population was reinforced, and certain that Venice eventually replaced Aquileia, destroyed by Attila in 452, as the first strategic and commercial centre in the Northern Adriatic. And if it is true that Aquileia was a glass-making or glass-carving centre, as is quite possible, Venice may well have acquired a tradition that was to stand her in good stead in the future.

The Lombards did gradually adopt orthodox Christianity and assimilate something of the Italian civilization, but their modes and their manners had evoked such detestation that when, by invitation, Charlemagne overthrew the Langobard kingdom (773) the world was the gainer and no Italian discontent.

In all this long continued strife learning almost perished in the Western Empire, and when learning dies the other arts will already have gone, and not last the art of fine glass-making, while pillage, plunder, and the mere lapse of time must have wrought havoc with the glass already in existence. How far the trade routes remained open seems to be doubtful, but under such conditions there could have been little demand upon the Egyptian and Syrian factories and, as will be seen, these lands had troubles of their own.

Whether, and to what extent, common glass continued to be made in Italy is a matter of opinion rather than of evidence. For only now, three parts of a century after the all-important official adoption of Christianity in 324 does the significance of that event become clear to the glass student. Hitherto the tombs have furnished material in plenty from which the evolution of glass-making can be deduced, while leisure and learning have bequeathed at least some contemporary comments on and references to it. The burial of glass was, however, a pagan practice which ceased as Christianity spread. By the year 400 the tombs largely fail us for specimens and by 450 even the Christian gilt glass is no longer found.

I am going to assume that despite all commotions, the relics of the Western Empire and the old provincial centres such as the Rhône valley and Catalonia still made common glass as and where possible. It is a reasonable assumption remembering the simplicities of its manufacture and the conveniences of its use, and the lack of any evidence is no argument against such an assumption. I think the probability is that the old traditional forms were adhered to, and if any such were deposited in late pagan tombs they would not be recognizable as post-4th-century glasses.

So far as Italy is concerned there is no evidence of any continuance of fine glass-making. Yet the successful self-reliance of the maritime cities may be remembered and the courage and tenacity of the Church in adversity had been notable. Throughout the 7th and 8th centuries the influence of the Papacy in world affairs had been increasing. Surely a certain state would have been maintained by the Popes, sufficient to attract a nucleus of craftsmen. If so, it is impossible that there should not have been glass-makers among them, and some colour is given to the possibility by Nesbitt's belief that glass mosaics continued to be made in Rome until the 9th century. But I know of no direct evidence.

The case is rather different in Northern Gaul. Of all the immigrant Germans, only the Franks from the Rhineland contrived to combine wisdom with force and thereby succeed in establishing a permanent state. By the middle of the 6th century their boundaries stretched from the Atlantic to Thuringia and from the Mediterranean to the North Sea. It is from the Seine-Namur-Rhine area of this relatively stabilized kingdom that clear evidence of continued glass manufacture is to be found. It was obviously in the northern regions far distant from Rome that paganism was likely to linger and ancient burial customs to persist. And so from Frankish tombs in Gaul and across the Rhine, and from Saxon graves in England and Southern Scandinavia, we get a series of glasses of distinctive and distinguished appearance, possessing what has been called 'a northern appeal'. They include unstable drinking bowls (Pl. 5c), and particularly the cone-beakers and their derivatives the 'claw-beakers'. They are glasses for the rich, and the finest of them will stand comparison with any hand-made glass since blown. They date up to the 7th and 8th centuries, when their story also closes. Specimens will be found in the British Museum and, one regrets to say, scattered in small local museums where their presence is hardly known and their importance likely to be overlooked. Few examples are in private hands.

For the poor there were palm cups (Pl. 4d), little beakers such as might cap a modern thermos flask. Their date is not easy of assessment but some are undoubtedly of the 5th to 8th century. Much more may have been made. Utility glass will not be expected to have survived unless deposited in tombs, and although the Seine-Rhine populace can hardly have been universally Christian, it may have become indifferent, or universally too poor to provide grave goods, or possibly the old custom died out irrespective of religious considerations.

As to glass, fine or common, being made in England between the 5th and the 8th centuries, evidence again is lacking. It is generally thought that the fine pieces referred to above were brought from the Continent. Even if that be so, it does not follow that common glass was not made in this country, although the case for this assumption is much less strong than for Northern Gaul. The same must be held to apply to Spain.

2. THE LATER ROMAN EMPIRE AND ISLAM

THE term 'Eastern Empire', so often and conveniently used, is really a misnomer until A.D. 800 when Charlemagne's Empire in the West could legitimately claim the title of 'Roman'. The Later Roman Empire is a preferable title for the eastern portion of the old empire. Its history begins with the establishment of Constantine's new capital (indifferently New Rome, Byzantium, or Constantinople) in A.D. 330. Its tradition and population were predominantly Greek. Its official language from the middle of the 6th century was was Greek. Its civilization and culture was inevitably Graeco-Roman. But its peoples were still Roman in the old political sense of the word and until A.D. 800 there was only one Roman Empire, varying indeed in extent and in power with circumstances, but still a single entity even if (as at first) there were two capitals and generally two emperors.

For this civilization, new-focussed on the ancient city of Byzantium, only the term Byzantine is permissible. Its importance as a world influence ought not to be overlooked.

For as the heir to the past, and as the greatest city of the world and the only one which had never been pagan, Byzantium naturally stood supreme in civilization, and from its situation it linked East with West and so was of immense importance commercially. As a state, the Later Roman Empire was always what we now call a world power, and almost always the first world power. The services it rendered for a thousand years as a bulwark to a somewhat undeserving West are inestimable.

For there was always an actual or potential menace from the east and the north. We have seen how the western provinces of the Empire were lost in the 5th century and partly and temporarily regained in the 6th. It was unfortunate on all counts that after a truce lasting some two and a half centuries and despite a very recent promise (how history repeats itself!) of eternal peace, hostilities with that rival empire of Persia, the Parthia of earlier times, should almost immediately have broken out (A.D. 540). It took nearly a century of consistently unfavourable war before the Persian power dissolved at the hands of Heraclius (A.D. 628). With a loss of the greater part of Italy, of all Syria and Egypt and much of Illyria, and with herself dangerously threatened (A.D. 626), it was by little that New Rome had escaped extinction. But the disappearance of the Persian power was an event of such magnitude that all and more than all might have been recovered. Time and the unexpected denied such rewards.

The surprise was the sudden rise of Mohammed, which must have seemed inexplicable to the Romans, so long and so often dominant in the East and now apparently without a rival. Christianity had permeated Syria and Egypt and had spread to Abyssinia; it was converting the Teutonic barbarians; it had its centres and an ever-increasing influence in Arabia. And Persia had, if not a religion, at least a beneficent philosophy.

To a thoughtful mind these facts must have demonstrated that paganism could never stand before the new faith. If then a non-Christian mind rebelled at the thought of Christianity, it might easily conclude that some alternative belief was imperative. Mohammed's was such a mind, and his teachings were in fact, if not in design, a competitive religion. Though they seem to have been tolerant enough on their inception, they were received as coldly as all new teachings are. But once established, not so tolerantly, their spread was as rapid as anyone could have wished. First haltingly preached in 610, the new religion so quickly became a political force that in twenty years Mohammed felt strong enough to demand the conversion of both Heraclius and Chrosoes III of Persia. As conversion implied submission, it is not surprising to find no record of the replies of those rulers. By the middle of the 7th century Islam controlled Arabia, Syria, and Egypt; quickly she added Persia and Armenia, and by the end of it dominated Africa, had besieged Byzantium (A.D. 673–7) and was shortly to do so again. Of all this territory only portions of Syria were recovered by the Empire, and these but intermittently.

A religion no more difficult to understand than Christianity, one which was satisfied with an affirmation of faith rather than a demonstration of it, and one, moreover, which encouraged conversion by the sword and rewarded the converter with the spoils, such a religion could hardly fail for lack of enthusiastic adherents. But as a world power Islam could and did fail just because of them and their mutual rivalries and jealousies.

With the defeat of the second attempt on Byzantium (A.D. 717–8) egress from the drier and desert lands was checked, and the constant indefinite warfare which followed for the next two centuries did nothing to promote progress on either side and much to retard it in the areas in which these mutual hostilities took place.

Generally speaking, the 8th century was for the Eastern Empire one of prudence and reform. Stepping ahead, we find that the 9th saw a resurgence of its power and a period of re-conquests. The 11th saw the beginning of a final decline, when the familiar and hereditary dangers on the north and east were accentuated by political aggression on the part of the Normans, and commercial aggression on the part of Venice. And at last the Franks and Venetians exploited the situation created by the Turks and captured Byzantium in 1204. It was not the end, but it was the beginning of the end, and the world cannot thank them.

What then of the glass of the Later Empire during these second four centuries? That Byzantium itself made, and continued to make, fine artistic glass can hardly be in question. It could not have been otherwise in a city of traditions, with skill at hand, and an hereditary delight in pomp and circumstance. If the elaborate embellishment of St. Sophia with coloured mosaic and window glass was possible, and there is no doubt of that, there must have been the artistry at hand to fashion fine vessels. Their identification, and particularly their dating, is another matter, and taking into account the subsequent vicissitudes of Constantinople and the cessation of the ancient burial customs, it is by no means surprising that important Christian glass of the 5th to 8th centuries is unidentified or lacking.

Glass of lesser importance but still of considerable merit was still being made in Syria, the favourite forms of the 4th century being continued in the 5th and first half of the 6th, that is, until the Persian War, without much development in style, colour, or decoration. Among such glasses are two-colour *amphoræ* and ewers in green and blue, or in amber and green. Pl. 5a illustrates a 6th-century water pitcher of a form that Ruth might have carried centuries before. Differentiation between a 4th and a 5th century specimen is likely to be difficult and the decision unimportant. The same would hold true for common utility glass.

For the rest of the 6th century and well into the 7th, the power and prestige of the Empire was sorely strained, as may well have been its credit, and the evidence does not contradict a suggestion that these unhappy circumstances meant, or coincided with, a certain decadence in Syrian glassmanship, wherein a coarser Arab influence appeared. If so, there was no time for any revival before the Empire had Mohammed as a foe in place of Chosroes and it took exactly the same time to neutralize the danger, that is to say another eighty-eight years (630–718).

War was more desultory then than it has since become, and Islam or no Islam, I do not think that enterprising Syrian glass-makers would easily have relinquished the market which the capital of the Later Empire offered, and there is nothing to show, now or later, that the domination of Mohammed and his successors implied direct interference with trade relationships. But it is a question whether Syrian glass-makers were any longer enterprising after nearly two centuries of trouble. So from 550 onwards we do not know whether Constantinople got what she wanted from Syria, any more than we know what it was she wanted. She may have been constrained to take what Syria could now make until time and her reconstituted power altered the situation.

All that is certain is that the change to Mohammedan overlordship had an early influence on Syrian and Iraqian glass-blowers, and eventually a profound influence. Distinctions in style are not always clear-cut, but that is why the Syrian glass we know, after the 6th century, is more and more coming to be termed Islamic, and not Roman or even Syrian.

The alternative term 'Arab' is an equally good title for the earlier types of Islamic glass. This betrays little evidence of the Semitic craftsmanship of the first four centuries, and it may be permissible to wonder whether the successors of the Ennions and the Artas did not migrate, as their kindred were later to do from Northern Gaul, under very similar circumstances. No market, no Semite, is still the rule, and the converse is no less true.

There is a good deal more ordinary Islamic glass than was formerly believed, and we may anticipate that much more yet will come to light. Its survival is partly due to its relative strength and coarseness, and partly to excavations on abandoned city sites. Certain types can be mentioned which seem to have been made with only unimportant variation over a long period, and with our present knowledge only the archæologist excavator can hope to date individual specimens with any exactitude. Something of this conservatism in design has already been seen in the pre-Christian glass of Egypt. But it adds to the difficulty of dating those forms and fashions which changed so little in so long a time, except for the worse, and as a result different writers give very widely differing dates to the same group-types.

One of the commonest group-types includes many little globular or cylindrical bottles (Pl. 6a) and some incurved hemispherical bowls, which generally look as though made of glass of mud. It is a hard incrustation which does not flake away at all easily, and beneath it the metal is clear or pale honey-coloured. The glasses are liberally trailed, sometimes with a sort of starfish pattern; flat circular prunts are also applied and both the trailing and prunting may be in purple, blue, or pale green. They may have looked very well when new. More fanciful are some *unguentaria* enclosed within a grille or lattice and mounted on the back of a horse (Pl. 6b). A 6th to 8th century date is reasonably correct for this group, examples of which were widely spread, from Jerusalem to the Euphrates.

Of quite different calibre is a group of little cut bottles of very thick glass (Pl. 7c). It has been suggested that they may be reliquary bottles because of their very small capacity. They are generally square in section, finished on the wheel, and cut with some elaboration on the sides and particularly beneath the base, which may be cut away to leave a pointed foot at each corner. Their metal is rather granular and ice-like and they come towards the end of the period, *c.* 700, and persist over perhaps three centuries. More elaborately-cut bottles are also later (Pl. 7d), as, in general, are glasses with engraved work.

As to the origin of all these specimens, to leave it vaguely as Syria is a convenience, but that ought not to be accepted too strictly. There seems to be no reason why the Palestinian area should not have been active, and since the Euphrates valley is a frequent finding place, glass of such simple kinds is likely to have been made there too. Egypt provided its frequently indistinguishable quota, without wholly forsaking a higher craftsmanship, but there is nothing to negative the conventional belief that the fountain-head of glass-making was still in Tyre and Sidon. The nomadic habits of the Arabs, and of glass-makers in particular, will help to explain the rest.

FOR FURTHER READING

DILLON, E. *Glass.*
EISEN, G. A. *Glass.*
LAMM, C. J. *Glass from Iran.* 1935.
POWELL, H. J. *Glassmaking.*
THORPE, W. A. *English Glass.*

CHAPTER IV
The Empty Ages
(A.D. 800–1400)

I. WESTERN EUROPE AND GERMANY

THE period now to be dealt with is generally regarded by collectors as one which cannot be represented in the cabinet except by the grace of good fortune and a purse long enough to command a Saracenic mosque lamp. It remains true that, taken as a whole, no age is so empty, and with some thousand years of civilization behind it the thought is a sobering one. It is also true that, in so far as European glass is concerned, the cabinet is likely to remain empty despite the most accommodating of purses.

The East, however, does now offer a fair range of interesting glass of good quality, quite apart from its expensive enamelled work, and, as time goes on and recognition is given to it, this Islamic glass will be more frequently seen. If provenances and dates can only be guessed at within a century or so and a few hundred miles, nobody is very much the worse, and in due course fuller knowledge will become available.

There may be hardly anything to find of European make, but there is still evidence that glass continued to be made. There are treatises on its manufacture, not very comprehensible, not always original, and never free from a certain alchemistic leaning. Fact and fancy are mingled in a truly medieval manner, but were there no other evidence the mere existence of such treatises would be enough to prove that glass was needed and was made.

In the West, in what is now France, the practice of burying glass in pagan tombs was finally dying out. Glass-making continued, though the Franks with a law and a church and an empire to sustain may have envied the profitable Semitic glass trade and have implemented their covetousness. In any case it seems that there were reasons strong enough to persuade these glass-makers to migrate in the 9th century (Dillon says 11th century) this time to Altare in Montferrat, not far from Genoa, a movement which had both an immediate and a delayed effect. The disorders consequent on the break-up of Charlemagne's empire doubtless contributed. Populations were rural, not urban; the local market was small; and the lack of law and order deterred movement, even a peaceful penetration by itinerant glass-blowers. On the other hand the Roman road system was breaking up and the transport of goods was becoming impracticable.

And so far as the Normandy-Picardy glass-makers were concerned, it seems reasonable to suppose that their migration was powerfully influenced by the depredations of the pagan northmen. It is at least significant that their exile corresponds so closely with the official existence of the Duchy of Normandy (911–1204) carved out by Rollo after a century of incursions and rapine. Rouen, Paris, and Picardy especially suffered, though the raiding went far wider than that, inland as far as Bourges, and coastwise to Bordeaux, and to Nîmes and Arles near the mouth of the Rhône.

Those who remained in the old glass-making centres, and any of the Franks who may have been tempted to exploit the trade, found fine glass-making beyond their powers. Deprived of technical skill and commercial Semitic enterprise, the stimulus was lacking. Markets fell away and the craft degenerated into the mere making of utility *verre de fougère,* i.e. a potash glass, using 'fern' (bracken) or beechwood ash as the alkali, presumably in the simplest of the ancient forms but of which we possess no recognized example.

Towards the end of the period, that is to say in the 14th century, there is evidence of a very considerable output of serviceable glass, and of some elaborate glass, all still seemingly *verre de fougère,* but again no recognized specimens exist. Latterly also, inventories demonstrate that royal and other owners possessed and prized a certain amount of fine glass. This, too, is lost and the descriptions which have come down leave us little wiser than before. The conventional view is that such pieces came directly from the East as gifts, or as souvenirs of a crusade. Doubtless some did, but there is no means of gauging the true quality of this inventoried glass. Some may have been made locally by straggling oriental craftsmen.

There is also that delayed effect of the Semitic expulsion to consider. When conditions permitted, those Altarist descendants began to migrate once again and their dispersion is generally dated to the 16th century. But that gives them an Italian home for some seven centuries, and of their handiwork during that extended period there is no trace. I would prefer to think that it was the 13th century at latest which saw this dispersion begin. It would account very easily for that large *verre de fougère* output in the Dauphiné in south-eastern France during the 14th century and also for at least a part of the inventoried glass. If that Laurence Vitrearius, who as we shall see settled near Chiddingfold in 1226, could be shown to be an Altarist the case would be proved. He is known to have come from Normandy, which had fallen to Philip Augustus of France in 1204, and it does not follow that he was a native of that Duchy, an early and likely goal for any Altarist whose forefathers had migrated thence.

In the Rhineland, and possibly elsewhere in the eastern areas owning allegiance to Frankish dominion, a *waldglas* tradition must have developed comparable to the *verre de fougère* further west and south. The one was generally based on the use of beech or other wood ash for the necessary alkali, the other on the use of bracken, but the resultant glass was much the same. It might be that one or two shallow cylindrical palm cups of the crudest, almost granular metal, belong to the 8th–12th centuries (Pl. 6c), but nothing is recognizable until we come to a very few examples, little sealed pots of heavy glass enclosing relics, found embedded in altars. One at least belongs to this period, being dated 1252. Others are dated to the end of the 14th century and to 1519. There are pictorial records of comparable and concurrent little prunted cups and an actual example of the mid-15th century. Later these developed into the prunted roemers and beakers of the Rhineland.

In the northern parts of Germany paganism lingered on, and more glass might be expected from graves in parts of Poland and along the Baltic shores. Indeed, eastern Prussia and Lithuania were not 'converted' until the 13th and 14th centuries, and then by the knightly Teutonic Order which had founded itself during the Crusades. Conversion in this case meant coercion and in due course a cohesion which turned the tables and wrecked the Order. Its practice of and services to real Christianity are not impressive. Kisa records a few grave glasses as late as the 10th century, but the paucity of examples suggests a virtual cessation either of the ancient burial customs or of any contact with glass-making areas, which latter would not be very surprising in view of the then state of Europe.

Then there are the Hedwig glasses, seven in number, preserved in mid-Europe. They are heavy glass beakers, coarsely cut with a decorative design given an Islamic origin or influence. Where the great disagree it would be unwise to pronounce, but it could be argued that they might be the work of some immigrant Egyptian working no earlier than the 12th–13th century, and possibly later.

In England no grave glass is known later than the 7th–8th centuries and as we find requests from English churchmen for French workers to make window glass it can be inferred that any such home industry had disappeared. It was not until the second quarter of the 13th century that Laurence Vitrearius, hailing from Normandy, established himself in the Surrey-Sussex Weald, and glass was again certainly made in England. Primarily it was window glass which was made, but there was naturally a certain output of vessel glass. It was doubtless a profitable business as Laurence was followed in due course, notably by the Schurterre family in 1343, again specializing in stained glass, and they by others. Of the vessel glass there remain only indecisive fragments discovered on the glasshouse sites. It is not possible to verify the window glass they made even though it is known to what churches it went.

Both in England and on the Continent the importance of the demand for window glass, and especially church window glass, must be given full weight. It went a very long way towards restricting the manufacture of vessel glass, indeed consciously or unconsciously the Church checked this latter by prohibiting the making of chalices in glass. This would be understandable even without having to remember the unexampled influence and power of the Church. Both rich and poor could do without beakers, jugs, and bowls, or get them in alternative materials, but there was no substitute for window glass. Comfort had to come before convenience, and that fact goes far to explain the paucity of even fragments of medieval utility glass.

Little can be said as to glass-making in Spain during these empty ages. It must be assumed that glass-making never quite ceased, and that under Moorish occupation, lasting until 1492, it displayed a strong Moorish influence, more important glassware being imported from the East. In the north, which had been liberated centuries before by Charlemagne, Barcelona was a powerful commercial and shipping rival to Venice and its glass is likely to have been designed under similar influences to, and might in due course even have competed with, the finished Venetian product, had not the discovery of America and the prospect of easy wealth diverted Spanish shipping to the Atlantic shores, to the detriment of steady trade and industry. No Spanish glass I know of can assuredly be dated within the period under review. The rather famous Barcelona glasses enamelled in rich green colours date for a little while from the end of the 15th century and are comparable with the early enamelled Venetian glass later to be described.

2. MOHAMMEDAN GLASS

ITALY contributes no recognizable glass of this period with the doubtful exception of that famous specimen in the British Museum known as the Aldrevandini beaker which is dated to *c.* 1300. Its inscription 'Magister Aldrevandin Me Feci' suggests that the glass is as good as could then be made or at least that the maker took pride in it. It is, however, rather poor work, surprisingly poor in view of Venetian connections with Syria, cognizance of the graces of Constantinople, the existence of a guild of glass-blowers in 1224, and records of an export trade in 1279. There was acquaintance, too, with the glass-makers of l'Altare in the (Genoese) Marquisate of Montferrat, competitors and rivals of Venice with similar interests in the eastern Mediterranean and (*c.* 1200) with far more territory. There were, moreover, glass furnaces at other places in Italy, such as Padua and Bologna.

It is rather surprising, too, to read that Murano craftsmen reinforced the Altarist workers in the 14th century. Perhaps this happened earlier because there was always the keenest rivalry between the Venetians and the Genoese, and from 1253 to 1380 often actual war. Perhaps it was simply that individuals crossed to l'Altare, not so much with the idea of co-operating as with a desire to escape the trammels at home and then to carry their art into new and more profitable fields abroad.

No example of Altarist work has come down to us either. But if Italy is void of any indigenous glass of the period, it is still to Italy that we must go to find the largest collection of medieval glass in existence. Elsewhere there are preserved in churches a few specimens to which tradition assigns romantic histories which we may credit or not according to taste. But at St. Mark's in Venice there are some thirty examples (I follow Dillon) of so-called Byzantine glass reputed to have been brought from Constantinople on its fall in 1204. Most of these are probably of eastern origin, but there has been plenty of time for error to creep in, particularly as regards dating. Tradition is notoriously misleading and with no more knowledge of the collection than any reader can as easily obtain, I would prefer to regard the series as an invaluable but as yet indeterminate accumulation of early glass. When this glass was tabulated and the record of it published in 1886, the world's knowledge of such glass was too small to permit of a reliable appreciation.

It seems to me beyond the bounds of probability that nothing remains of 13th and 14th century Venetian and Altarist glass, and one easy explanation offers. From the 11th century both Venetians and Altarists had been in touch with the age-old glass industry of Syria; is it not highly likely that they adopted Syrian styles and reproduced them at home faithfully enough to prevent our distinguishing the Asiatic from the European product? Time, and its waywardness in medieval days prevent the metal being any guide.

The 13th and 14th centuries were busy ones for the Venetians. They were occupied with carrying other people's goods and with territorial expansion, and certainly had weightier matters than glass to attend to, as will be seen. None the less, these centuries quite surely saw the establishment, rather than the mere foundation of their glass-making industry. Some relics of that industry should remain. Its production may have been simple and yet still in advance of any other in Europe. Its future could not then have been visualized; chance has played an unusually large part in the fortunes of Venice and the merit of its citizens was their power to exploit the unforeseen.

In the East, Egypt continued to make glass, to export it, and probably to export its glass-makers as well. Colour, cutting, and relief cutting may have been its specialities, but its glass was necessarily Islamic in character, and so many similar or identical types have been found in such widely separated places that I infer a great deal of it was either imitated or originated elsewhere.

In Syria, and the present day Iraq and western Iran, a goodly number of specimens have been found, as well as a vast number of fragments. The 9th and 10th centuries saw more of the heavy crystal-like glass of the preceding period. The square-cut footed scent bottles were continued, not impossibly with more elaboration of cutting. They were four-, six-, and eight-sided, heavy-walled and of small capacity, cut with or finished on the wheel. More important were certain globular bottles with a straight-cut neck, and types of shallow faceting on the body (Pl. 7d). All this is true cut work.

Wheel-engraved work is found on beakers and bottles, so coarse that it is fairly termed wheel cutting. Most of this work is confined to the simplest patterns, so simple that they can hardly be termed geometrical, but in rare instances there are naturalistic designs of a conventional kind, showing more imagination than technique.

It was perhaps a combination of this coarse engraving and the cutting already referred to which brought into being relief cutting or carving. This has had more than a little admiration on account of the reputed artistry of the modelling, which included a stylized form of a running hare-like animal. Dillon figures one glass, a bag-shaped vessel, mounted as a false ewer, but he gives no date for it. In Buckley's *Art of Glass*, Pl. 9, Fig. 78, another is figured and given a date, *c.* 1000, a thin-walled ewer, conjectured to be carved from a single block of glass, an elaboration one might think both needless and impossible. Present conditions have precluded an examination of either of these glasses, but the latter, especially, seems to have some affinity with a specimen of my own (Pl. 9b) which is certainly not carved but a heavy blown glass with trail work which is apparently, and perhaps in part, finished on the wheel, but is more probably carefully tooled. It shows a number of duck-like birds.

Mould-blown glass of the 10th century includes more bulbous bottles with a little bulb or bulbs in the cylindrical neck (Pl. 7a). Simple *unguentaria* had the same neck motif. Bag-shaped ewers with a thumb-piece to the handle were crudely moulded with indefinite designs, occasionally with an apparent inscription (Pl. 8b). Another form of ewer and bottle was made with the upper part in blue glass and the lower in what was probably intended for clear metal but which is rather pale green or pale amber (Pl. 8a). Sprinkler bottles in heavy green glass emerged in the 12th century, the bodies moulded as before, the necks with a vermicular collar at the base (Cf. Pl. 8d). Accompanying the mould-blown glass, and like it continuing a much earlier technique, were various types of vessel with applied ornament, of no particular merit, unless it be the trailed and cut work referred to above.

This glass must be regarded as Mohammedan glass, much of it made in Syria, but some perhaps fashioned in other localities as distant as western Persia, from imported 'pigs' of metal, and, in view of the hazards of transport, it may be that the latter method was more widely adopted than we know.

The end of the 11th century saw the beginning of the Crusades, which led to the establishment of a long coastal belt of European king- and countships, incorporating the ancient centres of glass-making, Sidon, Tyre, Hebron, and Tiberias. What effect this occupation had on the industry is problematical. There was booty and no doubt a certain demand by the more important expeditionaries for the curious luxuries they had never before seen. But the self-seeking proclivities of the Crusaders in general and the debased standards of the rank and file seem more likely to have checked the industry than to have promoted it. Indeed it is not beyond the bounds of possibility that the glass-makers withdrew to Damascus, of which there has yet been small mention, whence they could exploit the appetites of the invaders without residing within reach of their jaws.

A much more important result was the practical knowledge acquired by the Venetians in their capacity as shipping agents and purveyors in general to the crusading forces. They were not the men to let slip any opportunity and we can be grateful for their enterprise without admiring their methods.

In the 8th–9th century a simple beaker had appeared, as nearly Christian as Islamic. This was cylindrical and thin-walled. Pl. 7b shows a specimen with stringing and vertical bands of coloured glass and rings suspended from little loops on its sides. By the 12th century the beaker was much stronger and flared, and it gradually became taller and more flared. There are waisted forms also (Pl. 9d). The decoration included blobs or bands of colour and also circuits or zones in red colour as if drawn with a pen; this is now usually obscured by flaking or incrustation but originally it was merely decorative, or on occasion inscriptional or pseudo-inscriptional, in character. Gilding might accompany colour work.

There were Damascus-made sprinkler bottles of flat oval-bodied form with tall slender necks (Pl. 9c), which again reproduced a much earlier style, but with a device in true enamel colour on the shoulders, encircling the base of the neck. This was a technique to be found on other simple vessels, and in no long time it had fuller expression in a certain number of substantial flared beakers such as the 'Luck of Eden Hall' which may be early enough to have been brought away by one of the Crusaders. Others, and among them the superb "Hope" goblet in the British Museum, can hardly have been in time for that. Beyond saying that they have a Saracenic air about them, the question of individual provenance can be neglected here.

Then in the late 13th and 14th century came the splendid Saracenic glass, enamelled in glowing colours, a translucent blue predominating. It is chiefly mosque lamps (they are really lamp shades or lanterns) which have survived, but there are some bowls and vases. Their origin is taken as Aleppo and they are the only outstanding glasses of the Empty Ages of which a collector may hope to acquire a specimen. They are numerous, as rare glasses go, but museums prize them—Cairo alone has some seventy lamps, and the Metropolitan Museum of New York boasts as many as thirteen examples—so there are not enough to go round and prices are high. At the time of writing a fine vase or bowl may need an outlay of at least a thousand pounds.

From further east, that is to say the present Persia, the 12th and 13th centuries give us a few opaque glass bottles and vases (Pl. 10a), smoothly finished and delicately made, so well made indeed we might be excused for giving them a 16th–17th century date. Of 13th century glass, there remains at least one perfect bowl decorated on the inside only, in part with superimposed enamel colours which exhibit a different design when viewed from the outside. Lamm (Mittelalterliche Gläser) records its reputed discovery between Baghdad and the Persian border (Pl. 10c). There is no question but that the decoration is Persian in character if not in actuality. There is an ever-growing quantity of fragments which will in time extend our present knowledge.

There is no knowing into what these fine techniques of the Saracenic and Sassanian glass-makers would have developed had not history once more intervened, this time in the shape of Tamerlane. His shadow had appeared a century before over Damascus and such were the intricacies of eastern power-politics that he was welcomed as a providential ally. Damascus, it must be said, had had experience of Christian allies as well as Christian customers. But the substance, in 1402, had become wholly predatory, and Tamerlane's ubiquitous incursions culminated in the capture of Damascus and the enforced transfer of its craftsmen to embellish his capital of Samarkand. That they adapted themselves to their new quarters with—at least—artistic resignation is a reasonable speculation. To decorate glass in and for Chinese taste would have been no novelty, and some examples of this handiwork still exist.

To us, a more important result was the opportunity it gave Venice to usurp the ancient Syrian industry, and to develop without competition the glass techniques it had not omitted to acquire. One era had passed away. Another, that of modern glass, was in sight.

FOR FURTHER READING

DILLON, E.	*Glass.*
*HARTSHORNE, A.	*Old English Glasses.* 1897.
LAMM, C. J.	*Glass from Iran and Oriental Glass.*
THORPE, W. A.	*History.*
	English Glass.
WINBOLT, S. E.	*Wealden Glass.* 1933.

* Within whose pages something will be found on all phases of old glass.

CHAPTER V

The Rise and Fall of Venice

I. HER FORTUNES AND MISFORTUNES

IT has been noted how strangely the fortunes of Venice were determined by events never to have been foretold. Hardly any more unsuitable site could have been found for a great city than those watery islands and unstable lagoons of the north Adriatic. And it has been mentioned how refugees from Aquileia reinforced the original fisher-folk when Attila destroyed that city in 452. It is unlikely that these were the first refugees, for Goths and other barbarians had passed through the land with their customary thoroughness. Still, they had passed. The destruction of Aquileia marked a change in that it coincided with the fall of the Western Empire. If many of those unhappy refugees now gave up hope of rehabilitation, and sought security through their own unaided efforts, they were wise in their generation. The domination of the Lombards was still to come.

It was a case of safety first and those overgrown islets of the lagoons formed an almost unassailable refuge from the land-bound barbarians. And with Aquileia gone, Venice, as she may now be called, found herself the port of entry nearest to central Europe. Her citizens could and did control the traffic routes from Egypt, Syria, and the East, to mid-Europe and the Baltic. The amber of the North and the manufactures of Alexandria alike paid their dues in passing.

Whether the refugees from Aquileia brought with them their reputed knowledge of glass-making cannot be said. It seems possible, even if opportunities for practical use of it were limited. For it must have been a matter of immense labour and no common ingenuity to build such a city as Venice on such a site. It was indeed the last and the greatest example of European lake-dwellings, and seemingly its mere construction was the main preoccupation of its citizens, because history has little to say about Venice until the 9th century.

The Venetians could not be content with a static role. They very naturally and very quickly became carriers as well as merchants and developed first into a maritime power, landless and invulnerable, and later into a world power by conquest, negotiation, and an indifferently peaceful penetration, but were then more open to challenge. It was the lying athwart the north to south trade route that brought Venice her greatest opportunity.

The reasons for and the vicissitudes of the Crusades make strange reading, but little else was to be expected when the interests involved were so diverse and so conflicting. Not the least of these was the ambition of traders to found a controllable route to the East, and as the Venetians were by no means the least ambitious of these traders, their co-operation, upon terms, was whole-hearted. Had the primary effort been directed towards Egypt the course of history might have been a very different one.

So from the year 1096 the Crusades went forward, and Venice was there to provide shipping, services, and supplies to those who needed and could pay for them. It was a profitable business, though the terms of the bargains struck included some curiously indefinite provisions that Venice should receive a given proportion of the conquests made, provisions the self-seeking Crusaders could hardly be relied upon to implement or the Venetians be in a position to enforce.

But they sufficed to secure special privileges such as exemption from tolls, and in some cities special quarters were allotted to the Venetians, with churches and even a justice of their own. They could then carry on trade with both friend and enemy with true commercial dispassion, and in something like complete independence. By 1124, and at the height of Crusading successes, they were firmly established in Jerusalem, Acre, Sidon, and especially in Tyre. It is not necessary to suppose that all these establishments were abandoned when Saladin retook Jerusalem in 1187. There was no particular enmity between Christian and Moslem: even the respective leaders seem to have been on quite as good terms with their enemies as with their allies.

The only fly in this so-satisfactory Venetian ointment was the competitive activities of the Genoese, and for the next two hundred years the history of Venice is largely one of struggle with her rival for trade supremacy in the eastern Mediterranean. It explains the attack upon Constantinople with its resultant capture in 1204. Some time before, the Genoese and others had found it not difficult to persuade the Emperor Manuel I to dispossess the Venetians trading in Constantinople, and the latter's indignant declaration of war had been disastrous (1171). The negotiations must have been curious, but when a revengeful Venice succeeded in diverting the Fourth Crusade to Constantinople, the wheel of Fortune had turned once more, and she emerged from the adventure with great possessions stretching from the Adriatic to and into the Black Sea. Crete was bought from Boniface of Montferrat and Venice had suddenly become a world power. Even when the Ottoman Turks occupied Syria (1189–91) she was not ashamed to treat for and retain her ancient trading rights.

Much must have been learned by all these enterprising traders, including some knowledge of the technique of the Syrian glass-blowers. Among the goods of trade it was inevitable that glass would have formed a part, and it could not but have occurred to both Venetians and Genoese what advantages and what profit there lay in making such fragile wares at home. Each had at least a traditional knowledge of the art and probably an actual experience of blowing simple glass forms. Whether either of them could justly claim greater skill or could rival the finer styles of eastern glass cannot now be known. Probably they could not, and it would have been quite in keeping with her enterprise for

Venice to have included competent Byzantine glass-blowers among her loot from Constantinople in 1204, thereby assuring herself of practical tuition as well as theoretical knowledge.

For certain it is that as early as 1224 there was a glass-blowers' guild at Venice, that in 1268 they could make 'graceful objects' in glass, and that in 1279 they were sufficiently well known to attract German pedlar-purchasers, while other Venetians were working glass furnaces elsewhere in Northern Italy.

It is equally certain that when Tamerlane took Damascus in 1402, and virtually extinguished the Syrian glass industry by deporting its craftsmen, Venice was able to make the most of this further unforeseen stroke of fate and to replace the East as the world's centre of fine glass-making. How much such a favoured position came to be valued may be judged by the extreme measures the authorities took to promote a monopoly of the art. Substantial European competition was appreciably postponed by these measures, which authorized severe reprisals on workers who passed on the secrets of the industry. Nevertheless it was not often possible or politic to enforce such drastic edicts.

But until new evidence comes to hand it cannot be assumed that the Venice glass industry was a full success from its inception. It may be partly fortuitous, but it remains the fact that not until half a century after Tamerlane's capture of Damascus do we come across any fine specimens of known Venetian make, and then the design and the decorative enamelling are far removed from any known Saracenic style. Between any presumptive establishment of the Venetian industry *c.* 1200 and the first datable series of Venetian glass *c.* 1450, two and a half centuries had to elapse marked only by one possible specimen, the Aldrevandini beaker of reputed 1300 date (I count the Hope goblet as eastern). Two centuries had to elapse before there is any record of exportation to the Low Countries or England (1394–99), and even then such exports were insignificant glasses (see Pl. 12d).

It would appear therefore that over this long period fine Venetian glass was not made, and that Venice could not rival the wares of Syria. It may be that any Byzantine workers brought away from Constantinople were less skilful or less willing than had been expected. We have indeed no means of gauging their capacity. Moreover European potentates as a whole condemned the attack on the Eastern Empire, and were probably disinclined to put profits into renegade Venetian pockets as long as they could buy the glass of the East, and as for European populations, they had still some distance to go before becoming buyers of any good glass at all.

Accordingly, opportunity did not really arrive until Tamerlane eliminated Damascus as a competitor, and by that time Venice may easily have lost some of the experience and knowledge she had gained. And as Tamerlane was not the man to do things by halves, one may guess that his deportation of the Damascus craftsmen was complete enough to render negligible any influence these men might otherwise have had on Venetian progress. In such circumstances Venice would have had to learn quite a lot about colour and fluxes before she could produce a worthy rival to the enamelled Saracenic glass. That may not have taken the half century, 1402–50, during which we have no successful example, and indeed no example of any sort, but it is of course unlikely that we now possess the earliest of Venice's fine glass. It will be obvious enough that the true sequence of events is highly speculative.

In the naval war between the rivals the honours were not uneven, but Venice secured the last battle by counter-blockading the apparently victorious Genoese fleet in her very own lagoons. This action in 1380 settled the matter. The threat had been one of starvation and it was doubtless with regret that Venice was driven into a not unsuccessful attempt to become a land power, her peak being reached at the end of the 15th century. But the effort needed was great, and it coincided with less fortunate contests with the

Ottoman Turks, from 1453 supreme in Constantinople. Europe had no sympathy for monopolist Venice and demonstrated its feelings by forming the League of Cambrai against her. Venice could justly claim a great position and a world reputation, but she could not include extra-national goodwill among her acquisitions. It does not appear that this was a common commodity anywhere during the late Middle Ages, and Venice had done little to merit even a small share of the world's sympathy and respect. Her rulers, then, had to congratulate themselves on a lucky escape when the league which had pressed them almost to extinction fell to pieces on account of internal jealousies.

These reverses might have been foreseen. What could not have been foreseen was Diaz's discovery of the Cape route to the Indies. Fate had struck again, and this time directly at the foundation of Venetian prosperity, for the overseas route was not only quicker, but also safer and cheaper and the invaluable trade passed into the hands of the ocean-going nations, the Portuguese, the Dutch, and the English. Venice had been effectually by-passed and ceased forthwith to be a world power. The gradual loss to the Turks of her remaining possessions was then a foregone conclusion, despite her best and bravest efforts. The process was complete in 1716.

It is difficult to regret this 16th and 17th century decline because it coincides so exactly with the ascendant period of Venetian art, not only in glass but in painting and in other fields. It is as if Venice, recognizing her failure to dominate in commerce, had resolved in consolation to dominate in art. It will be conceded that her second thoughts brought her the greater glory.

2. HER GLASS

THE text-books describe the glass of Venice more fully than it is possible or necessary to do here. Its early and entirely documentary history has been referred to, the evidence being suggestive of a considerable output of simple serviceable glass which was nevertheless in advance of anything made elsewhere in Western Europe, other than (possibly) the products of l'Altare, as to which our knowledge is not even documentary, and of Catalonia, first heard of in the 15th century but then well advanced. It has been mentioned that the Catalans were by no means uninterested in the eastern trade.

As then this documentary history of Venetian glass begins about 1200, manufacture on a considerable though possibly unambitious scale must have been taking place at the same time. One likely reason why we know nothing more of Venetian glass prior to 1450 is that we have been looking for something distinctive, whereas the ordinary Italian production was almost certainly a *façon de Syrie*, and, when found, specimens have been confused with Mohammedan glass. Plate 12d shows the sort of glass I have in mind, a simple little phial, which was excavated in Finsbury, London, according to the label on it, and may even be one of the 'little bottles' recorded as reaching London from Venice at the end of the 14th century.

So far as we to-day are concerned, Venetian glass begins after rather than before 1450, two and a half centuries after the latest possible establishment of the industry. It begins with those richly coloured pedestal-footed goblets in Gothic style which will always stand in the forefront of the world's glass. Their makers relied on metal colour, heightening it with gilding and 'gemming', i.e. with little pearl-like spots of coloured enamel. Some few specimens such as the famous marriage cup by Berovieri in the Museo Civico at Venice were also pictorially enamelled and rank as commemorative glasses. Plate 12c shows an excavated wine cup which may be placed early or late in the 15th century according to taste. Its simplicity denies any safe dating.

Interesting and instructive as these goblets are, it seems almost a pity to have thus overwhelmed the beauty of the metal itself. This particular type of richly-coloured glass passed all too quickly, but it had its descendants in certain colourful imitations of ancient techniques. It is as though the traditional styles of Alexandria and Syria had arisen again, colour and glassmanship waging a losing battle against crystal and dexterity.

From the Berovieri side come vessels built up of millefiori canes, but not, as anciently, finished on the wheel. They were not particularly successful and indeed it remained for the 19th century to show what could be done with millefiori glass. Another derivative which arrived early and stayed late was chalcedony or *schmelz* glass, imitating marble or streaky stone. The colour was not merely on the surface but was a 'through' colour. Splashes of avanturine, looking like gold, might be added. The milk-coloured glass, technically *lattimo*, may perhaps be correlated with the foregoing. This might be anything from a dull opaque white to a more or less transparent and shaded opalescent glass, and it took gilding, painting (rather than enamelling), and splash decoration very well. Early Venetian examples of millefiori, chalcedony, and milk-glass are of some rarity.

All these styles were reintroduced in the 19th century and only in the case of the purplish-greenish *schmelz* glass is any confusion likely. The colour cult did not of course cease with the introduction of the clear alternatives but it cannot be said that it was very popular. The 16th century saw the other school arise and attempt the production of crystal-clear metal. Enamelling and gilding processes were still commonly used and so we find the scale-gilt and gemmed bowls (Pl. 11). These and comparable round dishes can have armorial coats enamelled in medallion-like style at the centre. Not every such coat however is genuine. These bowls in particular had a lengthy vogue, I believe, and they seem to me to represent a compromise between the colour and the *cristallo* schools. Some of a heavier greenish-grey metal rather crudely made and indifferently gilded (Pl. 19c) are not Venetian at all but 16th–17th century *façon de Venise*, and my own view is that they are of English origin.

Stem formations underwent a radical change early in the 16th century, the simple classic pedestal being supplanted by a hollow stem displaying a pair of lion masks (Pl. 12e). This stem was blown into a two-piece mould exactly as the ancient Roman 'Janus' bottles were, and it was very often *semé d'or*, i.e. dusted with gold. It was a delicate and impracticable stem but it achieved an extremely wide popularity and there is no reason to suppose its makers were concerned about its fragility. The same two-piece mould technique was also used for bowl forms though examples are hard to come by. Pl. 13a shows such a bowl, reminiscent of earlier Florentine *décor*. It has been firmly wedded to an important English stem and foot (Pl. 34b) of the late 17th century, a quite reprehensible union which has however so far defied dissolution.

Much more often the bowls were free-blown and range from the perfectly ordinary straightforward forms to wavy-edged widely flared styles which make such inconvenient drinking vessels that they are often termed *bouquetières* (Pl. 12e). There is no end to them. Decorative devices are used much less on such bowls than they are on ewers, bottles, vases, and the like. They include moulded fluting and applied work, such as ribbing, stringing and masking, gilding and possibly a little gemming also. Masking is the attachment of separate medallion-like facial representations to the glass. The Romans had used the head of Medusa (Pl. 4b). Venetians preferred a lion's head, doubtless in compliment to the Lion of St. Mark. Prunting was a similar process, virtually a seal of glass pressed to leave little points in relief (raspberry prunts) or some other variation.

Crackle-glass or ice-glass (Pl. 12b) was also a decorative process, the hot half-blown vessel being suddenly cooled and then reheated, expanded, and finished, when noticeable fissures are left all over it. Or the hot paraison—the incipient vessel—could have fragmentary glass rolled into the surface and then be fully blown and finished in the ordinary way. Vessels such as these probably looked better when new than they do now, with the dust of ages inextricably settled within the cracks and fissures.

Other techniques based on *lattimo* glass followed inevitably. For other articles than drinking vessels, bands of *lattimo* were applied to the gathering before manufacture was far advanced and then dragged into a series of festoons. Exactly this work is seen on very many of the English Nailsea flasks. From festooning and its obvious alternatives such as banding, we come to the true Venetian lace glass or *vitro di trina*, most notable because so striking and so often seen. All its many variations were being made from the latter part of the 16th century onwards. In its simplest form it is merely a spiral threading or narrow banding of opaque white enamel, a form of bowl decoration early enough to occur on glasses with the lion mask stem. Then the threads were multiplied and worked into true lacy bands in considerable variety and used to decorate the bowl or even to cover it entirely (Pl. 13b). The foot could be similarly made. The ultimate development was the intricate *netzglas* where two layers of lace glass were fused together in such a way as to leave the threads or canes forming a net pattern (*a reticelli*) each tiny square of which contained a minute air bubble.

It was so easy a step to replace some of these white threads by coloured ones that an almost infinitely variable series of coloured lace glass might have been expected. Examples do occur, usually with a ruby threading, but they are not common. There are however plenty of such beakers and ice plates to be found, of modern manufacture. The coloured threading was in the main reserved for decoration of the stem and was less in favour at Murano than at Amsterdam. The Venetian trend (Pl. 13c, d, e) towards the end of the 16th century was rather towards a much-convoluted stem in colourless glass, with 'wings' or 'ears' having a delimiting pinched trail in a lovely translucent blue glass. There were also simpler 'knop and pillar' stems, hollow and with wrythen ribbing.

No undue elaboration of bowl form occurs or indeed could

occur in intricate lace-glass or *netzglas*; the patterns would be too distorted. I do not think the glass-blowers were really happy until they hit upon the idea of *cristallo* bowls and convoluted stem-work. Then they could blow all the fantasies their imaginative hearts desired, and support them on equally fantastic and fragile stems. There was still a home market rich enough to buy them, or powerful enough to order them, and ready enough, it seems, to destroy them all in a single night of carousal. Were the glass-blowers not there to make some more?

Not many of these whimsical drinking vessels have come down to us, as can be understood, but there were glasses in the forms of animals, monsters, ships, windmills, birds, and human figures, in sufficient variety to permit of a belief that still odder things were made. They were essentially ephemeral things, fashioned for the hour and not for posterity. They were blown so extremely thinly, partly because they could not otherwise have been fashioned so well, and partly—and this applies particularly to the more ordinary wine glasses—because the *cristallo* was not in fact particularly clear, and because the thicker it was the less clear it became.

It may be well to remark here that the early Venetian *cristallo* is of a peculiar greyish tone and not so free from minute bubbles. It improved in both respects as time went on but it never approached the clarity of English lead or German soda-lime glass of the 18th century. I do not know that it surpassed the best of Roman clear glass, and the encomiums lavished upon it are justified only when a comparison is being made with the sort of metal previously current.

The convoluted stems may show something of the 'beast' motif. A serpent with a coiled tail may support a simple bowl or the 'wings' of a 'figure of eight' stem may be topped by a pair of grotesque heads which fancy may resolve into spitting monsters. Naturalistic floral devices were also used, but obviously the stem afforded less scope for a glass-blower's ingenuity than the bowl.

The decoration of ordinary bowls is confined to simple dip-moulded patterns, an over-all diamond design (Pl. 13e) being as attractive as any. There were the unobtrusive forms of applied work including loops suspending loose rings at the sides. A certain number are found with delicate 'diamond-point' or graver etching, generally with a repeat floral pattern incorporating birds and perhaps the vine. But even these simple designs are comparatively scarce; the point of course is that the wheel could not be used for engraving a very thin bowl, and even the graver had to be used with extreme care.

That so much remains to us is sufficient evidence of the quantity of glasses made. That hardly any specimen is of a commemorative character is equally good evidence that they were not expected to last. It will be seen how different in this respect were the glasses of England, Holland, and Germany.

Something of a decline is observable during the latter part of the 17th century. Not only were the territorial and trading losses disheartening and impoverishing the home market, but other nations had contrived to lure away Italian glass-blowers and had learned how to make their own glass. That cut very deeply into the export trade of Murano and by the year 1700 that trade was confined, so far as blown glass was concerned, to a relatively small trickle to such eastern markets as were left to the former universal providers of fine glass. There remained the still-important mirror-plate business, itself not untouched by competition, and the age-old manufacture of beads in which Venice still excelled. But one does not live on beads alone: the profits were inadequate and the glasshouses of Murano otherwise so stricken that glass collectors to-day hardly recognize an 18th-century Venetian glass at all. No doubt some were still made in the best-selling lines; to distinguish them from true 17th-century glasses seems not to be attempted.

There is one exception. Whereas Venice had formerly taught the world, there came a day when one Briati determined to investigate the secrets of the all-too-successful Bohemian competition. He worked disguised for three years in a Bohemian glasshouse and on his return to Venice, about 1736, he achieved a good deal of success for himself without noticeably advancing the welfare of Venetian glass in general. He gained especial note in making *vitro di trina* at least equal in quality to the earlier glass of the same kind. But his money was more probably made out of his lustres or what we now term chandeliers.

However, all came to nought with the fall of the Republic in 1797 and not until 1838 was there any attempt to revive the industry. Then a considerable measure of success was achieved and is being achieved. This modern glass with which the name of Salviati is so popularly linked receives little contemporary recognition, but some of it has much artistic interest and the time to collect it is, after all, when it is still to be had, and particularly while it can be properly identified and labelled for the benefit of those to come. The volume, the diversities, and the similarities of all modern glass will puzzle future students sorely unless some such record is made.

To close this short summary, it ought not to be assumed that the glass Venice exported so widely was identical with that used at home. No doubt odd specimens of the latter sort reached foreign countries by one means or another, but much of it was inherently unsuited for export, irrespective of considerations of foreign taste. The Venetians were business men, and business men try to make what their customers want. That would be a fair assumption even if we had not the correspondence between Greene of England and Morelli of Venice, *c.* 1670 (of whom more anon), wherein the one sends specific designs with his orders and the other more or less fulfils the instructions given. These glasses were, in a sense, English glasses made in Venice. There is also evidence that the requirements of the German market were studied, and it is easy to appreciate the difficulties involved in discriminating between Venetian glass for export and *façon de Venise.*

Plate 14 shows just such a problem. It is an outstanding glass and when offered for sale it deceived everybody to some extent by being fitted with an ancient copper foot, which presumed breakage. But other glasses which it closely resembles in form have foot-mountings, for reasons of stability. There is the Hope beaker and the Palmer-Morewood glass (Hartshorne, Pl. 22) both of the 14th century, and the covered Lehmann beaker (Muhsam Catalogue, II, 115) of about 1592, though the latter is less flared. The glass in question is free from damage and is enamelled most skilfully with the arms of Fugger, a family whose exploits as the super-Rothschilds of the 16th century in commerce, finance, statesmanship, and the arts deserve the much that has been written about them. The metal has a greenish-grey tinge and contains many tiny bubbles. The enamel colours are distinct and can stand comparison in all respects with the very best of acknowledged German work. Exceptionally, they are laid on perfectly smoothly and in part on a background of gold-leaf. Its importance—it is dated 1584 though the glass itself may well be much earlier—and the fact that it has never been described before may excuse this detailed account of it.

FOR FURTHER READING

Buckley, W. *European Glass.* 1926.
The Art of Glass. 1939.
Dillon, E. *Glass.*

CHAPTER VI

The Revival in Western Europe

I. THE TURN OF THE TIDE

WE have followed a tide of glass-making, rising in the East about the time of Christ, flowing through Italy to Spain, Gaul, and perhaps Britain, in the 1st and 2nd centuries, and reluctantly receding, leaving at best a few stagnant pools here and there as a relic of what had been.

With its going went what was left of the by no means negligible civilization installed by Roman power. For its going, and for the thousand year hiatus in our glass history and all that that implies, we have primarily to blame the men of the Oder, the Spree, and the Vistula. Time has cast a cloak of romance over the barbaric invasions, but history has left an evaluation of their real meaning in its negative record.

Then we have seen the tide rise a second time in the East and flow quickly to Italy, and we have measured its subsequent strength and depth there. The further spread of that tide has now to be followed.

It will be remembered that the Semitic glass-makers of Gaul gave up the unequal struggle and retired, some of them, to l'Altare. It is not so apparent that the glass-makers from the Rhine end (Liège, Aix and Cologne) followed suit, and if there was one pool left behind by the first wave which was wider and deeper than another, I suggest that it was the Rhenish pool. There the density of population was surely as great, and the Church as firmly and ambitiously established as anywhere north of Italy, and the vast influence which the Church had on glass-making can hardly be overstressed, even if it did not encourage vessel glass.

When the tide began to flow again, it was not the Venetians

who set the isolated pools rippling again. It was the Altarists (especially), and the Lorrainers. The story makes confused reading and if we had not a portion of the Altarist archives we should know very little indeed. These records have been extracted by Schourmann, and they may innocently mislead us into thinking there was at first no other influence at work. They suggest for instance that the Lorrainers, who will soon feature in glass history, were among Altarist pupils. That need not presuppose that the Lorrainers were altogether ignorant of the art of glass-making, but it does infer a liberality of action entirely foreign not only to Altarists but to all others of the glass-making craft. Above all, such men desired to keep their secrets to themselves. Some were prepared to make glass, on terms, for anyone who wanted it, but it is very clear that they all refrained from teaching the craft to others, and to this natural reluctance one may trace some of their troubles with imperious customers who expected a good deal more than they actually got.

Count Raymond of Toulouse with his Provençals, and Godfrey of Bouillon and Baldwin his brother with their Lorrainers, had together forwarded the First Crusade and had ruled in Tripoli, Jerusalem, and Edessa. Richard of England, Philip Augustus of France, and Frederick Barbarossa of Germany had been concerned in the Third Crusade. Baldwin, Count of Flanders, had had his own adventures and associations with Dandolo, Doge of Venice, in the Fourth. No important part of Western Europe was therefore ignorant of the arts of the East, and nearly every western potentate was ambitious. Their cities were growing, their trade progressing, and their manufactures being established. That they were eminently desirous of adding glass-making to the list goes without saying, and if ambition had not dictated, comfort certainly would have done so.

One may guess that the new tide began to flow into Western Europe somewhere between the establishment of French power over the Normans in 1204 and the middle of the century, and that is borne out by the recorded arrival from Normandy of our Laurence Vitrearius about 1226. It is not difficult to believe that some of the earliest Altarists would immediately have directed themselves towards their ancestral home in Normandy. The first phase, however, must be attributed to individuals without much knowledge and its first effects were probably insignificant.

Subsequently, and perhaps considerably before 1400, accredited Altarist craftsmen began to permeate France, and, in somewhat lesser degree, the Low Countries. Whether, and if so how soon, Lorrainers followed this example, we are unable to say, but from the fact that John le Alemayne, presumably a Lorrainer, was at Chiddingfold in 1350, it seems they may not have been less enterprising. Their natural field lay northwards, where the peoples were at least as anxious as the French to learn the art of glass, and at least as able to pay for their knowledge. They may also have moved eastwards into Bohemia although the reverse process has been suggested to account for their origin.

It is largely an academic question, for in spite of all this far-flung activity even less is known of 13th to 15th century glass in Western Europe than of the glass concurrently produced at Venice. It is therefore quite impossible to guess whether it differed. If it did, it is much more likely to have been a difference in quality of metal than any striking difference in style. The important point is that it cannot have been better than the not so very good glass which Venice was then making, and it may have been notably worse but for all that better than the hereditary *verre de fougère* and *waldglas*.

For these early Altarists and Lorrainers, window glass was the primary and most profitable business. The world could not have too much of it and utility vessels were a side-line. Among the latter, I conjecture that lamps (that is to say, oil-containers), phials, and bottles took precedence over drinking vessels. They come into view during the 14th century, and there may be more specimens than is realized.

The difficulty is one of recognition, as anyone who tries to date a parcel of old phials, will discover. Unless the circumstances of the find are incontrovertible, the simplicities of form and similarities of metal over three centuries may easily confuse.

And so, for the first phase of the new tide of glass, the term 'late medieval' is appropriate. There could be no *façon de Venise* until after 1450 because until then Venice had established no recognizable fashion of her own.

A very different and much more important phase set in with the 16th century, by which time the Murano glass was deservedly famous, and the western potentates were more anxious than ever not only to possess it but to see it made within their own boundaries. Equally, the authorities at Venice were most anxious to retain a monopoly of their superior knowledge and skill. But money talks, and the discovery of the Cape route in 1486 had entirely changed the commercial situation. Portugal, the Low Countries, and Britain were well on the way to becoming the world's traders. Their merchants were rapidly ousting the land-locked Venetians and Genoese from their earlier predominant position, with Antwerp, Amsterdam, and London clearly marked out as world ports of the future, to serve influential towns that had grown up inland.

And so, enough persuasion was forthcoming to induce ambitious Murano men to circumvent the prohibitions laid down by their masters and to travel north to work in more powerful states and to compete with Altarists already established there. What these men did not know of the possibilities of profit, they could easily guess, and if sometimes their guesses were over-optimistic and too little regardful of local difficulties, that too would only be in accord with human nature and normal commercial experience.

For competitive Altarists and Lorrainers, also advanced in the lore of glass-making and now *gentilshommes verriers* who might work and trade without prejudice to their acquired or assumed nobility, there were other inducements. Britain was fast becoming a Protestant country, and more important, was a comparatively tolerant one. That suited those Huguenots and others whose religious tenets carried an inherent risk. Britain, too, was not unused to war but her soil had remained inviolate for half a thousand years. Artisans as well as gentlemen glass-makers may easily have thought that as considerable an advantage as did those others who streamed to America in the 18th and 19th centuries and there made American glass in all the pure European styles and in many more of hybrid origin. Britain in the 16th century bade fair to provide not only security but an ever-expanding market. British ships were annoyingly ubiquitous wherever profitable trade was to be found, and distressingly indifferent as to how they found it. Britons held the obnoxious theory that the seas were free, particularly to those who had the better ships and the tougher sailors. They were making settlements and founding colonies in places so remote and so little known that popular belief turned their rivers into silver and their sands into gold. The prospects were eminently favourable.

In general, the development of glass-making in all western countries was much the same as in England, and need not and indeed cannot here be separately described. In some, development went far, in others less far, but nowhere was more progress made than in England, or so at least we think, without the least discredit to very much fine continental glass.

2. FRENCH, NETHERLANDISH, AND LOTHARINGIAN GLASS

THE second phase, from 1500 to 1700, is important because it brought with it glass *façon de Venise*. Many Altarists and some Lorrainers felt, or were compelled to feel, its influence, so perhaps the term *façon d'Italie* would be a better one, for the flights of fancy of Murano were considerably modified to suit a more stolid and practical north, and it was not only

Murano men who were concerned in the matter. Only the green Lotharingian glass, with its prunted beakers and roemers, firmly retained an individual style.

Spain seems to have stood relatively unimpressed by the need for glass, and showed little anxiety to develop it. She had had her early furnaces, and by the 15th–16th century Catalonia was making good glass, the green-enamelled work of Barcelona being the most famous now, perhaps because the best known. It was not far removed from the Venetian, and Barcelona might indeed have supplied the western maritime cities of Italy and all those of Sicily and Sardinia more easily than could Murano. It seems that she would not, for her glass-making history becomes undistinguished, and one may conjecture two reasons. First, the transatlantic obsession, and second, Castilian scorn for meticulous trade, an apathetic refusal to contemplate progress, and perhaps a certain prideful disdain of competition. The void was naturally filled by others, and although our information about glass in Spain is very inadequate, I conclude that the Spanish Netherlands exported a certain amount including crude greenish or straw-tinted glasses (Pl. 17a) to suit Spanish taste. Subsequently, in the 18th century, Holland, Germany, and England all catered for the Spanish market, and when the royal factory of La Granja de San Ildefonso was opened in 1728, its workmen were largely foreign, and production so like the foreign article that differentiation between the Spanish-made and any competitive copy is largely a matter of guesswork.

France, for all her early traditions and despite the widespread Altarist influx, failed to make good. There are a few enamelled glasses of the 15th–16th centuries (Pl. 12a), but she can show nothing to compare with the output of Murano, Liège, Antwerp, and the Rhineland. The industries of France were agriculture and war, ill-assorted steeds for the chariot of any state. Whatever was won on the field of battle was more than offset by the losses on ten thousand fields of peace. The people suffered on both counts, and it is the people who buy glass and the burgher who buys fine glass.

There was Burgundian glass with a distinct reddish tinge belonging to the 16th–17th centuries and later, and as might be expected there was a Normandy and also a Poitevin production. Little known as it is here, it must be regarded as essentially utility glass of much more interest than merit.

Most writers find it convenient to consider under one head the glasses made in what we call the Netherlands or the Low Countries. Those however are really geographical terms. The peoples who lived there were already quite sharply divided by racial and cultural differences, so that despite the changeful vagaries of their political allegiances and boundaries, it may be simpler to separate them as they are separated to-day, into Belgians and Dutch, and to deal with the glass they made accordingly.

It must be appreciated, however, that each party made quite a lot of glass in competition with the other (Pl. 16), to the confusion of the buyers of the day and to the bewilderment of collectors now. And Murano's own contribution to the Netherlandish markets adds a further problem. It sounds like free trade all round. Actually glass-making was carried on much as in England, under a licence which policy might recommend or interest obtain. Such licences often carried certain material benefits such as subsidies or freedom from tolls, and might be supported by interdicts on competitive foreign glass. It does not follow that the licences were always granted without some consideration or that the attached benefits were invariably implemented. Among other vicissitudes of glass-making in the 15th and 16th centuries, internal competition greatly affected profits, but that these were potentially important can be inferred from the recurring attempts to realize them.

In Belgium, the chief centres were Antwerp and Liège; the glass-masters of the former place, among whom Pasquetti, Mongarda, and Gridolphi were prominent, preferring a *façon de Venise* of more convenient design than the true

Murano glass, not without idioms of their own such as the Neptune masks and the little turquoise eyes to their raspberry prunts (Pl. 15d). Liège followed fairly closely, but in the 17th century under the Bonhommes moved towards what Baar calls an Altarist style. This again is a simple *façon de Venise* but with more applied work, gadrooning to the bowl, and a finial with pinched wings to similar covers. The stem might have a series of hollow knops often ribbed (Pl. 17, b, c, d), or have one or two hollow quatrefoil knops (Pl. 18d).

Both these places were well situated geographically and politically to obtain *barilla*, the soda derived from a Spanish coastal plant, an ingredient widely regarded as an essential factor if clear glass was wanted. English crystal and Bohemian *cristallo* put Antwerp out of business at the end of the 17th century. Liège continued for another hundred years making undistinguished glass, including those always unfortunate bowls or baskets of trailed glass which are so frequently attributed to Bristol.

The Dutch records show that glass was made in many places, none of which gained the eminence attaching to Antwerp and Liège. Among the first to establish the industry were Amsterdam and Middelburg, and these places certainly made a *façon de Venise* (Pl. 15c), more perhaps with the idea of competing in the Belgian market, whither it was openly or surreptitiously sent, than because it suited national taste.

The Dutch preference was very much for the green prunted beakers and roemers. Beakers we have met, more or less cylindrical vessels, tall in relation to width, and now with various types of prunt applied to the walls. The earliest form of these prunts is a flat circular blob without much trace of the up-pointed 'thorn' left when the tool depositing the pad of glass was drawn away. In the 16th century the thorn was accentuated of set purpose (Pl. 15a), and occasionally looped. In the 17th century, the familiar raspberry prunt (Pl. 15b) became common alongside a form of blunt triangular 'thorn' or 'beechnut' (Pl. 16c). The base was provided with an indented or even a clawed band. This developed on the roemers into a 'spun' foot, formed by winding a trail of glass round a wooden core. At first only a matter of two or three coils, the foot gradually became taller, with a score of turns in the coil, and its narrowness left a good deal to be desired in the way of stability.

The roemers were most distinctive vessels, derived from the beaker, the transitional form being conical at top and cylindrical below. In the 17th century the cone became a cup, the cylinder was narrowed and became a hollow stem, which carried the prunts, and the coil foot was added beneath. When inverted such a roemer looks very much like a bottle or carafe. There had indeed been a great development from the crude heavy 'Igels' of the 15th century and before, such as were imbedded in altars. A further but not so early a series is found in certain *cristallo* beakers, with an applied ring at the base to improve stability, and often with a band of fine stringing round the rim (Pl. 18a).

In all cases, metal improvement kept pace with design, the green glass in particular giving a strong impression of control, as opposed to the inherent greens of the old *waldglas*. Its finish and texture was good and it contained no more of the tiny air bubbles than was inevitable with the firing methods of the times.

But it was not so much the Dutch to whom credit must be given for these outstanding developments as the inhabitants of Lower Lorraine, of, or formerly of, the Aix-Cologne district, that is to say, the ancient Rhenish pool. They had no doubt spread over a wider area, and though there seems to be no definite evidence, it will accord with the probabilities if we assume that Upper Lorraine, the wooded country south of the Ardennes and west of the Vosges, was no less able to make this Rhineland glass. Hence the better term Lotharingian which is often applied to it.

The Dutch, I think, were glass lovers rather than glass makers, perhaps of necessity. Nature had not been kind to their land in the provision of fuel. England, far better wooded, found it politic to forbid the use of wood as fuel, and although there is some doubt as to the pertinence of the reason given, viz. a possible shortage of oak for shipbuilding, the same circumstances would have applied in still greater force to Holland without there being the same resources of coal as an alternative fuel. Consequently there is no purely Dutch glass of merit. The manufacture was carried on in many places such as The Hague and Maastricht, besides those already mentioned, but somewhat intermittently and unobtrusively. In the latter half of the 17th century and in the 18th, when it may be supposed that better communications eased the fuel problem, a good deal of utility glass was made, some very crude, some fairly good but none really fine. Among the best are some wines of clear metal, in Altarist style, and perhaps an answer to the Bonhommes. One peculiarity is the provision of loose rings hanging in Syrian fashion on the outside of the bowl.

One of the characteristics of an intelligent and industrious nation is the power to rise above circumstances. The glass-loving Dutch were intelligent enough to perceive the way out of their difficulties, industrious enough to take the trouble, and artistic enough to make it worth their while. They realized that if they could not compete in actual glass-making, they could still tap a rich market by specializing in the decoration of other folks' glassware. So from the last quarter of the 16th century, and for all we know still earlier, they applied themselves to engraving, first with the diamond point or steel graver and later on with the wheel, and by so doing they conferred distinction and often historical value upon many glasses otherwise of no great account.

This work will be referred to further on. The best of it lives unexcelled, and some of it seems inimitable until it is remembered that what man has once done, he can do again. It has been suggested that some of the work was that of gifted amateurs. Even so, the varied and personal nature of many of the engraved designs is almost proof of a commissioned order of a commercial nature. In wheel-engraving the Dutch had no competitors save the late 17th and earlier

18th century artists of Nuremberg and the Bohemian area, whose execution may sometimes have equalled that of the Amsterdam shops but whose artistry never did. These parallel styles may possibly go some way to substantiate a theory that the German production was helped by eastward-moving Lorrainers.

FOR FURTHER READING

BUCKLEY, W. *European Glass.*
The Art of Glass.
DILLON, E. *Glass.*

CHAPTER VII

German Glass

THE account, which follows hereafter, of the decorative processes applied to glass must say so much of German work that it may serve also as a description of German glasses, albeit to say a glass is German is very nearly meaningless. Germany to-day is not what it was, and some small study of its historical vicissitudes suggests that it never was. The term 'German' therefore is here applied to the people, lands, and glasses of mid-Europe lying north of Italy and east of the Rhineland (Lotharingia) the glasses of which have already been mentioned. That of course covers what was until 1918 known as the Austrian Empire, including Bohemia, or Czechoslovakia.

These interior Germanic countries may have owed something to stragglers from the Rhineland, but without question their knowledge of glass-making came mainly from Italy. We already know their pedlar-purchasers were fetching glass from Venice in the 13th century. Buckley, in his *Art of Glass*, gives data as to various known glasshouses and some dates at which they were working. Not all these places are easy to identify, and the dates given are not necessarily those of their establishment, but enough remains to suggest that glass-making may have penetrated by two routes. One of these ran more or less northwards from Venice to Trent (1468), then over the Brenner to Hall in the Tyrol (near Innsbruck—1534), onwards to Munich (Upper Bavaria—1584) and Nuremberg (Middle Franconia—1542), further to Lauscha (Thuringerwald—1597), and thence, in a north-westward direction to Cassel (Hesse—1584).

The other route from Venice ran north-eastwards, to Villach (Carinthia—1468), and Vienna (1486), though some sort of glass was being made there in 1428. The intermediate town of Graz is heard of in 1650. From Vienna, the penetration would have been to Prague and thence fan-wise to the wooded boundary ranges of the Erzgebirge and Riesengebirge, and into Silesia. The northern glasshouses of Hanover, Brunswick, and Brandenburg were later; Potsdam's requisitioning hand was not stretched out until 1674.

It has to be admitted that this theory of the spread of glass-making is nothing more than a reasonable speculation, and doubtless as incomplete as are the records themselves. For all that, glass-making did come to Germany from Italy, and the earlier the glass and the nearer to Italy that it was made, the more Italian it was in style. This was very natural seeing how often it was actually made by Italians or Italian-trained workmen.

Otherwise the great majority of German glasses had an enduring characteristic of trying to impress; they wanted to be original, whereas they succeeded only in being different. It is doubtful whether any drinking glass made east of the Rhineland could claim originality of form, even whether that was possible. Originality in form and convenience in use were no longer compatible objectives, and in some cases, such as the greater *humpen* and *passgläser*, neither was achieved. In others, the classic lines of the forms adopted were marred by superfluities. In particular, the bowl too often overshadowed the foot. A tall stem, or a bowl necessarily rather heavy in order to accept the decoration imposed upon it, was often given too light a foot. In such cases the result was a glass unbalanced in both senses of the word, and if too high a centre of gravity was countered by extra width to the foot, as in some Nuremberg goblets, its beauty was still further impaired. The determination to be different is apparent throughout the whole of German glass, but it does relieve the collector from the necessity of recognizing more *façons de Venise*, other than the *netzglas* of Bohemia, of fine technique, but still somewhat Germanic in form.

Other than the palm cup and *maigelein* (Pl. 6d), which

derived from the Rhineland if not in fact made there, we are unable to recognize, or do not now possess, any German glass made before the 16th century. Then the Tyrolean glasshouse at Hall came into being. The glasses most safely attributed to Hall came from the royal Austrian collection and are (we hope) preserved among the treasures of the Kunsthistorisches Museum of Vienna. They displayed a strong Italianate tendency, but, in the absence of corroborative data, a similar attribution for comparable specimens can only be speculative.

Nuremberg made tall goblets of character in the second half of the 17th century and continued them into the 18th (Pl. 25c), otherwise the earlier German glass is essentially beaker-like and utilitarian in form, if not always so in size. It remained so until the 18th century when, as I suppose, something more polite was called for, and glasshouses adopted the classical wine or goblet with conical or round funnel bowl and inverted baluster stem (Pl. 25d), with free local differences in proportion and treatment.

Bohemia, Silesia, Saxony, Thuringia, Hesse, Brandenburg, and many less important areas made much the same kinds of glass in their different styles, which are confusing to English collectors and not always clear to German ones. Some baluster (Pl. 26b) and plain-stemmed English designs were copied, with characteristic German insistence upon disguisement. The frequent provision of a cover may be symptomatic of this, or it may reflect a convention that an uncovered vessel silently invited a refill, a covered one satiety.

Whatever criticisms may be levelled against German design, due credit must be given to German metal. The tinted forest glass used for the *humpen* of Bavaria, Franconia, and Thuringia, was perfectly in keeping with the hearty enamelling so often applied to them; indeed, when this metal died out the enamelling did not long survive.

From 1650 to 1730 Nuremberg made its towering goblets with multi-collared stems, and many smaller beakers, in an adequate *cristallo*. Meanwhile Bohemia and Silesia gave a clarity to a hard soda-lime metal which was nowhere bettered (Pl. 26d). Between 1740 and 1750 Lauenstein in Hanover duplicated Ravenscroft's experiments and failures, but eventually produced a really fine lead metal (Pl. 26b), short-lived and worthy of a better fate.

Credit must also be given to German chemist-glass-makers for their attention to coloured glass. Johann Kunckel produced what is usually termed 'ruby' glass at Potsdam in the late 1670's; this has a somewhat cold colour, rather red-ink or red-currant-like and very different from the later raspberry-coloured ruby glass of Bohemia and elsewhere. It must be distinguished from the cheaper 19th century 'flashed' ruby glass, which is clear glass given a thin skin of coloured metal. Kunckel also made a good green and perhaps a blue, though there was no particular novelty or superiority in these. Buckley credits him with agate glass also, made in ingenious variety in the early 19th century in Bohemia as well as Potsdam, under the term of 'hyalith' glass. German opaque white glass was also the subject of much experiment and, when compared with Bristol white, small success. There was made, I do not know where unless in the Dresden area, a considerable quantity of well-fashioned tea-ware in good decorated milk-glass. The commonest examples are cups and saucers with close spotting in blue (Pl. 23a); these were probably decorated in Germany, and also those with blue, purple, and green combing. Others were painted in the manner of porcelain (Pl. 23b), and I suspect that the Dutch were responsible for much of this work, thereafter exporting it to the most suitable market.

But most of all to the credit of Germans was their painstaking, industrious ingenuity in decorating the glass they made. Not everyone will approve of the profuseness with which this decoration was frequently applied. They may dislike its intensity and regard it as a further manifestation of the German determination to impress. On the other hand, it is not everyone in the 20th century who can form a fair judgment on foreign work of the 17th and 18th centuries;

certainly the best of it, whether enamelling, painting, or decoration with the wheel, does and will rank as a high artistic achievement under handicaps now easily underestimated.

The aftermath of the Napoleonic wars saw a period of strained design everywhere, and it is not too much to say that German extravagance went further than all the rest. Not so much could be done to the bowl because it had still to serve the decorator's convenience, but there was hardly any limit to the fanciful treatment of the foot. Production everywhere had to be stepped up for commercial reasons; the individual craftsman no longer controlled the pattern by his art or influence, while education had not yet succeeded in bringing design into industry. Yet where a remaining craftsman had a free hand, he could still correlate proportion and line, and produce a vase or vessel which might be Victorian but which was none the less a work of art not necessarily fated to be spoiled by cutter or decorator.

FOR FURTHER READING

Buckley, W. *As before.*
Dillon, E. *Glass.*
Hartshorne, A. *Old English Glasses.*

CHAPTER VIII

Gilding the Lily

1. PAINTING AND ENAMELLING

FROM very early days men had painted upon glass, a simple matter in itself; the difficulty was to render the painting permanent. Consequently, we find two kinds of painting. First, where the colour is laid on with some sort of fixative, such as varnish, and is sadly impermanent. This is known as 'cold painting', and it appears at intervals all through glass history. Being impermanent, it cannot be known how much the technique was used; some was probably the handiwork of individual amateurs, and some was not intended to last, as witness the Sunderland rolling pins and the souvenir ware, crudely painted and splashed over with a cheap varnish. Traces of better work appear on a few Irish finger bowls of the early 19th century.

The second kind of painting required a high degree of technical knowledge, for here the paintwork was fired after being laid on, and so rendered permanent. Obviously, the colours had to fuse into the body of the vessel without the latter being affected, so that questions of materials, fluxes, and temperatures ruled the result.

It is usual to divide this fired work into enamelling and painting, the former term being apparently used to cover the opaque or semi-opaque heavily laid work, somewhat in relief, the latter term for more transparent and smooth work, but I find it impossible to draw any hard and fast line between the two.

As we have seen, the art of enamelling glass in colours was first brought to perfection in Saracenic times, at Damascus and Aleppo (Pl. 10c). Its practice in Venice, for all too short a time, has been noticed, as have a few French and Spanish glasses in the same tradition. Here was an art which must have appealed strongly to the German temperament, one which had perhaps a barbaric appeal, for in the middle of the 16th century, it was enthusiastically adopted and practised with every kind of assiduity. It must be admitted that it was an art well suited to forest glass.

Convention evidently decreed that the German enamelled glasses should be dated and for that its collectors may be grateful. The earliest record is one of 1541, but any 16th-century specimen is something of a prize. The enamelling maintained its vigour until about 1670, and continued into the second quarter of the 18th century, but by then it had lost its earlier robust character though by no means its artistry (Pl. 21b). Whereas the Italian enamel colour was painted on evenly, the German artists preferred to lay it on heavily, without attention to smoothness.

The quality of German work largely depended upon the subject depicted, the *Reichsadlerhumpen* for instance, which are a tribute to the Emperor, being particularly well done (Pl. 20a). These showed the crowned double-headed eagle displayed, its wings bearing the names and arms of the constituent states of the Empire, and the best of them also carried the figure of the Christ upon the Cross. The *Kurfürstenhumpen* were more irregular in execution, though generally worthy glasses; they showed the Emperor and the seven Electors. Glasses depicting the 'Ten Ages of Man' fell into the same category. There were many armorial glasses of fine quality, mostly with a string of initials to denote the owner's name and titles besides which our modern abbreviational conventions seem simplicity itself. *Apostel-gläser*, depicting the Twelve Apostles each with his insignia, are too rare to warrant comment (Pl. 20b). Lastly, among the aristocracy of enamelled German glasses were what may be termed 'guest glasses', ceremonial and individual vessels, featuring the owner in some way or other, and used (as an inscription sometimes makes plain) to compliment both host and guest, especially a first-time guest (Pl. 20c). It is worth noting how often it is the glass itself which is regarded as speaking, a compliment in all cases strictly uniform and unimpeachable.

So far as the foregoing types are concerned, I think Dillon's strictures upon the quality of German enamelling are much too severe. He is on safer ground when criticizing the many guild, betrothal, and family glasses, and glasses with crudely comic scenes. In these, the drawing and colouring rarely merit praise, but it takes all sorts of glasses to fill a collector's cabinet, and many are both interesting and informative. There was less variety with the *Fichtelgebirge* glasses, which showed a studiously conventional view of the padlocked Ochsenkopf, whence flow four rivers. The treasures this mountain was alleged to contain were as unreal as the stags' heads which peep symmetrically from its bright green slopes. I suggest that this and other crude work was done on the glasshouse sites, the fine work in such towns as Augsburg, Nuremberg, and Dresden.

The foregoing are nearly all *humpen*, a more or less cylindrical beaker sometimes but a few inches in height, sometimes requiring both hands to lift. *Passgläser* (banded glasses) were narrower cylindrical vessels on a pedestal or a ring foot, divided into zones by horizontal trails of glass or bands of colour. Some of these were very well enamelled with a playing card, the zones of liquor having some relation to the gains or forfeits incurred in the game. Usually it is the queen or knave which is displayed on the glass (Pl. 21c).

In the third quarter of the 17th century a competitive school of painting made its appearance, using glasses in a *cristallo*. These were small and convenient in use, a low beaker on a hollow bun-shaped foot being a favourite model which may be assigned to Nuremberg and Lotharingia. One such example of painting, or enamelling, in white heightened with black shows the equestrian figures of two of the seven Electors, Pfalz and Brandenburg, with a castle (? Juttenbuhl) on reverse, inscribed *Heijelberg*; it was obviously one of a set, and I take it to be quite as early as the well-known work of Johann Schaper (1621–1670) who worked at Nuremberg, painting landscapes with battle scenes or ruins, and armorials, chiefly in black or sepia (Pl. 21a). His style was quickly imitated by others and continued with less and less success (Pl. 21d) until a still more delicate school of painting arose in the early 19th century. Meanwhile in the early 18th century, the Preisslers, father and son, had initiated a style of drawing in black and gold in imitation of engraved work.

Vignettes in bright colours were painted on Bohemian glasses and bottles in the third quarter of the 18th century (Pl. 22d). Conversation scenes were popular; series of designs portraying the months of the year were also in demand. As a whole it is pleasant decorative work and little more. It may, however, have had an influence on the later work of William and Mary Beilby, which must be mentioned, in greater detail perhaps than its importance warrants. William, I believe, worked first in a thin smoothly spread white enamel, drawing simple decorative designs of the fruiting vine and hop and barley (Pl. 22a). A fine needle was used to delineate the veining of the leaves and other details whilst the enamel was still soft. This was, I think, an attempt to imitate the then very popular wheel-engraved 'flowered' designs. Not much of this thin 'wash-enamel' work will be found. The rest is in a much thicker and densely white enamel (Pl. 22c, e). The same decorative designs were continued as before and festoons of various kinds were given to the rims of simple glasses. This work is attractive but less important than certain others decorated to order for presentation.

Much more ambitious were scenic representations of classical ruins, pastoral subjects, and a series of sports and pastimes (Pl. 22e). There is a certain sameness about them, but they are scarce and highly esteemed by English collectors. Then there were some armorial glasses and decanters, painted in colours with great care; sometimes a signature was added, with or without a date. Amongst these were a few goblets with the Royal Arms, presumed to have been painted on the birth of the Prince of Wales in 1763. An undue enthusiasm has lifted values to inordinate heights, but it must be agreed that the Beilbys, brother and sister, are our only English enamellers known by name. There were a few other anonymous attempts almost unknown to collectors, among which the portrait glasses of Prince Charles Edward in colours are an outstanding example, less for their artistry than for their association value and extreme rarity.

Michael Edkins, painter and gilder rather than enameller, worked on opaque white glass at Bristol about the same time. His decorative designs were both artistic and finely executed, and they multiply many times the value of the glass he employed (Pl. 22b). He had unknown imitators, or pupils, whose work was hardly less proficient and it can only empirically be separated from his own.

On the Continent cheaply made and crudely enamelled glasses gradually became common after 1750. They were mostly peasant glasses and they had a considerable popularity. Many canister bottles, clear, white, and blue, come from mid-Europe, that is to say the Tyrol and the Swiss-German border (Pl. 23c). They all had conventional scrolls or foliage and some a human figure or figures, caricature-like in effect if not in intent, and there might be a sentimental motto. Painted tankards came from Holland ("Hansie in de Kelder") and elsewhere. Spain enamelled on both white (Pl. 23d) and clear glasses, and after 1800 every glass-making country produced its cheap decorative and souvenir ware. Our own Tyneside was no laggard in this respect and permitted itself no small artistic licence in design.

The work of Joseph Mildner will be mentioned later, but he may have been the stimulus for another school of German painting which used a thin transparent enamel and had a decided preference for pastel tints. Among the purists in this style the names of Samuel Mohn of Dresden, and Gottlob Mohn and Kothgasser of Vienna are the best known. Samuel and Gottlob were partly contemporary, working between

1805 and 1818. Kothgasser had a longer career, signing and dating glasses mainly between 1814 and 1830, and his work is naturally less difficult to find. A peculiarity of all these beakers is the care with which the gilt or other bordering was painted.

All these men preferred simple glasses of the small beaker type, and produced a quite extraordinary range of subjects. Scenic representations of famous places and buildings were their mainstay, selling for quite modest sums; they produced portraits, some by S. Mohn being also in silhouette, while biblical, allegorical, and sentimental designs were popular. There were some delightful floral designs. One of Kothgasser's beakers depicted an unexpectedly attractive witch astride a broomstick; another represented fish in an aquarium (Pl. 23e). Playing cards, owls in a tree, and Venus admiring herself in her mirror, added to the variety of subjects. Taken together, they are evidence of the fey side of Teutonic imagination.

A more commercially-minded school of painters carried on their tradition. Some floral designs on mid-18th century overlaid glass were finely but not imaginatively done. Portraiture on the later florid Bohemian vases was undistinguished and did not repay the trouble so clearly taken. I suspect that economic considerations had transformed the artistic into a hack decorator.

2. ENGRAVING

ENGRAVING is older than painting and we have seen something of its practice in ancient times. Egypt and Rome provided incised work done by a hand tool. Rome engraved, or incised, glasses on the lathe, using flint or wheel, and developed this into flat cutting. Rome also carved glasses, but how to draw the line between wheel-engraving, cutting, and carving is another matter. To-day, collectors recognize several kinds of engraving:

(a) 'Diamond-point' engraving, executed by hand, using a diamond or graver (Pl. 24).
(b) Stippling, which is similar work of a more delicate kind carried out in dots, using perhaps a little hammer, or in very fine and very short lines. In the latter case, of course, it approaches (a) (Pl. 25a, b).
(c) (Surface) wheel-engraving. This can be anything from very coarse to exceedingly delicate, according to the skill of the worker and the type of wheel used. A stone wheel gives a coarse effect; a copper or bronze wheel gives a sharper cut, whose delicacy is determined by the size and, no doubt, by the quality of the wheel; the finer this is the more delicate the work can be (Pl. 26).
(d) Carving in low-relief. This is done with the wheel and it usually has a polished finish; generally speaking, the finer the finish, the better the work (Pl. 28a).
(e) Carving in high-relief. Again the wheel is used, the design being made to stand up from the body of the glass (Pl. 28b).

Diamond-point work appears on early Venetian glass, an intricate decorative border on bowls, and dishes, and a conventional floral design, sometimes incorporating birds or animals, being found on drinking glasses as well (Pl. 24c). It was a hazardous technique for the frail 16th–17th century Venetian glasses, and also, I fancy, too laborious a task for impatient Latin craftsmen. But it had some appeal for Germans, eminent copyists by instinct. The Hall glasses of the Tyrol are engraved in Italian style, whether by Italians or German trainees cannot be said.

More individual are a few *Reichsadlerhumpen* and comparable glasses, some of which are figured by Buckley in his *European Glass*. German diamond-point work, however, was not persisted in because enamelling and wheel-engraving had a still greater appeal.

The Italian decorative diamond-point work was copied

in both France and England, the one artist common to both countries being Anthony de Lysle, to whose hand we owe identification of the Verzelini goblets of the late 16th century; such glasses are however very rare.

I cannot separate them, but it was the Rhinelanders and the Dutch who made the most of the possibilities of diamond-point work, and it might be true to say that they drew upon glass as naturally as Schaper and the Mohns painted upon it. They produced pictures where others had only reproduced designs (Pl. 24b). The art was not an easy one. It was one thing to engrave upon a flat surface and quite another to achieve an artistic effect upon a glass bowl which had varying contours. There was, consequently, an engaging air of careless abandon in the scenes portrayed, and meticulous accuracy was avoided because unattainable; the result pleased the artist and his public as much as it now pleases us, as witness the dancing peasantry and the Lion of Holland on the Buckley glasses (*Art of Glass*, Figs. 353 and 357).

Some Dutch portraiture was more sedate and I think the less impressive for being more life-like. A more painstaking accuracy found expression in the so-called 'calligraphic' glasses notable for the elaborate slender scrolls which masked some motto and which might cover the whole glass. Anna Roemers Visscher (1583–1651) was the first we know of to work in this style; in some eyes she ranks as its finest exponent, and is, incidentally, the first woman artist in glass we have record of. Among men, van Heemskerk (1613–92) is a familiar name, but all signed work of this period is rare.

In addition to these artistic styles, the Dutch produced much pleasant decorative work of a minor character in the Venetian tradition, roughly hatching in the outlined flowers and animals of convention to give body to the design (Pl. 24a).

Of English work there is nothing of importance until just before the middle of the 18th century, when the Amen glasses were made anonymously, and two allegorical designs by one Chapman. Francis figures one of these in his *Old English Drinking Glasses* on Pl. lx, but neither they nor the Amen glasses display professional skill, and their value is historical, not artistic. Other diamond-point glasses were spasmodically made, and indeed still are. They were essentially for commemorative or presentation purposes and the only series to be found consists of some mid-19th century rummers with vignette armorials, coaches, and hunting scenes. They are interesting rather than meritorious, and suffer from the inclusion of a doggerel sentimental verse in a minute and crabbed handwriting.

Stippling was only successfully accomplished by the Dutch, and indeed not seriously attempted by any other nation. A few names are known, notably Frans Greenwood (1680–1761), and David Wolff, who worked between 1784 and 1795, but there must have been many other similar specialists, no less capable as I think, whose names remain unknown. The identification of the many stippled glasses which exist is confused by doubts and over-hasty *dicta*. The technique was simple, the image desired being produced by a series of tiny punctured dots upon the surface of the glass (Pl. 25a). They provided the high-lights in the picture, the intensity being achieved by varying their closeness; the shadows and background were obtained by leaving the surface more or less alone.

It must have been an assiduous business, requiring great skill and patience, but the results well rewarded the artist. The pictures seem at first sight to be breathed upon the glass, so delicate are they. Consequently collectors seek them, and signed examples are costly, but mere signatures should not sway a buyer unless he can be sure they are genuine.

Some artists added a few very fine lines to the design to represent some outline or to assist with a head of hair. Others used more lines and fewer dots, and some relied entirely on fine lines and eschewed the dots altogether (Pl. 25b). In such cases the result is better seen on the glass, and I do not know that the technique was any less skilful.

In the majority of cases, English lead glasses from Newcastle were preferred, partly because the metal was softer and would take dots or lines with less effort, and partly because it was more lustrous and better fitted to emphasize the unworked shadows.

Surface engraving with the wheel, like the other decorative technique, was practised anciently but was then mostly of the crudest description. Seeing what skill the craftsmen of the first four centuries displayed in cameo cutting and gem engraving, it is surprising how far surface engraving lagged behind. It can hardly be fortuitous that no single celebrated specimen of surface engraving is recorded by our text-books until the early 17th century, and if some reason be sought, I can only suggest that the manufacture of the essential tools, for instance, the tiny wheels, had until then not been achieved.

It must be conceded that until the 19th century, surface wheel-engraving of quality was the province of the Dutchman and the German. It was not a technique suitable for the frail Venetian or *façon de Venise* glassware, consequently any would-be technician had to wait until there was a sufficiently heavy glass for him to work on. Caspar Lehmann is the earliest such, working in Prague for the Emperor Rudolf II, and signing and dating a beaker in 1605. This displays a far-advanced skill. There are two more anonymous glasses dated before the Schwanhardts, father and sons, assumed the mantle of Lehmann and, from 1622, engraved glasses at Nuremberg. They improved upon Lehmann's technique by polishing their engraving. No less competent were their followers, Schwinger (d. 1683), H. W. Schmidt, and Killinger (d. 1726). These men used the tall multi-knopped multi-collared Nuremberg goblets (Pl. 25c), whose relatively thin walls required a delicate hand, and heavier tumblers suited to low-relief work, and bun-footed beakers.

The work of this Nuremberg school is at first generally

fine, and sometimes superb in its drawing as well as its technique. It deteriorated in the early 18th century, displaying a flatness and lack of perspective and proportion.

Bohemia and Silesia have been credited with surface engraving of the mid-17th century, but it had little merit. The engraved work of this home of glass-making is undistinguished until the first quarter of the 18th century, when it succeeded in displacing the Nuremberg artists. It abandoned the pictorial style in favour of conventional designs composed of ribbon or strap work, foliage, and scrolls. Flat-cutting, as well as high- and low-relief work, came in at the same time. The technical excellence of this Bohemian and Silesian work was unsurpassed; some of its mid-18th century portraiture is superb and closely akin to the earlier Nuremberg work, but the general characteristic of much Bohemian and still more Silesian surface engraving is a superfluity of conventional patterns, enclosing armorials or vignette portraits, with a wealth of intricate detail and meticulous workmanship. Its execution was no doubt greatly facilitated by the hard metal of the soda-lime glasses used. It should not, of course, be forgotten that side by side with this quality work there was a large output of undistinguished engraving; it seems indeed that comparatively few Bohemian-Silesian glasses escaped some form of treatment.

In the early and middle years of the 19th century, Bohemia in particular turned out a series of delicately engraved glass in competition with the glass-painters of the day. The designs showed a wide range of subject, portraiture, memorial (Pl. 27a) and family glass, battle scenes, hunting scenes, and of course topographical glasses. The figure and animal drawing had in many cases nothing to learn from any earlier artist, and the standard of execution was generally high. The name of Anton Simm (Pl. 27b) is among the many of those far more familiar to Continental collectors than ourselves. The urge to decorate is manifest in all other German glasses, although the character of the decoration was generally lower. None the less, there were few glass-making centres which did not produce some fine work. Thuringia, Brunswick, a somewhat indeterminate district known as West Germany which may mean Baden, and the Lauenstein glasshouse in Hanover (Pl. 26b), all come to mind as having produced some really fine engraved work, but their normal production was inexpensive glass, much of it for export.

There are still a considerable number of German-type glasses in existence engraved with the imperial arms of Russia, appertaining to the reigns of Elizabeth Petrovna and her successors (Pl. 26c). They include a monogram, and some a portrait as well. Foreign efforts had been made to manufacture glass in Russia, fairly early in the 17th century, but it seems that Peter the Great (emperor, 1689–1725) established the industry. Several factories came into being in the middle of the 18th century, probably through German enterprise, and it must be from these that the series referred to owe their existence. The imperial glassworks at St. Petersburg were not established until 1792.

There is a superb portrait of Elizabeth, executed in low-relief and not necessarily in Russia, but the majority of these royal glasses were rather carelessly surface engraved and often heightened by black enamel or gilding. One assumes that the royal consumption of glassware was considerable, and, from the generous capacity of the bowls, its household a thirsty one.

The only serious challenge to German surface wheel-engravers came from the Dutch. Their craftsmen engraved many notable glasses from the second quarter of the 18th century. As in Germany, much of their work lacked skill, but much more of it had some historical or social interest. Family affairs evidently loomed largely in Dutch eyes. The best known Dutch engraver was Jacob Sang and he and his school produced many glasses of eminent quality and appeal (Pl. 44d). They chose English lead metal glasses and found no difficulty in adopting the German strap work, conventional scrolls and floral motifs, with a restraint and sense of proportion which left the main design in due prominence.

Some Dutch landscape and shipping scenes are notable for their accuracy and perspective, than which hardly anything could be more difficult on a curving surface. Some 'copper-plate' inscriptions with the wheel indicate a control few now possess with the pen. Sharp curves with the wheel were difficult indeed, so much so that in England the graver was often employed to connect the easier upstrokes and down-strokes of the lettering.

English surface engraving can hardly be called anything more than pleasant until the early 19th century. Such work as is found on early glasses is mainly the work of Continental engravers, and a purely English school did not arise until about 1750, when simple decorative designs were given to small wine glasses. The trade name for this was 'flowered' (Pl. 53a), though even conventional flowers were in a minority among the many designs chosen. Probably the fruiting vine was the commonest motif. A little later, portions of the design were given a high polish, as in most of the roses of the Jacobite glasses. The hop and barley design was especially effective when rendered in this fashion.

Various English commemorative glasses, such as the Privateer glasses, needed greater skill but they cannot be ranked as high works of art. Not until about 1765 could any English work stand in company with that of the Continental experts, and not much of it even then. The early 19th century saw some improvement and a good many rummers will be found with finely executed work (Pl. 27c), but it still lacked draughtsmanship and artistic inspiration.

There was a certain amount of engraving on American glass, from the latter part of the 18th century. On the whole it most nearly approached English work in style and execution, but its workmen were so often Dutch and German that Continental feeling was frequently apparent in both the glass and the engraving. Writing with only an academic knowledge of American glass, I think it must be as difficult to-day to distinguish between many European-made and

American-made specimens as it was to separate Italian for export and the various *façons d'Italie* in the 17th century.

The contributions of France and Spain to wheel-engraved glassware of any kind are of very small importance.

It is not easy to say when surface engraving becomes carving in low-relief, but in general acceptance the latter term covers engraved work which is deep and wide, leaving the surface of the glass with a number of concavities. Such work was polished in greater or less degree and it required a high degree of skill to produce any sort of artistic result. Generally speaking, I think the results obtained were unsatisfactory, and the technique was not widely used, perhaps for that reason. Bohemian, and probably Silesian craftsmen also, developed this technique towards the end of the 17th century. What appear to be Nuremberg beakers were engraved in similar fashion at about the same time, though some of these may actually be Bohemian.

Better results were achieved at Potsdam (Pl. 25d) by Winter and Spiller in the last twenty years of the 17th century, at least as far as the engraving was concerned. The glasses themselves were heavy-walled goblets and tumblers of small distinction and very liable to decay and crizzling, a fault here so bad as to arouse surprise, for ordinarily there was no difficulty in making perfect soda metal glasses. The carving at Potsdam was deeply cut but not always highly polished. One such glass and the odd cover, the remains of a pair of covered beakers, was elaborately engraved to commemorate our own King William III, and his consort Queen Mary. It is difficult to estimate how good the carving was, so pronouncedly is the glass decayed. Other houses in Brandenburg working on similar lines seem to have given a higher polish to their work.

The technique occurs at intervals on Bohemian glasses (Pl. 28a) and comes into prominence again in the 19th century, when amber glassware was deeply carved with stags, trees, and hounds. Though stereotyped, these were naturalistic designs, and many exhibit a high degree of skill. Overlaid glass was also carved through the colour, in an effective fashion, Karl Pfohl in the 1860's specializing in animal forms. These later glasses of pretence are characterized by the most careful finish in themselves, with fine cutting to stem and foot, and evidently ranked highly in the eyes of their makers, as they still rank on the Continent, and as they will eventually rank in England.

Carving in high-relief was an obvious corollary of the foregoing to anyone searching for novelty, but it required more skill and time than the result justified. Certainly much of both was put into the fine specimens which remain. They are all 18th century German work and far from common (Pl. 28b). A curious alternative was provided by engraving a convex cameo medallion portrait; this was attached to the bowl by some transparent adhesive and the rest of the glass was engraved in the ordinary way. No doubt this saved time, but it was not altogether satisfactory because the cameos were liable to crack across, having perhaps a different coefficient of expansion, and also to come away entirely.

Their appearance is very different, but the technique of the modern cameo-cut French vases of Gallé and others is very similar (Pl. 28c). In these the vessel was overlaid with glass of various colours, but not necessarily evenly overlaid. The body might have layers of coloured glass, or patches, or both. The artistry consisted in removing the unwanted glass so that the design, floral or scenic, would be left in high-relief. A spray may be left with green leaves and blue flower; shading could be accomplished and a skyscape developed in the background. Much of the task of removing unwanted glass was accomplished by hydrofluoric acid, but the wheel, and no doubt other tools were required to complete the design. The finish could be polished, or matt, or satiny. Webb & Sons did similar work in England, often with greater care in design and workmanship, but, I think, in less impressionistic fashion (Pl. 28d).

3. OTHER DECORATIVE TECHNIQUES

ATTEMPTS to replace the wheel and to engrave glasses by the aid of hydrofluoric acid cannot be said to have been made before the end of the 18th century; a record that acid was used by Heinrich Schwanhardt may be corroborated by a single unsigned panel dated 1686, and something was accomplished with flat glass from about 1700, but the Frenchman Marcassus de Puymarin is the first we know of to experiment with drinking glasses. We have his publication but not his glasses. There were subsequently German exponents of the art, and eventually English ones, commercially minded. Very little is known of these men or of their work, which is scarce; I will only say that it comes on rummers with wide cylindrical bowls, now known to be English (Pl. 27d). They have the word 'Patent' acid-etched on the pontil. Late work included portraits of English notabilities, such as Disraeli; they were not high art and rank as honest souvenir ware, but more ambitious attempts have met with less success.

The technique of the Christian 'gold-glass' of the 3rd and 4th centuries was revived in the first quarter of the 18th by Bohemian artists. It was precision work, two walls being used for each vessel, one fitting exactly into the other. The inner wall projected a quarter of an inch or so above the outer, and this projection was thicker than the rest, and was cut with a flange so that it would rest upon the outer wall. Before insertion it was ornamented with gold leaf and etched with a needle; silver leaf and colour could be added. The joint between the rim of the outer wall and the flange of the inner had to be an exact one; it was cemented by some colourless adhesive and masked by a further decorative band of 'inserted gold'. Finally the complete vessel was submitted to the wheel and cut with fairly narrow vertical flutes from base to rim; hence the term 'many-sided' which is frequently, but erroneously, applied to the little beakers

(Pl. 29a) and graceful goblets made in this fashion. The base of the beaker had a circular disc cut away from the outer skin; another disc was given a simple ruby and gold 'insertion' and cemented into place.

The designs chosen correspond with those on surface engraved glasses, hunting scenes being extremely popular. The weak point of the technique lay in the jointing, especially the base joint, and in the disfigurement which occurred if the two skins of the vessel were not an airtight fit; in that case an ugly air bubble would spoil the effect, and few glasses are entirely free from this failing. They were, and are, extremely effective glasses and popular abroad, if not in England.

Towards the end of the 18th century, Mildner produced a variant of the technique. He cut away an oval from the wall of a simple beaker and inserted designs in gold, silver, or colour, and often a combination of them. He worked at Gutenbrunn between 1787 and 1807, making a large number of monogram and armorial glasses, with some portraits in colour or silhouette and a few topographical and conversation scenes. He signed and dated his glasses on the inside with commendable precision. As before, the joint was masked by a decorative border.

The possibilities of gilding seem to have been less explored than might be expected, for hardly anything looks better, to my mind, than a finely gilt glass. The main methods of applying the gilding were the same as those for painting, that is to say, either with a fixative or by a firing process. In the first, the gilding retained its brilliance until worn away, which will be soon or late according to the efficiency of the fixative and, of course, the extent to which the gold is subject to wear. In the firing process, the gilding was reasonably permanent and was presumably brilliant when newly burnished, but it becomes dulled by age.

The first method was commonly in use on the Continent

in the 16th century. The Venetians used oil-gilding, as it is called, under the rims of dishes, where it had some protection from wear, and although its brilliance was somewhat marred by the greyish tint of the metal above, it was, I think, the most satisfactory plan. On bowls, and on the German *humpen*, it had perforce to be laid on the outer surface and was more vulnerable. This, too, was the normal English practice, though I know of no instance of its use here before about 1750, unless it be on any such standing bowls as had been made in the Venetian 16th–17th century style (Pl. 19c).

English wine-glasses may be found, belonging to the third quarter of the 18th century, with oil-gilding in the simple floral style of the Bristol painters. There are wines and goblets with the fruiting vine, and ales with the hop and barley (Pl. 29b). From perhaps 1745 it had not been rare to gild the engraving put on by the wheel and traces of such work may be found, but specimens in anything like their original condition are exceptional.

Fired gilding was a Continental practice very common in the 18th century (Pl. 26a), particularly on the rims of drinking glasses. As stated, it was much more lasting but tended to lose tone, and it has a mechanical look which displeases. Not many fired-gilt English glasses will be found, but they do exist, and were perhaps made for export.

Something must be said about cut-glass, a comprehensive account of which has yet to be written. Its practice in Roman and Islamic lands has been briefly noticed. In modern times it was re-introduced by Bohemians at the end of the 17th century, facilitated by the adoption of water-power to drive their machines and no doubt by improvements in abrasive and polishing materials. The art spread quickly throughout Germany, and in due course brought German glass into countries hitherto almost ignorant of its existence. Western Europe provided an accessible market, the Low Countries a wealthy one. This German commercial scramble took place during the second quarter of the 18th century,

England receiving its quota without much enthusiasm, as I judge, despite its novelty.

No doubt it served to put fresh ideas into the heads of English glass-makers who themselves began to advertise cut-glass, not all necessarily English. There are records enough, but as there are hardly any pre-1750 glasses both made and cut by Englishmen, I infer that the home market was unresponsive and the output insignificant.

In any case, the Excise Act of 1745–6 put a crippling weight tax on the contents of the glass-pot and finance forthwith dictated a drastic reduction in the size and weight of the glasses made. Cut glass suffered especially since the metal lost in cutting paid duty, so that the Act almost prohibited anything but very simple cutting where ornament-value compensated for duty losses, or luxury cutting where cost did not matter. The Excise of 1777 doubled the duty and nearly halved the weight of all ordinary production lines; it also included 'enamel' glass, spelled the doom of the filigree stem, and ushered in the age of small Georgian glasses (Part II, xiii) plain or perfunctorily cut.

But the duties did not apply to Ireland. Those of 1745–6 were important enough to induce a good many English glass-masters to set up furnaces in Ireland, counting freedom from duty and the too-inquisitive exciseman full compensation for an attached prohibition of export, which difficulty may not have been so insurmountable. The Act of 1777, however, almost coincided with a grant to Ireland of free trade (1780), wherein may be traced the influence of the quite loyal Irish Volunteer movement. This enabled Irish-made glass to go to America, and go it did, to the extent that the Irish home market was content to use cheap English dutiable glass and thus permit a greater part of its own non-dutiable production to go abroad, not only to America, but to the West Indies and to England herself.

So from 1780 until 1825, when Irish-made glass was first taxed, the success of the Irish factories was phenomenal. But the glass they made was Irish only in name; it was really

English glass made in Ireland for purposes of convenience, and made by English or English-trained glass-makers upheld by English capital. It was by no means the first time that English glass had been made in Ireland under precisely similar auspices but it was the first time the venture had reaped a due reward. Accordingly, there was nothing to prevent the same glass being made in England, if cost did not matter, and undoubtedly London in particular had a large output of luxury cut glass; how large it is difficult to ascertain. But it does not receive the same cachet of public approval simply because so much of it is automatically and inconsequentially dubbed Irish.

The style of cutting changed with the years and a volume of illustrations would be necessary to figure the patterns evolved. It may be possible to declare that a certain specimen is Irish, but rarely to decide upon a Dublin, Cork, Waterford, or other origin. It is still more difficult to assign English cut work; a London or Midland origin is as likely as any other. There is much misdating of the later cut glass. Good Irish and English work was still being turned out after 1850, but it passes for late Georgian glass.

Following precedents, the Dutch had already adopted, and I think improved on, the German cut-stem work. In the early 1760's they were importing glasses from Newcastle and faceting the stem and bowl-base in a manner unsurpassed by anyone; the bowl itself was reserved for engraving or had already been engraved. These were a special, not a production line. When Irish flat-cutting came in, the Dutch did it equally well on a tinted soda glass which could, and does, easily pass for the mythical bluish Waterford. The rectangular, triangular, and polygonal canister bottles they made for travelling cases are still fairly frequent. Some of this is very good and authentic work.

After 1815, Bohemia developed some fine cut work on goblets and beakers, though it may not be to English taste; the French Baccarat factory did the same, and the metal of both is superlative. Both however lacked the lustrous quality of the late 18th century lead glass of Britain.

The 20th century has seen something approaching systematic forgery of early cut glass, yclept Irish. The deceptive pieces are not without merit, but their production must be deplored, and their purchase guarded against. Wisdom will discount fairy stories about *trouvaille* from Irish castles and ancient manors, and dictate their closer examination, particularly when sets of candlesticks, wall-lights, and chandeliers are in question. None the less, there exists fine Irish glass in Ireland, though it is not necessarily for sale.

Of mould-blown glass, Ireland produced a quantity for cheapness sake, about 1820–30. Decanters are still reasonably common; some are marked with the factory name, and are sought for by collectors. Modern finger bowls with 'Cork Glass Company' on the base are often seen and will no doubt again be purchasable wherever bargain hunters congregate. Modern decanters with the same marking have been blown from the original moulds and are very deceptive. There were also Irish spirit bottles, decanters, and goblets which were blown into a two-piece and three-piece mould, an ancient technique, also widely practised in the United States. Scotland, or perhaps Tyneside, copied the one-piece mould-blown Irish decanters in a soda glass which varies from quite good to bad.

Press-moulded glass followed, an American invention which was quickly adopted in France. This can give some extremely elaborate patterns of glass, inexcusably costly by any other method, and the resulting vessels have an exceptional brilliance. It is a mechanical art, but not necessarily an unworthy one.

Another 19th century innovation was what is known as *crystalle ceramie*. It is to an Englishman, Apsley Pellatt, that the credit must be given for developing and indeed perfecting the technique, for which he took out a patent in 1821 at his works in Falcon Street, Southwark.

A refractory material, often pottery ware, was moulded into the required form, and this was embedded in the solid glass and so rendered impervious to exposure or change. There was no difficulty in enamelling the device in question, and so we find cameos, or *sulphides* as the French term them, apparently in silver, gold, or enamel; portraits, figurines, armorials, medals, and even landscapes. Pellatt's work is good but not easily recognizable. That of the Frenchmen Desprez and Andrieu is equally good, and some at least is signed. The Baccarat factory, I think it must have been, specialized in armorial devices with gold and colour. Much more frequently to be found are beakers and other objects (Pl. 29d) with representations of the Christ or the Madonna and Child, more indifferently moulded than they need have been to satisfy a welcoming if indigent public.

It was a short step from this *crystalle ceramie* work to attempt to enclose designs composed of coloured pastes in a crystal prison, and in most eyes a greater success was achieved. The two techniques were occasionally combined.

So we have a somewhat bewildering series of decorative paperweights, and other utility items such as door-handles and vases. The basis of one main type was a series of coloured canes arranged with care in some sort of pattern, or enclosed haphazardly. In another type, flowers, vegetables, moths, snakes, and so on, were hand-fashioned before enclosure in the weight.

It was a French triumph of skilful ingenuity, emanating perhaps from the Saint Louis factory, for I have an obviously immature specimen with the factory marking SL and date —45. Progress was very rapid, for there are good St. Louis vases dated in the same year. Baccarat was making and dating millefiori weights in 1846 and doubtless Clichy was making its own models, though it did not date any. These Clichy weights are generally distinguishable by a hallmark in the shape of a pink and green 'Clichy Rose' which is never forgotten, once seen. By 1849 the era of dated weights, and presumably of good French weights, was over.

Competitive English attempts were piteously inadequate; some pallid examples are attributable to Birmingham and London, but that is all for which I can find any evidence. Some factory workers found spare time to put flower-pots and bubbles into door-stops of bottle glass. These can hardly be taken seriously and most examples seen are completely modern.

It would require a further volume and more knowledge than the present author possesses to deal with the later 19th century developments, and the processes by which glass of graded colours and new surface effects was made (Pl. 30a, b). Some of it is likely to be ephemeral, in a utilitarian age; some also is most attractive, both to the eye and the touch, and has a high decorative value. Of the quite modern American, Swedish, Czechoslovakian, French, and Viennese glass, the same may be said. English glass-makers perforce competed in an almost international search for novelty, but catalogues, price-lists, and illustrations of our modern productions are strangely hard to come by. Perhaps it was the repeal of the Excise Acts in 1845, perhaps it was the wealth and solidity of the early Victorian era which swayed some English glass-makers at the Exhibition of 1851 towards weight, size, and elaboration, in a variety of supposedly antique styles, as well as in some modern continental ones, Bohemian for instance.

It was, however, an unnatural phase, and it brought its own remedy. A reversion to simplicity rewarded those manufacturers who found it possible to relate design to the exigencies of commercial production, and who did, in fact, import modern Art into modern Industry.

There is much in all this glass, continental or English, which is worth attention. It may or may not appeal, but it is foolish to condemn an article merely because it is modern.

Nobody will deny that, among all peoples, appreciation of inherent art is quickest in the French. This cultured nation finds it worth while to maintain a museum devoted to contemporary workmanship, partly no doubt to encourage the manufacturer, partly to educate the people. Paris has therefore a series of the chosen work of modern makers, including glass-makers, and a collection which is already documentary. It would be a noteworthy event if some English museum could find the means to bring together a representative series of our post-1850 glasses; having done so, it would not be difficult to keep it up to date, and so assure posterity of a similar documentary collection for which it will be more than grateful.

FOR FURTHER READING

II. III.	BUCKLEY, F.	*History of Old English Glass.* 1925.
I. II.	BUCKLEY, W.	*Art of Glass.*
II.	do.	*European Glass.*
II.	do.	*Diamond Engraved Glasses of the Sixteenth Century.* 1929.
II.	do.	*Monographs on Greenwood, Schoumann and Wolff.*
I.	DILLON, E.	*Glass.*
III.	JANNEAU, G.	*Modern Glass.* 1931.
III.	MCKEARIN, G. S. and H.	*American Glass.*
III.	PELLATT, A.	*Curiosities of Glassmaking.*
I. II.	THORPE, W. A.	*English Glass.*
I. II. III.	do.	*History.*
III.	WESTROPP, M. S. DUDLEY	*Irish Glass.* 1920.

I. *Enamelling and Painting.* II. *Engraving.*
III. *Other Decorative Techniques.*

CHAPTER IX

Glass-making in England

I. THE PIONEERS

ALTHOUGH there are indications that glass may have been made in a few places in earlier days, the documentary history of English glass begins with a record of one Laurence Vitrearius—*sc.* Laurence the (? window-) glass-maker—coming from Normandy about 1226 and settling himself at Dyers Cross, near Pickhurst, with such success that in a few years he was making glass for the abbey at Westminster (*c.* 1240).

Granted that he had to go somewhere, the question arises—why to Pickhurst? To-day this is a tiny hamlet a mile or so from Chiddingfold, lost in sparsely populated wooded country, halfway between Guildford and Petworth. It is difficult to assess the relative importance of these places in medieval times but neither can have been much more than a village. Pickhurst lies on the western outskirts of the ancient forest of Anderida, some ten miles as the crow flies from the Roman Stane Street running from Chichester to London, but—in the 13th century—what miles and across what country! That a foreigner intent on making glass in England should then have arrived here without some inside information seems unlikely; that he should also have hit upon Pickhurst by chance or search seems almost incredible, and so I shall infer that glass-workers, indigenous or otherwise, had already established themselves in the Chiddingfold area. A fragment of vessel glass found at Vann (three miles north-east), and below the level of all else, might support this conclusion. Dyers Cross is shown by Winbolt as a road fork, a few hundred yards south and west of Pickhurst.

There Laurence worked, apparently with more than one

furnace, and there he prospered. He was succeeded by his son William, now 'le Verrir', who may have laid more emphasis on the firm's vessel glass. He too was successful, and it was partly due to him that Chiddingfold received a Royal Charter in 1300.

Whether success bred apathy or whether other circumstances intervened, we do not know, but half a century later the Schurterres had captured the Wealden industry. It is here that our John le Alemayne appears, apparently more as a factor than as an actual glass-maker, to take his part in an industry which was still based on the production of window glass and whose vessel glass was still simple and severely utilitarian. In their turn the Schurterres had to meet the competition of the Peytowe family (1435), and the industry was still active in the first half of the 16th century.

Until now, each new arrival had probably succeeded by virtue of greater technical knowledge. During the third quarter of the 16th century (1549–75), still better equipped glass-makers reached England, Protestant Lorrainers headed by Carré, including Hennezel, Thisac, Thiétry, and Houx, and Catholic Venetians represented by Giacomo Verzelini. Carré's was the moving hand and he obtained a licence in 1567. He followed tradition, and policy also, so far as to set up furnaces in the Alfold, Surrey, area, but broke new ground establishing a glasshouse in London itself, where he intended to produce quality drinking glasses in *cristallo*. It was the obvious thing to do. Alfold, and for that matter Chiddingfold, was then more uneconomically situated from a transport point of view than almost any part of Britain to-day. Proper supervision must have been very difficult, and above all the Spanish barilla could only be imported by sea. Its further transport to Wealden sites in the depths of Surrey and Sussex, over roads and tracks which were always hazardous and often impassable to wheeled vehicles, was necessarily tedious and expensive. It was an ambitious and yet sensible scheme, and Carré has the honour of having established modern glass-making in England.

But the success of it was not to be his, perhaps with justice, for his relations with his business associates seem open to a good deal of criticism. His intervention alarmed the older Wealden glass-makers, and there were forceful protests from the Wealden ironworkers who, also, had claims on the available fuel. Change is always resisted in rural England and strangers suspect. Whether justly or otherwise, the importunity of the ironworkers largely prevailed, and so Carré's Lorrainers dispersed, with or without men of the older tradition, first to the woods of Hampshire (Buckholt—*à bouque haut*), then on to Gloucestershire (Forest of Dean and Woodchester), to Blore Park near Eccleshall and Stourbridge in Worcestershire, to Cheswardine in Shropshire, and eventually to Newcastle-on-Tyne.

Most of these places lie in districts where coal is found or easily obtained, and their choice cannot have been entirely fortuitous. That some popular or particular resentment was the immediate cause of this migration is likely enough; that it was the deciding factor is much less certain. There can, indeed, hardly have been any decisive shortage in 1567, and what the glass-blowers used was the 'lop and top', suitable for nothing but firewood. The Edict forbidding the use of timber as fuel did not appear until 1615, by which time not only were glass-makers established in coal-providing areas, but new furnaces had been designed (1611). The only possible and the only natural conclusion is that the glass-makers were aware of the advantages of coal fuel long before the authorities, and had made their dispositions accordingly. State edicts are liable to lag behind events. It seems not to be recorded when continental glass-makers first used coal. If the needs of Antwerp and Liège glass-makers had already pressed their local coal deposits into service, Carré's Lorrainers and others would have been aware of it, and ready enough to follow suit.

Some of the newer Surrey-Sussex furnaces carried on working until the end, but the initiative had passed elsewhere, and if anybody suffered it may have been less the glass-makers than the ironworkers themselves who had so strongly raised the issue. They would have been well advised to follow the lead given to them. They had already been prohibited from using wood as fuel in certain parts of the country (1558), and this ordinance may well have disposed them to quarrel with the glass-makers. The building of more Sussex ironworks was prohibited in 1584, but it was a long time before ironworkers as a whole took kindly to the idea of mineral fuel.

It is not quite certain whether Carré saw his *cristallo* glasshouse in Crutched Friars in full production. He probably saw it started about 1567, with the help of the Lorraine men, and was so disappointed with the result that he enlisted Venetian workers instead. They arrived in June, 1571, but Carré died eleven months later and Verzelini reigned in his stead.

It is no disparagement to say that Verzelini reaped where Carré had sown. There were still pitfalls in plenty for the most welcome of manufacturers, and Verzelini was a stranger, unknown to his customers-to-be, and suspect by the strong group of English merchants whose business was the importation of glass from abroad. The connection is unproven, but when in September, 1575, the Crutched Friars glasshouse was in full operation and was destroyed by an unexplained fire, Verzelini demonstrated his own view by promptly seeking protection from the Privy Council. The London glass merchants protested with equal promptness, but without success, for on the 15th December, 1575, Verzelini secured a royal licence giving him the sole right to make Venice glasses in England for twenty-one years. It further prohibited the importation, by anyone, of foreign glass, thereby securing Verzelini from outside competition, and affording the country a timely period during which it could assimilate a knowledge of fine glass-making.

This licence and his own qualities determined Verzelini's success. He avoided Carré's mistake of trying to make different kinds of glass at one and the same time in London and remotest Surrey, and his late opponents, who, after all, were only concerned with selling, will have done as they were to do a century later, that is, patronize the home manufacturer as soon as he could provide the goods they wanted. If Verzelini made any mistake, it was one which affected his successors rather than himself. He seems not to have moved with the times in the matter of coal fuel, and under the circumstances then ruling it is not easy to see that he could have done so. His twenty-one year licence was apparently determined on his retirement in 1592. He took with him the respect of his community, and a fortune to match.

Sir Jerome Bowes took over the men and obtained a new licence, more extensive than the old one in that it included the sole right to import Venice and Murano glasses if he so wished, or a limited obligation to do so if he did not so wish. It was, however, operative for twelve years only, and an annual rent was exacted. A soldier by profession, Bowes had small knowledge of glass, and probably did little more than pay his way. His glasses would naturally be in line with those of his predecessor. His licence expired in 1604, but seems to have been temporarily renewed in 1606, and other somewhat ineffective grants were made before the Edict of 1615 opened an entirely new chapter in the history of English glass.

Between Laurence and Carré more than three centuries had elapsed, and it might be thought that some specimens of the period would have survived. If they have, they have not been recognized except for one or two trivialities of almost timeless glass. But from sites in the Surrey-Sussex Weald and elsewhere, a great number of fragments have been collected. Mostly it is window glass, but there are the bases of drinking vessels and the necks of little bottles, and something has been done by practical men towards reconstructing such pieces, rather unconvincingly I think. Pl. 19a shows an early *verre de fougère* glass of unascertained origin, with a hollow-blown high-kicked foot, the formation of whose bowl it would have been impossible to guess at. This rather thinly-blown piece has a sheared rim and is made in a coarse, bubbly, green metal, only half-translucent, with many tiny flaws which look like black flecks in the glass. They seem to originate in the larger surface bubbles which have burst. It is just such a glass as would suffice for a peasant's cider or home-brewed.

There are other fragments of vessel glass and many pieces of flat glass which as a whole are too small, too erratic, and sometimes too affected by long burial to be of any guidance. These relics have been recovered from the old glasshouse sites, chiefly from the earlier ones compactly situated around Chiddingfold, and from the later ones, more scattered, lying east and south-east, rather nearer Stane Street. Some of the sites seem to have been in use more or less continuously over the centuries. Dating accordingly becomes difficult, and the matter is further complicated by the possible finding of cullet brought from elsewhere.

To summarize, the Wealden production is primarily one of window glass. Of vessel glass, there is the earlier coarse metal which Winbolt describes as milky-green and semi-opaque. But there is also a later type of metal of the Carré period, to which too much praise can hardly be given. The fragments betray excellent workmanship, the metal is homogeneous and free from bubbles, while its texture and finish is surprisingly good. Its counterpart is found in a number of *bénètiers* (Pl. 19b) attributed to Antwerp, and of the same period, and if Carré's Surrey glass was as similar in style to his Antwerp glass as it was in metal, distinction between the two might be very difficult indeed. This particular metal is by no means a *cristallo*. Its colour varies with thickness and the range of bluish and greenish tints is wide. Latterly it was a rather deep blue-green, not unlike that found in Spanish coastal glass of relative and later date. In fact, the whole range of tints rather recalls the varying colours of 17th–18th century Spanish peasant glass. There are some fragments of crystal glass, somewhat like early

Mohammedan crystal, but whether they were made on the sites is uncertain.

In view of the brevity and mischances of the Carré régime in London, little is to be expected and nothing is known. All we can guess is that his styles would have been Altarist and not Venetian, and if his crystal was as attractive as his *verre de fougère,* its absence is indeed to be deplored.

With Verzelini we fare better, but still disappointingly. His was a high-class trade in the Venetian tradition, and five glasses can be attributed to him, three others being doubtful. It seems that their metal is not the equal of that which Carré made. All five are engraved with the diamond point and in much the same style. All carry dates between 1580 and 1590. Only two are undamaged. The engraver was almost certainly one Anthony de Lysle, hailing from France, and but for his work it is problematical whether the glasses would ever have been recognized as English at all. Of the Bowes period a single specimen survives, again engraved and dated 1602 by de Lysle. It is a meagre tally for so distinctive and important an output over almost forty years, and it ought not to be regarded as a complete one. On the Continent many more glasses of the period have survived, despite an equal fragility or a greater clumsiness. The conditions for survival were probably more favourable in England than elsewhere, her people no more careless than foreigners.

No doubt, the question is primarily one of recognition, and we are much too apt to think in terms of drinking glasses only. These were, in fact, not only a relatively small part of Verzelini's production, but the more vulnerable part. The table of a wealthy nobleman needed more than goblets. It needed, and possessed, a much larger proportion of bowls and dishes than is called for to-day, and how far this is true may be learned from the Kenilworth Castle inventory of glass items belonging to the Earl of Leicester in 1588. Mr. Thorpe quotes it, and there are at least three times as many bowls and dishes as there are drinking glasses. Not all of them were necessarily for the dining-table, but many were, and Pl. 19c represents a type of bowl which Verzelini and Bowes may very well have supplied. It can be traced from Venice in the early 1500's to England in the late 17th century, with not a few connecting links.

Many fragments of high-class work have been found, particularly the stems of drinking glasses, and while it may be impossible to allot any certain dating, or to distinguish between what was made here and what may have been imported, they have this importance, that they tell us to think of good English 16th century glass as a definite *façon*, more that of the Low Countries than of Venice. It is no use at all searching for something outstandingly different. We may in time come to recognize certain small points as indicative of English make, but the general appearance will remain conventionally 'Venetian'.

2. MANSELL

BOWES the soldier was succeeded by Mansell the sailor. Not quite at once, because two or three other licences were current when the coal-compelling Edict was issued, only Bowes being placated by an annuity he did not live long to enjoy. It was to Sir Edward Zouche and his partners that a new and comprehensive patent was issued, in effect conditional upon his using coal fuel, although the drafting merely prohibited wood. And it was an already augmented and prosperous Zouche Board that Sir Robert Mansell joined in 1615. Three years later he had bought out his fellow partners and was in full control.

The story of Mansell's career has been recorded elsewhere in such detail that repetition is superfluous. Suffice it to say that he was what we now term a financier, but he was—indeed he had to be—an organizer of no common order as well, and during the forty years of his domination he transformed an unstable and scattered art into a genuine industry. His was a harsh monopoly, the sort of thing now regarded with so much abhorrence. It did indeed bear hardly upon the small man, and particularly upon any such who may already have been habituated to the use of coal fuel. The alleged sins of the state being visited upon its favoured nominee, Mansell had to meet opposition both legal and illegal, and sabotage as well. The situation was regularized in a characteristic fashion when the government cancelled a re-drawn monopolistic patent granted only the year before, and replaced it by equally effective Letters Patent, in 1624. The point is that at that time, and under the conditions of 17th-century society, only a harsh monopoly could build up a coherent industry capable of competing on terms with Italy and the Low Countries. The importation of Venice glasses was intermittently prohibited, and they were always dutiable, despite constant representations from the Venetian ambassador. A few favoured people received special permits to import for their private use, and no doubt some unscrupulous people disregarded the regulations altogether and smuggled foreign glasses into the country. Mansell had not much to fear from foreign competition.

We can easily infer that glass in quantity, and of quality, was now recognized as so essential a commodity that we could not afford to rely upon a foreign production which might cease entirely in times of trouble, and which was certain to be expensive even in times of peace. Mansell must therefore be regarded as the individual who, for no unimportant monetary consideration, was privileged to pull the essential chestnuts out of the foreign furnaces for the ultimate benefit of the community. Carré and Verzelini had shown how it could be done. Mansell developed their plan on the large scale, and whatever criticism is levelled against him ought more properly to be levelled against the government which empowered him, for good and sound reasons of state, to act as he did.

There is no evidence that Mansell made his own fortune in the process. On the contrary, it is likely that he conferred far greater benefits upon the industry, and indirectly upon the country, than ever the industry conferred upon him. It is an experience not unknown to many subsequent financiers and organizers in other walks of life.

Mansell's disability was, naturally enough, the same as Bowes', a lack of knowledge of glass itself, and so he was largely in the hands of his workmen. After some years of disappointment with a series of Venetians of whom Miotti, in 1619, was the best, he procured a company of Altarists from Mantua. These included Da Costa and Dagnia, in 1630, and later on a few more highly qualified Murano men joined him, among them Brunoro and Mazzola, in 1637. His first concern was of course to arrange for supplies of coal to serve his Broad Street furnaces. This he brought by sea from the then independent Kingdom of Scotland, an arrangement so suggestive to Scottish ship-masters that they were easily induced to raise their charges from 14s. to 24s. per ton, a figure which presumably included the cost of the coal but which was nevertheless prohibitive.

It fell to Lady Mansell, in the temporary absence of her husband on an expedition against Mediterranean pirates, to counter the pirates nearer home by resorting to the coal of Tyneside. It is a measure of the progress the Tyne has since made, that this was regarded as a surprising alternative in 1621, and it is a reason for gratitude to the much-abused monopolist. A glass enamelled by Beilby of Newcastle in the third quarter of the next century with the simple wording 'And The Coal Trade' may reflect something of the close connection between glass and coal.

Scottish glass-makers at Wemyss in Fifeshire were a further source of trouble, filching his workmen and generally exploiting their nuisance value, until Mansell bought them out lock, stock, and barrel, in 1627. There is nothing to show that the suborned workers liked the climate of Scotland any better than that of London, but they would, as always, go anywhere for a large enough bribe, and with the same mental reservations to leave as soon as they thought fit.

Theirs was a monopoly of skill, and they proved it to be just as vicious as any other kind of monopoly, more easily exploitable and less easily checked. It remains a major problem to-day.

That Mansell continued so long in business proves that he learned much as time went on, not only about glass but about the foibles of his workmen. It is moreover complete evidence of his business acumen. That his output was important is shown by his control of glasshouses from Purbeck to Fifeshire, and from Milford Haven to Lynn. It is shown by his trade lists and by the fact that he was able to export his wares. He initiated (wine) bottle manufacture, developed medicine bottles and mirrors, and did not disdain to make beads. I trace a certain criticism regarding the artistry of his glass, one that can hardly be proved or disproved because of the lack of evidence. But it cannot be expected that he troubled himself much with questions of art. People wanted glass of all shapes and sizes, useful glass, utility glass, inexpensive glass, and Mansell was there to supply them. I suspect that if we had a good range of his manufactures, it would not be very different from what America made in the first half of the 19th century. Even in a nobleman's household the requirements of the kitchen need to be satisfied before the banqueting hall can be properly served.

A small output of high quality Mansell drinking vessels need not, of course, be excluded. The skill was there, the metal was there, and the market was there. So must the glasses have been, however little they interested the financial magnate responsible for them. Unfortunately they are not here now, or else we cannot recognize them. Pl. 31a shows the only good glass likely to be of Mansell origin, and its preservation is doubtless due to the fact that it is a chalice, following a contemporary silver form, and made (so one supposes) to replace a silver one melted down to sustain one side or the other in the Civil War. It displays uncommon dexterity in manufacture, good design, and beauty of line if not of appearance, but that is because the bowl is double-blown, the walls enclosing a now dulled silver foil, with a pontil mark at the base inside them. The metal is neither Venetian nor Netherlandish, and it is tinged on the foot with an iridescence not due to burial or decomposition.

It is not clear when Mansell's monopoly lapsed, but it is certain that the Civil War and the Commonwealth régime seriously affected trade and business, his among the rest. The iconoclastic proclivities of ignorant if sincere men may well be in part responsible for the absence of examples of Mansell's work. There are those to-day who enjoy the destruction of what they do not comprehend, and it is too much to suppose that men were any less prejudiced three hundred years ago. I follow Thorpe in thinking that about 1650 there was a reversion to older practice, with scattered glass-makers blowing glass where and how they could, if not within the letter of the law, at least without disturbance by it. In other words, the monopoly dissolved through natural causes. It had done its work and needed no maintaining. Sir Robert's bolt was shot, and he died in 1656.

Complete Mansell glasses other than medicine phials are, as stated, virtually unknown, and we have to guess at their forms. His list is non-descriptive, but from other sources we know that he made cylindrical beakers ('beer-glasses'), some probably with trailed horizontal cordons round the walls. He may reasonably be suspected of having made serpent-stemmed and winged wine glasses in Italo-Netherlandish style. He may have used filigree or *lattimo* ornament, and there is no reason why he should not have experimented with colour (see Pl. 31b).

Of fragments, there are many which must have come from his glasshouses. They are scattered in various museums, and rarely are the circumstances of their provenance at all precise. Generally speaking, it is the stem which survives, and we do find a large number of the mould-blown lion-mask stem such as Verzelini used, and some strong hollow cigar-like stems which were later (Pl. 31c, d). Mansell must have used both types and variations of both types. It is hardly possible to say more.

3. THE GLASS SELLERS COMPANY

THOSE glass-merchants who gave Verzelini so much trouble may or may not be identifiable with the Glaziers and Painters of Glass, now the Company of Glaziers, whose history goes back to 1328 and whose first charter was granted by Charles I in 1638. The company denies the soft impeachment, but be that as it may, there is evidence that a glazier might sell glass just as a hosier might sell hose, and it does not seem at all improbable that some glaziers were also glass-merchants. As a company it had never been either rich or influential, and it suffered much from unauthorized competition. The Glass Sellers Company as such comes into view in 1637 with a protest against the alleged badness of Mansell's glass, probably in concert with the Glaziers Company. In 1664 it received its charter.

The Restoration of 1660 was wisely and widely welcomed because the people had discovered that progress was impossible under a party which ruled by the boot, and whose supporters were in the main characterized by intolerance and stupidity. A genial blackguard may be a pleasanter ruler than an intolerant bore. That Cromwell raised the power and influence of England to as high a relative point as it has ever reached in our history meant little to the peasant who had to deal with his sententious—and, can it be doubted, his frequently hypocritical—unlovable troopers. It meant still less to the trader whose trade was lost or bridled. A democracy of the 17th century had triumphed over a monarchical tyranny, which was good. But an eternal dictatorship appealed to nobody, so Charles came back to his throne, and a standing army has never since been acceptable to Englishmen.

With Charles back, a new enthusiasm was immediately apparent, and nowhere was this more decisively exhibited than in the arts and sciences. England, already far behind the Continent in such matters, had twenty years of leeway to make up as well. A charter to, and a quick transformation of, the Glass Sellers, was one of the results. Imbued with the prevailing spirit, their policy became constructive and helpful, and until the end of the century the company exercised a control which was none the less real for being discreetly disguised. It shows the strides the industry had made that the company, as a seller, could in effect dictate what the manufacturer should make. It chose wisely, and could afford practical encouragement, and of course it relieved the actual glass-makers of much anxiety by offering a ready market and a steady market for their wares.

It was as much to run with the now-fashionable scientific hound as to hunt the profitable hare that George Villiers, second Duke of Buckingham, usurped the position Mansell had held. He was perhaps drawn into the affair by one John de la Cam, who persuaded the Duke to finance a scheme for making 'rock crystal' glass, and, of course, to procure the necessary patent. The Duke obligingly complied, and for the next fourteen years (1660–74) he had a finger in every pie containing glass. Naturally he knew nothing about glass in itself, and when people who did, Clifford and Powlden, and Thomas Tilson, also obtained licences—but not patents—to make particular kinds of glass, the Duke enlisted them in his own service and turned their licences into patents, to their mutual advantage. It was the same when John Bellingham proposed to make mirrors by a secret process. The Duke gave him a handsome salary, put him in charge of the Vauxhall plate glasshouse, and secured the patent for himself.

Whether these transactions were profitable, we do not know. Very likely the Duke was equally ignorant, and content that things should go on as they were in the habit of doing, provided nobody troubled him unduly. He had plenty of other duties, and pleasures, to occupy his thoughts. I think we may infer that the Glass Sellers quietly stepped into the breach which would normally have been caused by the Duke's absences and inattention, and guided his various managers in the way they should go. On the all-important business side, as retailers, the company men best knew what the public wanted, and when it could not get its ideals realized, they were courageous enough to find an experimentalist, and wealthy enough to back him, as we shall see.

We know very little about the Duke's glass, except that it was good glass as things then went, and that it could be extremely thinly blown. We do not know that all of it was like that, but we have that one pointer. Of existing specimens, the 'Royal Oak' goblet of 1663, commemorating the marriage of Charles II and Catherine of Braganza, is the most famous. There is the 'Exeter' flute with a bust portrait of Charles II and the sprouting oak stump, and there is the 'Scudamore' flute, with the Royal Arms and those of the Scudamore family. Both these date from shortly after 1660, and all three are quite likely to be from one of Buckingham's glasshouses. Their form is certainly Netherlandish, but that proves nothing, as they were also international. Minor Buckingham glasses have yet to be recognized.

In the meantime, the demand for good glasses began to outrun supply. The prohibition of foreign glass had lapsed, and we find one John Greene, a prominent member of the company, corresponding with Alessio Morelli of Murano (1667–73), and directing what they should make and how they should make it (Pl. 32a, b). We are, indeed, fortunate in having some of this correspondence, and still more fortunate that Greene's designs, lettered and life-size, have been preserved. Some of these designs will be found in various text-books, but there are over four hundred of them in all, and we await their reproduction *in extenso* with impatience and, at present, small hope. Morelli had yet to learn that the customer is always right, and his interpretation of Greene's orders left a lot to be desired. Or so Greene thought and plaintively wrote, and considering that he had to contend with appreciable breakages *en route* (which will surprise nobody who has handled one of Morelli's glasses) it was natural that the company should embark on a policy of research at home.

The man selected, or who came forward at need, was George Ravenscroft, a man of intelligence and scientific attainments, and of sufficiently independent mind and means to accept guidance but not direction. It was a good and timely choice. Dr. Merret had translated Neri's *Art of Glass* in 1662 and had given Englishmen a much-wanted guide of which Ravenscroft will have made full use, and from which he may have drawn his inspiration to use lead as a flux.

In 1673 Ravenscroft built a glasshouse in the Savoy and shortly afterwards applied for a patent. It was granted in May, 1674, by which time the Duke's patents were expiring and Ravenscroft and the company had come to terms. There was a second glasshouse, primarily an experimental plant, at Henley-on-Thames, a location which must have had something more than isolation to recommend it but one seemingly ill-situated from a fuel point of view. It was at this house that another Da Costa was working in 1675. Ravenscroft knew what was particularly wanted, a metal which would combine strength with clarity, something which would resemble rock crystal and yet have the tractability of glass. His first experiments were on long-familiar lines, and they gave him a crystal-like metal which was both thick and clear, but it was subject to surface decomposition. Plate 32c shows such a specimen, perhaps the only existing one. It is free of any trace of lead and its mere existence suggests that the decomposition, or "crizzling" as it is called, was a progressive disease. Its form is derived with considerable exactitude from the Egyptian *œnochoe* of Chap. I.

Before long Ravenscroft thought of introducing oxide of lead into the batch, and the crizzling trouble was reduced, but not overcome. Further experimental work on the proportions of the mixture led him to think that success had been achieved, and in June, 1676, the Glass Sellers Company announced that earlier faults had been remedied and that future supplies would be satisfactory. In May, 1677, the now famous 'raven's head' seal was adopted, to distinguish the new glasses from the old, and a fresh three year agreement was executed between Ravenscroft and the Company, providing for a supply of the perfected glasses to, and their purchase by, the company.

Shortly after, and rather unaccountably, Ravenscroft gave the necessary six months notice to determine this agreement, and unless there was some unrecorded gentlemen's agreement whereby Hawly Bishopp carried on work in Ravenscroft's name at the Savoy, and that would be the less surprising alternative, we must conclude that the glasshouse ceased work altogether until Ravenscroft's patent expired and Bishopp could legitimately take over. The determination of the agreement need not have meant that Ravenscroft, or Bishopp as his deputy, did not go on as before—though no longer by obligation—making the much-wanted glasses, at least until Ravenscroft's death in May, 1681, which practically coincided with the expiry of the patent.

The satisfaction demonstrated by the use of the seal was perhaps a little premature, because most of the sealed glasses are (at least now) crizzled, as are a number of specimens of the Hawly Bishopp era which ensued. It seems to me that the seal was therefore quietly dropped. At all events, only nine or ten sealed specimens are known, against many more unsealed ones, and logically the so-called perfect glasses ought to outnumber the imperfect ones because recognizably bad glasses would have been destroyed. There are a few lead glasses which "sweat" profusely, that is to say they cloud over with a semi-sticky moisture. It can be washed off, but will return, and I regard this as an intermediate stage in the progressive disease.

Looked at as a whole, I think that Ravenscroft succeeded early in making a perfect lead metal. Pl. 33a shows such a specimen, which corresponds with one of Greene's designs and with a broken example (in greenish soda metal) in the London Museum. It is, incidentally, conclusive proof that Greene acted as he threatened Morelli he would act, viz. place his orders at home instead of at Venice. It is also the only known specimen to link Greene and Ravenscroft. Now this is a light glass. The metal is thin, and for that reason did not satisfy the company. What I think Ravenscroft found so difficult was to make a thick strong glass of equally perfect metal. They may have looked good enough when they came from the annealing oven—hence the optimistic seal—but in time a good many of them developed the old troublous fault in some degree.

If the proportions of the salts and the lead were correctly related, as eventually they were, a perfect glass would result. Otherwise crizzling may have been more apt to occur in heavy glasses than in light ones, even though at any moment in an experimental period mere chance might produce an occasional pot of perfect metal. It is a notable fact that, two generations later, the Lauenstein glasshouse in Hanover, the first we know of to make lead glass on the Continent, had exactly the same troubles that Ravenscroft experienced.

Bishopp officially took over the Savoy glasshouse in February, 1682, and had his own agreement with the company. If anything was still wanting, either in the metal itself or the power to repeat it at will, the credit for the discovery must be his. It is quite likely his in any case. Ravenscroft had made the essential discovery, but I cannot help thinking that it was Bishopp who rounded it off. By May, 1682, new flint glasses, as they were called, were in full production, and members of the company were selling them to the public at prices of 6s. a dozen for light or 'single flint' ones, and 12s. a dozen for 'double flint' glasses, i.e. strong ones. reputedly made of two gatherings of the metal. Pl. 33d shows one such simple glass, very slightly crizzled. The prices soon came down.

Apart from the sealed Ravenscroft specimens and similar

unsealed examples, it is seldom possible to be certain whether Ravenscroft or Bishopp was the maker (Pl. 33b, c). The years 1674 to 1681 were years of trial and error, and the glass of this period is often and quite fairly termed 'experimental lead'. On the whole it was utility glass—jugs, tazzas, bowls and other items, with stemmed drinking glasses in a minority (Pl. 34a, b). The Bishopp metal seems to me rather whiter (less coloured), rather less heavy, and naturally less crizzled. A few commemorative ceremonial goblets with hollow quatrefoil knops are very likely to be his work (Pl. 34c). It only remains to add that the new metal was thought good enough for export, and the Continent thought it good enough to engrave. A very few notable specimens have survived, the latest to be recorded being a sealed roemer engraved (apparently in diamond-point) with the Arms of Poland. The foot bears an inscription and what appears to be a battle scene. It was a gift to John Sobieski in 1677 from the City of Danzig, where it is, or was in 1939. This particular piece must be a Ravenscroft glass, perhaps the first example to be found with the plain seal (the illustration is not clear) which is known to have preceded the 'raven's head' by a few months. Recently I have had another. There were a very few other seals, with which fragmentary specimens have been found, notably one in soda metal with a female figure using a bow, conjecturally the make of Bowles and Lillington. All sealing, however, was short-lived.

By 1685 the new lead metal was being made almost as a matter of course, and the Glass Sellers Company could congratulate itself on a forward policy which had indeed returned it dividends beyond all expectation, and which sufficed at one stroke to put English glass in a premier position. It was to hold this position for a hundred years. At the same time, the celebrity of lead metal should not lead us to suppose that soda metal was abandoned (Pl. 32d). Lead glass was preferred by all manufacturers whose business it was to make fine quality glasses, but there are precisely similar types to be found in a soda metal which can be very good indeed and which is often not recognized as soda metal at all. For utility glass and cheap glass, a great deal of soda metal continued to be used, particularly in the north. It presents an almost untouched field for the collector and its investigation will bring out some surprising facts.

With 1685 a new era in English glass begins, and it is from this date that most collections commence. Something of the many types and fashions will be described in subsequent chapters.

FOR FURTHER READING

BUCKLEY, W. *Diamond Engraved Glasses.*
HARTSHORNE, A. *Old English Glasses.*
PERCIVAL, M. *The Glass Collector.* 1918.
POWELL, H. J. *Glassmaking.*
THORPE, W. A. *As before.*
WINBOLT, S. E. *Wealden Glass.*

PLATE 1. Egyptian glasses in *pâté de verre*, conventionally 500 B.C.
a. *Oenochoe*, white body, purple decoration
b. *Oenochoe*, purple brown, with palmette decoration
c. *Amphora*, lapis lazuli blue, pale blue and yellow decoration
d. *Alabastron*, as c.

PLATE 2. Roman Glass, 1st to 4th century
a. Thin clear glass beaker with " thumb pressed " body and sheared rim
b. Footed wine cup in greenish glass. c. Small blue mould-blown bottle
d. Ice-green press-moulded drinking bowl, heavily ribbed beneath
e. Amber drinking bowl, groved and finished on the wheel
f. Vase in near-clear glass, stringing and zigzags in dark green
g. Flat mould-blown *unguentarium*. h. Small purple white-marbled bottle

PLATE 3. Roman Glass, 1st to 4th century
a. Many-sided mould-blown bottle
b. Dropping-bottle, simulating a cactus, in yellowish glass
c. Janus bottle, greenish glass
d. Closely wrythen *unguentarium*, greenish glass
e. Handled and looped *unguentarium*, stringing in dark green

PLATE 4. Gallic Glass, 1st to 4th century
a. Ewer, trailed handle. Amiens
b. Ewer, Medusa mask. Amiens
c. Frontinus bottle, marked FRON. Seine area
d. Palm cup, spiked kick in base. Rhine area

PLATE 5. Glass of the 5th to 8th century
a. Large *amphora* or water pitcher, blue on green. Syria 6th/7th century
b. Tripod *unguentarium*, blue on greenish. Syria 5th/8th century
c. Drinking bowl, clear bluish metal, excavated at Faversham. 7th/8th century

PLATE 6. Islamic and early German Glass

a. Trailed bottle, amber on amber. Islamic, 6th century
b. *Unguentarium* with cage or grill, set on horseback; amber and blue on amber. Islamic, 6th/8th century
c. Small drinking or other bowl of granular glass. German, 10th/12th century or Irak, 9th century
d. *Maigelein*, with smooth black incrustation. German, 15th century

PLATE 7. Islamic Glass, 8th/10th century

a. Mould-blown bottle with bulbed neck. Islamic, 8th/10th century
b. Ring beaker, blue on greenish. Syria, 8th/9th century
c. Small wheel-cut bottle. Islamic, 8th/9th century
d. Facet-cut bottle. Islamic, 9th/10th century

PLATE 8. Islamic Glass, 10th/13th century
a. Parti-coloured mould-blown bottle in amber and blue. 10th
b. Mould-blown ewer. 10th century
c. Shallow mould-blown bowl in rich blue glass. 12th/13th cen
d. Sprinkler bottle, green on pale amber. 12th century

PLATE 9. Syrian and Islamic Glasses

a. Thin-walled "snake thread" dropping bottle. Syria, 3rd/5th century
b. Heavy-walled dropping bottle, with trailing finished to simulate carved aquatic birds. Perhaps Syria, 5th/6th century
c. Damascus sprinkler bottle, blue enamel device at base of neck and decorative body band in red colour. End of 13th century
d. Beaker, banded red and gold decoration at top and bottom. 14th

PLATE 10. Glass made in Iran or for the Iranian market
a. Sprinkler bottle in ivory white glass. 12th century
b. Wine bottle, green and red, with nail-shaped stopper. Perhaps 14th century.
c. Standing bowl, Aleppo "*rotreliefierte*" type. C. 1260

PLATE 11. Scale-gilt and jewelled Venetian bowls
a. First half of the 16th century
b. Second half of the 16th century

PLATE 12. French and Venetian Glass

a. Marriage goblet, enamelled in colours, with DE BON ♥ LE VOUS DONNE and Latin Biblical quotations. French, 16th century
b. Crackle-glass vase. 16th/17th century
c. Wine cup, gilt and jewelled rim, blue foot. 15th century
d. Phial of Syrian 11th/12th cent. type, in green, "excavated in Finsbury"
e. Goblet, lion-mask stem 16th/17th century

PLATE 13. Venetian Glass
a. Bowl of a goblet-vase, from a two-piece mould. See pl. 34. 16th century
b. Covered vase, in *latticinio* glass. 16th/17th century.
c., d., e. Wines of the 17th century

PLATE 14. Flared beaker, with the Fugger arms in coloured enamel, partly on a gold ground. Dated 1584. Set in an ancient copper foot for stability

PLATE 15. Rhineland and Antwerp Glass

a. Beaker, Lotharingian. Later 16th century
b. "Unbreakable" beaker. Lotharingian. Dated 1663
c. Goblet, ribbed and horizontally strung, lion-mask stem. Perhaps Dutch, 16th century
d. Goblet-vase, part in crackle glass. Neptune masks on bowl and stem. Antwerp, 16th century

PLATE 16. Glass of the Low Countries

a. Goblet, the knop moulded and *sémé d'or*. Liége, 16th/17th century
b. Tall wine. Antwerp, 16th/17th century
c. Goblet, with "beech nut" moulding. Amsterdam, 16th/17th century
d. Goblet-vase, mould-blown bowl showing pair of opposed lions. Antwerp, 16th/17th century

PLATE 17. Glass of the Low Countries
a. Trick glass, perhaps Spanish Netherlands. Early 17th century
b., c., d. Wines. Belgian, 17th century

PLATE 18. Glass of the Low Countries

a. Thin-walled beaker of international form. Holland, 17th century

b. Small "hour-glass" ewer in *latticinio* glass. Antwerp, early 17th century

c. Tazza, stepped and ribbed bowl. Belgian, 17th century

d. Goblet, with spiked gadrooning, one quatrefoil and one pear knop. Liége, c. 1680

PLATE 19. Glass of indecisive origin

a. Peasant goblet in *verre de fougère*, sheared rim and double-blown foot. Perhaps 15th/16th century

b. *Bénitier*, probably by Carré of Antwerp and London. 3rd quarter of 16th century

c. Standing bowl, the rim with blue circuits and formerly gilt, foot rim overlaid with blue. Presumed English, late 16th/early 17th century

PLATE 20. German Enamelled Glass

a. *Reichsadlerhumpen* dated 1592 b. *Apostelglas* c. 1600 c. Ceremonial beaker and cover dated 1641

PLATE 21. German Enamelled and Painted Glass

a. Bun-footed beaker, painted by Schaper with armorials. Landscape and ruins on reverse. Mid 17th century

b. *Humpen* and cover, enamelled with the arms of Frederick Augustus, King of Poland and Elector of Saxony, c. 1740

c. *Passglas*, dated 1723

d. Beaker, painted in black. 18th century

PLATE 22. Painted Glass

a. Ale, with wash-enamel decoration by Beilby, Gp. X, 4g
b. Bristol opaque white vase and cover, painted by Edkins or his school. 3rd quarter of the 18th century
c. Wine, with vine border in white enamel by Beilby, Gp. X, 3g
d. Bohemian scent bottle, with enamel decoration in colours. 3rd quarter 18th century
e. Wine, with fox-hunting scene by Beilby in white enamel, Gp. X, [illegible]

PLATE 23. Painted Glass

a. Cup and saucer in blue-speckled milk-glass. German or Dutch, 18th century
b. Cup and saucer, black and yellow decoration. 18th century. (See Chap. VII)
c. Canister bottle, painted in colours. Central European, c. 1775
d. Tumbler, good milk-glass, enamelled in colours VIVA CARLOS III REY DE ESPAÑA
e. Beaker, "Fish in an aquarium" attributed to Kothgasser, c. 1820

PLATE 24. Diamond-engraved Glasses

a. Bowl, with monsters and floral repeat. Dutch, 16th/17th century

b. Roemer, with fishing scene. Lotharingian, etched in Holland, early 17th century

c. Wine, with conventional floral repeat. Italian or Dutch, 17th century

PLATE 25. Stippled and Engraved Glasses

a. English wine, stippled in dots ; probably by Wolff, late 18th century
b. English goblet, stippled in line with the arms and ordination of Adriaan Wittert. Artist unknown, 1765
c. Nuremberg goblet, with continuous landscape scene. c. 1720
d. Potsdam goblet, engraved with the arms of George I as Elector of Hanover and (reverse King of England). c. 1715

PLATE 26. Surface-engraved Glasses

a. Gilt and engraved Zechlin goblet, c. 1742. (See Chap. XI)
b. Lauenstein goblet and cover, glass of lead, with arms of the Emperor Francis I, c. 1760
c. Engraved and gilded goblet, monogram of Catherine the Great of Russia, 1762–96
d. Silesian goblet; with scenes illustrating the linen trade. c. 1755

PLATE 27. Surface engraving and acid engraving

a. Bohemian beaker, with Napoleon in silhouette, c. 1821
b. Engraved beaker, by Anton Simm, c. 1835
c. Square-footed rummer, showing the arms (modernised) of the burgh of Leith, on reverse a variant of the royal Scottish arms, the sinister pennant having a Jacobite flavour, c. 1800
d. Acid-etched Rummer, bluish lead glass. English, 1840–50

PLATE 28. Engraving in low and high-relief

a. Beaker, with David and Goliath, engraved in low-relief. Bohemian, 1st half of 18th century
b. Goblet and cover, engraved in high-relief. Silesian, c. 1740
c. Vase, overlaid and cameo-cut. By de Vez, modern French
d. Vase, overlaid and cameo-cut. Webb and Son, England, c. 1910

PLATE 29. Other decorative techniques

a. Bohemian beaker, with "inserted gold" decoration, c. 1740
b. English ale, with oil-gilt hop and barley decoration, c. 1760
c. Figure of St. Peter, in coloured *pâté de verre*. French, Nevers, 17th century
d. A devotional emblem, with *crystalle-ceramie* decoration. Paris, 1830–40

Plate 30. Modern Glass

a. Modern French vase in tinted glass. Lalique

b. Satin glass spill vase in shaded blue and silver. English, late 19th century

c. Victorian raspberry-red vase, mounted as a ewer. Attributed to Birmingham, 1840–50

PLATE 31. English 17th century Glass
a. Chalice, double-blown bowl with silver foil inserted. Mansell period, c. 1642
b. Goblet, lion-mask stem and deep emerald bowl. Antwerp or London
c. Strong hollow cigar-shaped stem. Mansell period, excavated in London
d. Hollow lion-mask stem. Mansell period, excavated in London

PLATE 32. English 17th century Glass

a. Wine, a close approach to one of Greene's patterns, attributed to Morelli of Venice, c. 1670
b. Posset pot. Perhaps Venetian, for the English market, c. 1670
c. Jug in soda metal, heavily crizzled. Early Ravenscroft period, c. 1674
d. Goblet, distinct traces of lead, probably from the use of lead cullet. Presumed English, for the Dutch market, c. 1700

PLATE 33. English 17th century Glass
a. A Greene pattern in uncrizzled glass of lead, presumably by Ravenscroft, c. 1675
b. Flute, with horizontal blue milled trails, glass of lead, c. 1680
c. Quatrefoil-knopped wine, glass of lead, c. 1680
d. Wine, crizzled glass of lead, c. 1680–82

PLATE 34. English 17th century Glass

a. Large goblet, glass of lead, in Netherlands style, c. 1685 (cf. pl. 31b)
b. The stem and foot of a quatrefoil-knopped and winged goblet. Glass of lead. Hawly Bishopp period, c. 1681. (See pl. 13a)
c. Quatrefoil-knopped goblet, crizzled glass of lead. Engraved with the arms of the Province of Utrecht. Hawly Bishopp period, c. 1681

PLATE 35. Some types of decoration to English 18th century wines
a Moulded ribbing
b. Moulded wide fluting
c. Diamond and/or honey-comb moulding
d. Leaf or petal moulding (?)
e. Scale cutting
f. Panel moulding

PLATE 36. Further types of bowl, rim and foot

a. Bowl moulded with wide fluting: denticulated rim: foot, pressed radial grooves
b. Overstrung foot (enlarged)
c. Folded rim: milled thistle foot
d. Tavern dram with corrugated bowl

See also

i Faint fluting, pl. 54 c, 59d.
ii Wrythen bowl, pl. 62j
iii Part-wrythenbowl, pl. 63d
iv Swirled ribbing, pl. 63a: (merges with ii)
v Flammiform gadrooning, pl. 63b
vi Plain gadrooning, pl. 62a
vii Sunk gadrooning: as vi, but no horizontal ridge, *cf.* i
viii Oversewn foot, as (d) above, but with fine threading
ix Lynn bowl, pl. 58d

PLATE 37. Baluster Glasses

a. Goblet with cipher of George I, Gp. I, 1a
b. Goblet with cipher (T 5 E) for Prince Thomas Emanuel, Count of Soissons, 1702–29 etc., etc. Gp. I, 2a
c. Wine. Gp. I, 8
d. Cordial. Gp. I, 11b

PLATE 38. Moulded Pedestal Stems

a. Wine, hand-forged stem. Gp. II, 1a
b. Wine, thistle bowl. Gp. II, 1a
c. Wine. Gp. II, 3d
d. Wine, engraved in diamond point with the arms of the Province of Utrecht, strolling players on reverse. Gp. II, 7c

PLATE 39. Moulded Pedestal Stems
a. Wine. Gp. II, 5
b. Sweetmeat, denticulated rim. Gp. II, 7b
c. Wine, engraved with the arms of the Seven Provinces. Gp. II, 7c
d. Champagne. Gp. II, 9a
e. Covered goblet or sweetmeat. Gp. II, 11c

PLATE 40. Balustroid Stems

a. Low champagne. Gp. III, 1a
b. Trinket glass (?) with folded and spired rim. Gp. III, 1c
c. Wine. Gp. III, 1
d. Wine. Gp. III, 1c
e. Wine. Gp. III, 2c (but with base knop)

PLATE 41. Balustroid stems
a. Wine. Gp. III, 3a
b. Wine. Gp. III, 3b
c. Champagne. Gp. III, 4b
d. Ale. Gp. III, 4a

PLATE 42. Balustroid Stems

a. Early Jacobite wine with Rose and single bud, before 1741. Gp. III, 5
b. Wine. Gp. III, 7
c. Wine. Gp. III, 9b
d. Wine. Gp. III, 9e

Plate 43. Balustroid Stems
a. Wine. Gp. III, 10d
b. Ale. Gp. III, 10n
c. Wine. Gp. III, 10g
d. Goblet. Gp. III, 10b
e. Toastmaster's glass. Gp. III, 10a
f. Wine, plain gadrooning. Gp. III, 10j

PLATE 44. Light (Newcastle) Balusters

a. Wine. Gp. IV, 1a
b. Wine. Gp. IV, 1b
c. Wine, engraved with the arms of the Admiralty of the United Provinces. Gp. IV, 1j
d. Betrothral or marriage glass (?) ("I love but one"); Dutch engraving, probably by Sang. Gp. IV, 1l

PLATE 45. Light (Newcastle) Balusters
a. Wine. Dutch engraving. Gp. IV, 1m
b. Wine. Gp. IV, 2b
c. Wine. Gp. IV, 2
d. Goblet. Gp. IV, 3d

PLATE 46. Light (Newcastle) Balusters
- a. Wine. Gp. IV, 4a
- b. Wine. Gp. IV, 5
- c. Wine, Dutch-engraved, " Het Welvaaren Van De Leepelaer." Gp. IV, 6a (but knops at base)
- d. Wine. Gp. IV, 7a

PLATE 47. Light (Newcastle) Balusters
a. Goblet, Dutch-engraved. Gp. IV, 7h
b. Wine. Gp. IV, 7
c. Gin. Gp. IV, 8
d. Wine. Gp. IV, 7l. (See Chap. XI)

Plate 48. Composite Stems
a. Wine. Gp. V, 1b
b. Wine. Gp. V, 1c
c. Wine. Gp. V, 2e
d. Champagne. Gp. V, 2h (but no base knop)

Plate 49. Composite Stems
a. Wine, Dutch-engraved. Gp. V, 2l
b. Wine. Gp. V, 3b
c. Wine, Dutch-engraving ; with coat of Holland. Gp. V, 4a
d. Wine, Dutch-engraving. Gp. V, 4

PLATE 50. Plain Straight Stems
a. " Williamite " cordial, Irish. Gp. VI, e
b. Newcastle wine. Gp. VI, f
c. Wine, panel-moulded bowl and foot. Gp. VI, g
d. Georgian Wine or Dram. Gp. XIII, 5Ag
e. Toasting glass. Gp. VI, f

PLATE 51. Air Twist Stems

a. Wine. Gp. VII, 1b
b. Wine. Gp. VII, 1a
c. Jacobite wine, with two-budded Rose, Star and "Redeat" on bowl: Oak Society. Gp. VII, 2c
d. Jacobite semi-cordial, with two-budded Rose, and "Redi" with twin oak-leaves on foot. Gp. VII, 2c
e. Cordial (Cf. pl. 53b). Gp. VII, 2a

PLATE 52. Air Twist Stems

a. Jacobite " Audentior Ibo " wine. Gp. VII, 4c
b. Wine, with the arms of the City of Norwich. Gp. VII, 4d
c. Wine, probably of Newcastle origin. Gp. VII, 4h
d. Wine, saucer-topped bowl. Gp. VII, 4b

PLATE 53. Air Twist Stems

a. Wine, with domed foot and "flowered" decoration. Gp. VII, 5c
b. Cordial, faint-fluted bowl and folded foot (cf. pl. 51e). Gp. VII, 5f
c. Small goblet. Gp. VII, 5d
d. Wine, bowl honeycomb moulded at base. Gp. VII, 6a
e. Cordial. Gp. VII, 6e
f. Toastmaster's glass. Gp. VII, 6d

PLATE 54. Hollow Stems. Incised Twist Stems
a. Sweetmeat. Gp. VIII, 1a
b. Wine. Gp. VIII, 2a
c. Wine. Gp. IX, 1a
d. Wine. Gp. IX, 2 Ac
e. Wine. Gp. IX, 2 Bb

PLATE 55. Opaque Twist Stems

a. Wine. Gp. X, 1 b i
b. Wine. Gp. X, 1 a iii (but with base knop)
c. Jacobite wine, with Rose and two buds : soda metal. Gp. X, 2c
d. Champagne, folded rim. Gp. X, 3b
e. Frigate or Privateer glass (" Success to the Lyon Privateer "). Gp. X, 3d
f. Wine. Gp. X, 3

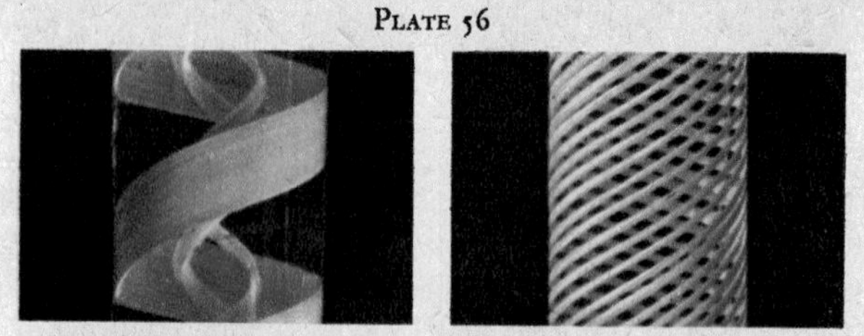

1. Pr. of Spiral Tapes or Threads/Single Close Multi-ply Spiral Band: *also* 1, 3, 4 or 8 *do.* Threads: Pr. of *do.* Bands: Pr. of Solid Spiral Bands 2. Multiple Spiral Twist

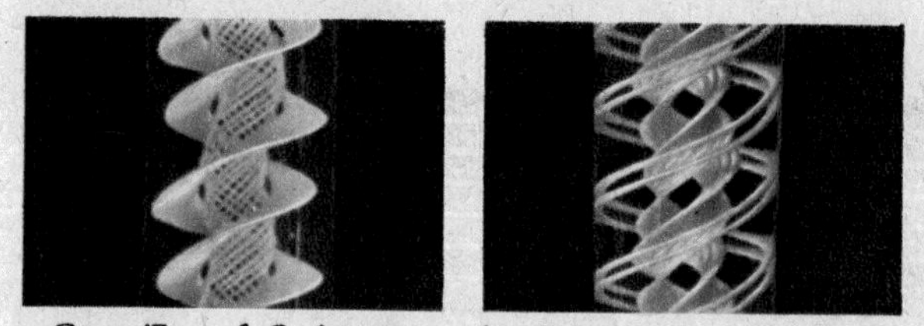

3. Gauze/Pr. of Corkscrews: *also* Gauze with Core: Twin Corkscrews 4. Pr. of Multi-ply Spiral Tapes/Pr. of 2-5 ply Spiral Bands: *also* Four *do.* Tapes: Four 2-3 ply Spiral Bands

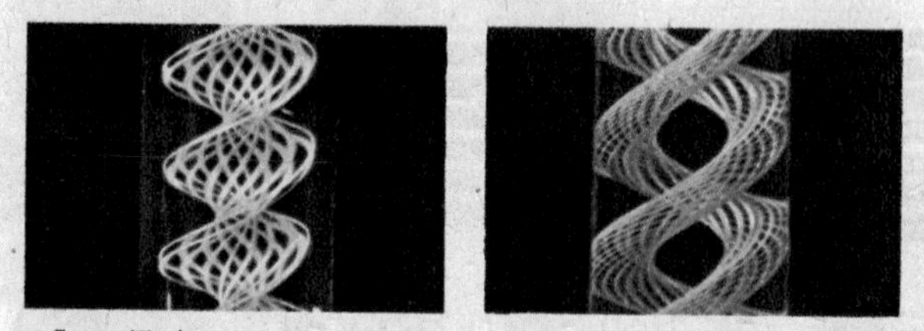

5. Lace Twist 6. Pr. of Spiral Gauzes: *also* Three Spiral Gauzes

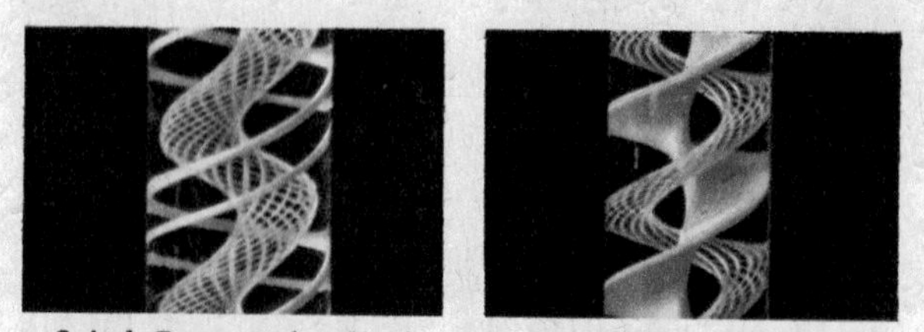

7. Spiral Gauze and a Single 2-ply Spiral Band: *also do.* and a 3-, 4-, or 5-ply Spiral Band 8. Spiral Gauze and a Corkscrew

PLATE 57

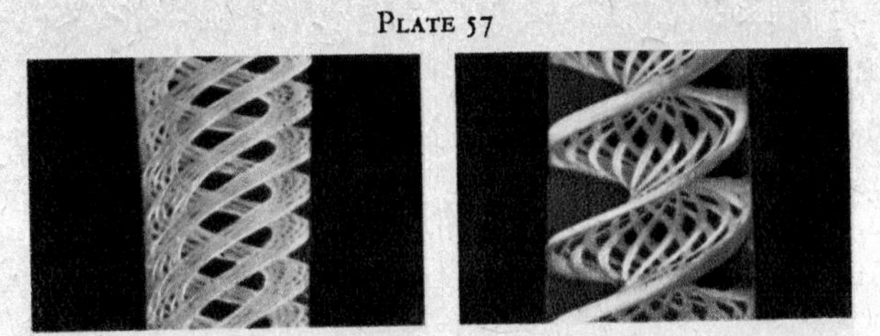

9. Four Spiral Gauzes 10. Lace Twist Outlined

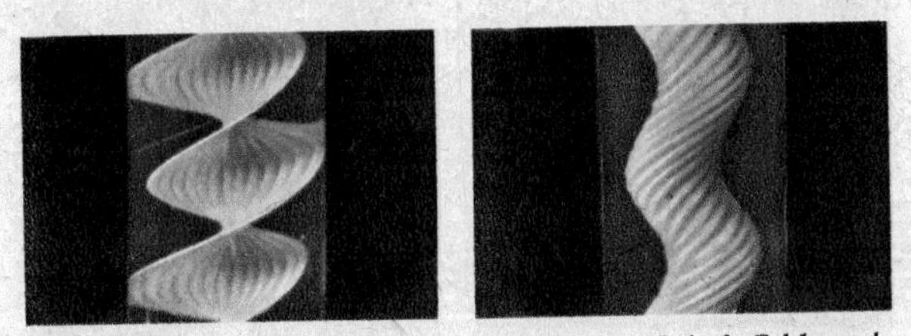

11. Multi-ply Corkscrew: *also* Pr. of *do.* 12. Spiral Cable: *also* Pr. of *do.*: Vertical Cable

13. Spiral Gauze with Core: *also* Pr. of *do.* 14. Pair of Multi-ply Spiral "U" Bands

15. Corkscrew/Single 6-10 ply Spiral Band: *also* Pr. of 6-10 ply Spiral Bands 16. Vertical Column/Four Corkscrews/Single 10-20 ply Spiral Band: *also* Vertical Thread: Screwed Vertical Column

PLATE 58. Opaque Twist Stems

a. Wine, with opalescent stem. Gp. X, 3h
b. Dram, terraced foot. Gp. X, 4
c. Champagne, with plain gadrooning. Gp. X, 4b
d. Lynn (or Norwich) wine, with three horizontal ridges. Gp. X, 4g
e. Ale, ribbed bowl and foot. Gp. X, 4k
f. Ratafia. Gp. X, 4f

PLATE 59. Mixed Twist Stems
a. Wine. Gp. XI, 1 A i
b. Wine. Gp. XI, 1 B ai
c. Wine. Gp. XI, 4 D b
d. Wine. Gp. XI, 5.

PLATE 60. Faceted Stems

a. Wine. Gp. XII, 2 b b. Wine. Gp. XII, 1 Ba

c. Wine with scalloped firing foot. Gp. XII, 2c

d. Ale, engraved with hops and barley. Gp. XII, 2c

e. Goblet, with English engraving. Gp. XII, 3

f. "Britannia" wine, commemorating the Treaty of Paris, 1763. Gp. XII, 3b

PLATE 61. Jacobite Glasses

a. Disguised glass, with Rose, two buds, butterfly, and grub. Gp. VII, 2c
b. c. Front and Reverse of Mourning glass, with Forget-me-nots. Gp. VII, 5a
d. Wine, with Rose and two buds, Oakleaf, and *Fiat* on bowl; Prince of Wales plumes on foot. Gp. VI, f
e. Wine, with engraved and polished Rose and single bud. Gp. XII, 3b
f. A later wine. See Chap. X. Gp. XII, 2b

PLATE 62. Other Rudimentary Stems
a. Dwarf ale, with plain gadrooning. Gp. XIII, 2a
b. Dram, thistle foot. Gp. XIII, 2a
c. Jelly, flanged rim. Gp. XIII, 2a
d. Jelly. XIII, 3 Aa
e. Jelly. XIII, 3 Ac
f. Jelly. XIII, 3 A
g. Jelly. XIII, 3 Bb
h. Jelly. XIII, 3 Cb
j. Dwarf ale. XIII, 4 Aa ii

PLATE 63. Other Rudimentary Stems

a. Dwarf ale. XIII, 4 Aa iii
b. Dwarf ale. XIII, 4 Aa vi
c. Dwarf ale. XIII, 4 B
d. Dwarf ale. XIII, 4 Da, part wrythen
e. Geo. wine. XIII, 4 Ec, wide fluting
f. "Thistle" dram. XIII, 4 Fd
g. Geo. ale. XIII, 4 Gc
h. Rummer. XIII, 4 H a, wide fluting
j. Rummer. XIII, 4 Hc

PLATE 64. Other Rudimentary Stems

a. Geo. wine. XIII, 4 K
b. Dram. XIII, 4 N
c. Geo. wine. XIII, 5 Ac
d. Tavern dram. XIII, 5 Ac,
e. Dwarf ale, deceptive bowl. XIII, 5 Bb
f. Rummer, hollow domed and square foot. XIII, 5 B
g. Rummer, solid domed and square foot. XIII, 5 Bd
h. Rummer. XIII, 5 Bf
j. Rummer. XIII, 6 A, vertical ribbing

CHAPTER X

Jacobite Glass

NOBODY who writes about English glass can escape a mention of our Jacobite glasses. Scores of articles have been compiled on this difficult theme, and a wealth of sentiment lavished upon the romantic adventures of Bonnie Prince Charlie, to the extent that a glass collector unfamiliar with our 18th century history might get an entirely fanciful view of it.

With apologies to those who know, let it first be said that the term Jacobean is only attributable to objects of the reign of James I; that the epithet Jacobin refers to those who favoured the anti-monarchical ideas of the French Revolution; and that a Jacobite is a partisan of James II or his descendants. We commonly extend this last term to cover propaganda and objects sympathetic to the Stuart cause.

Let it also be said that seldom has a claimant to a throne had fewer real adherents than the so-called James III, James Francis Edward, the Old Pretender. And few of royal blood can ever have done more to antagonize what supporters he had, or less to draw new ones to his side. His own attempts in 1708, 1715, and 1719 had all failed dismally. His son Prince Charles Edward, born in 1720, inherited a hopeless cause, and if anything in our island story is certain, it is that no power on earth could have replaced a Stuart permanently on the English throne.

Abroad, the Papacy, Spain, and particularly Louis XV of France were either anti-Protestant or anti-Hanoverian or both, and ready enough to exploit the nuisance value of Jacobitism for their own ends, but none was prepared to risk backing it with any real strength.

At home, experience had already shown that any movement in Ireland was anti-English and anti-Protestant rather than pro-Stuart. The resources of that island were in any case too pitiful and its determination too uncertain for it to be much more than a benevolent hindrance. The idea that the Scots wanted a Stuart and not a Hanoverian is pure fantasy. The majority of those who dwelt in Scotland were anti-Catholic, and while a goodly number were sufficiently anti-Union to move them to the Stuart side, the desires of most were those of the common man, peace and a stable government. The Highlanders, a race apart which in the 17th century was regarded as a race of hereditary cattle-thieving savages, cared neither for Stuart nor Hanoverian. Their loyalties were exclusively to their chieftains, who had never bowed to kingly authority in the past, and had not the smallest intention of doing so in the future. Their upholding of the Stuart cause arose primarily out of clan jealousies, and neither those who espoused it nor those who stood aloof or opposed it had more than a perfunctory interest in the ultimate fortunes of the Pretenders.

And, since it was the English throne which was being sought, it is not too much to say that success depended on the English Jacobites. It would seem that James misled himself as to the real state of affairs, or was misled by over-enthusiastic or unscrupulous agents. It was characteristic of him to expect all and provide nothing, not even intelligent liaison. Louis, it appears, was more realistic.

As it was, in both the major attempts, the English Jacobites failed the cause. In 1715, they had indeed little chance of influencing the issue. They seem to have been taken unawares, and some of the English Catholic squires may easily have deceived themselves. They might inveigh against the wickedness of the usurper; they might find it great fun to play at treason; to drink toasts to the King over the Water; to organize their clubs and their coteries; and generally to plot and plan with an assiduity which might seem real enough, but which did not mislead the government. Especially was this the case after 1745.

After all, these dining, drinking, and fox-hunting squires

enjoyed their freedom and their estates in a time of increasing prosperity. It was one thing—and in England a very common thing—to rail at king and ministers in security, and quite another to implement an over-stated antagonism by rising in arms in support of a House they well knew had no backing from the people at large. Justice brings the thought that they might quickly have risen in arms had Louis been rash enough to land French troops in James' support, but then only to repel, not to further the invader and his *protégé*.

In short, outside a small body of sincere and loyal men, the Stuarts had no reliable supporters. What cards they had they played badly. The 1745 attempt was made almost in defiance of Louis' advice, and headed by a young and inexperienced man of twenty-five. Once committed, he needed to be fool indeed not quickly to have realized how insecure his backing was, how selfish most of his immediate adherents, and how uncertain his more distant friends. If he was forlorn and apprehensive in the days of his reign in Edinburgh, all the reasons stood beside him. It must have been with deep foreboding that Stuart obstinacy and princely intuition were permitted to override sound advice, to order action to replace festivity, and to commence the march which ended ingloriously at Derby. Yet it may have been as good an alternative as offered in a hopeless case.

To facilitate understanding of what follows, it is necessary to explain the 'Jacobite theory', which is here entirely recast. The standard Jacobite glass is engraved with a very stable Rose, having either one or two buds. They are commonly known as Rose glasses. Other emblems may be present, and of these the principal are a Thistle, an Oak Leaf, a Star, and the word 'Fiat'. Portraits and Latin tags are among devices of a more specialized nature.

All is based on the Rose, and years ago this was explained as follows: the large Rose was alleged to stand for James Francis Edward, the Old Pretender. Of the two buds, the larger one on the dexter side (the left as the glass is faced) is about to open, and this was said to represent Prince

Charles Edward, the Young Pretender. The other bud, on the sinister side (the right as the glass is faced) is unopened, and this was said to stand for Prince Henry Benedict, the younger son. Most of the glasses with the two-budded Rose precede those with the single bud, and the disappearance of one bud was said to coincide with the acceptance by Henry of a Cardinalship of the Church of Rome in 1747, whereafter he was no longer considered a possible heir to the English throne, and eliminated from English glass.

Subsequent writers have generally subscribed to this theory, some I think without much conviction. Among the most obvious difficulties is the existence of a few single-budded Roses (Pl. 42a) which are earlier than any two-budded Roses and which date from Prince Charles' legal infancy. There are also very many two-budded Roses which patently date long after 1747, the year Henry became a cardinal. It had to be conjectured that the engraver was carelessly working in the old tradition, putting two buds where only one was permissible, but nobody seems to have remarked that it is invariably the larger Charles Edward bud which is missing and not the small unopened Henry bud. There are other difficulties, and in short the theory is untenable, and another has to be formulated in its place.

The late Rev. J. G. Knowles once enunciated the basic solution in a paper read to the now defunct Arundel Society of Manchester, but he carried his exposition to no distance. Quite lately, Capt. W. Horridge, to whom I was indebted for the hint which threw an entirely new light on what had already become a widely open question, has been responsible for a pamphlet containing his own conclusions, based on a wide knowledge of Jacobite glass and Jacobite history. His account and explanation of the subsidiary Jacobite emblems diverges rather considerably from the story given here, but there is and, I think, must be, unanimity on the basic proposition. That is the important fact, the truth of which is surely vouched for by its simplicity. It is this.

The Rose did *not* represent James Francis Edward. It represented the Crown of England, just as it did on the counter-Jacobite glasses of the Hanoverian Georges. The one side claimed it, and the other possessed it, but it was the same Crown and to all intents and purposes the same Rose. The traditional connection needs no stressing when there is a 'Rose and Crown' in half the villages of England.

The earliest standard form of Jacobite engraving showed the Rose with a single unopened bud on the sinister side (Pl. 42a). For a short time this bud represented the Old Pretender, and so far Horridge agrees. But either in 1735 (when fifteen) or in 1741 (when twenty-one), his son Charles Edward came of age, and on the evidence of the types of glass used I think it was at the latter date that the Prince was deemed worthy of inclusion in the emblematic design. By this time Jacobite hopes were running high. It was deemed necessary to distinguish between father and son, so the former was represented by an expectant opening bud on the senior dexter side, and the latter took up the position and emblem his father had previously enjoyed on the sinister side. For the engraver it meant merely the addition of the dexter opening bud.

It is to be particularly noted that Henry was not represented in any way at all, either on the Rose glasses or on any other type of Jacobite glass, save only in some instances on the 'Amen' glasses, and then only by afterthought as it were. This accords perfectly with his unimportance in the eyes of even the most zealous Jacobite. From 1741, let us say, there was no change in the Rose and buds design for a quarter of a century. Then in 1766 the Old Pretender died, and properly to mark the change it was only necessary to omit the dexter bud, leaving the design as it had been on its inception. Further comment is needless. The crudities of the old theory vanish, and we are left, not only with a straightforward explanation, but with a new standard by which to assess the date of many interior-twist glasses. The rule is often—but not always—broken in cases where the thistle and rose form a wreath round a portrait of Prince Charles.

That is my explanation. Horridge thinks that on the two-budded Roses the larger bud always represented Charles; that the smaller one still represented James; and that such glasses were favoured by the many Jacobites who considered that Charles, not James, was the real hope of the Cause. He further credits the equally common single-budded Roses to those who still regarded James as the rightful king. I have to dissent, partly because such a state of affairs suggests impolitic comparisons, if not differences, but chiefly because it offers no explanation of those numerous single-budded Rose glasses patently made after the death of James. If the larger bud represented Charles how is it there are no late Rose glasses with that bud alone?

Given that explanation, some account of other Jacobite glasses can be proceeded with. The half century which included the risings of 1715 and 1745, and the other abortive attempts, and which concluded with the battle of Culloden Moor in 1745, is marked by comparatively few Jacobite glasses, but by just how many cannot be certainly known. There are a few early memorial specimens imprisoning a coin of Charles II or James II, still fewer individual records and disguised glasses, but there is only one stable type exclusively of this first period. It has already been referred to as being engraved with the first single-budded Rose. It never has any additional emblems and is very easily recognized, being a wine with a small-waisted bowl, a compositely-fashioned knopped stem with tears and a domed and folded foot. As mentioned, this type cannot be later than 1741* and is unlikely to be earlier than 1730.

Until recently, the Amen glasses, of which something over a score of genuine specimens exist, were regarded as the earliest stable type, and as having been made between 1720 and 1725 to commemorate the birth of one or other of the

* Or 1745, if it be assumed that Prince Charles was included in the design only after his arrival in Scotland.

two Princes. It was, however, recently shown that (as regards the engraving) not one of them could be earlier than 1735, that all were almost certainly post-1740, and further evidence since to hand makes it very probable that the whole series is post-Culloden.

An Amen glass is a glass engraved in 'diamond-point' with a royal crown, the cipher IR direct and reversed and incorporating the figure 8, together with (as a rule) either two or four verses of the Jacobite anthem, concluding with the word 'Amen'. They are essentially private glasses, expressions of personal loyalty to James the King, Charles Edward the Prince of Wales, and sometimes also to Prince Henry by particular mention. A few are dated, the Dunvegan Castle glass to 1747, the Mesham and the Drummond Castle glasses both to 1749. Some very dangerous forgeries were put into circulation in the 1930's.

It is possible that a few glasses bearing the word 'Fiat' may belong to this first period, but it is very certain that the great majority do not. They are quite numerous, a collector's favourite, and therefore fairly expensive. There are good forgeries and a motley collection of reproductions. 'Fiat' has been stated to be the peculiar Word of the Cycle Club, founded in 1710, reconstituted in 1724, but only glass-conscious (so far as we know) in the time of Sir Watkin Williams-Wynn, the second, from 1745 onwards. But the 'Fiat' is far too often and too differently found for it to be peculiar to the Cycle Club, and it is best regarded as a general 18th century Jacobite slogan, suggestive of enterprise but still quite non-committal (Pl. 61d).

After two centuries it seems clear enough to us that the battle of Culloden Moor, the ignominious flight of the Prince, and the subsequent penetration and pacification of the Highlands, together spelled final doom to Stuart hopes. Contemporary Jacobites, however, seem to have thought otherwise. Whether they were stimulated by defeat in the past or by hopes for the future, preparations were widely made for a further attempt, said to have been expected in 1750. Perhaps 'preparations' is too strong a word; our modern term 'propaganda' is more suitable, for while there is no evidence that the Pretender made any factual preparations at all, and indeed that side of it rested wholly with Louis XV, there was certainly much underground activity of a wordy sort among the English Jacobites.

It is to the two or three decades after Culloden that so many of our Rose glasses, all or nearly all our Fiats, and all our Portrait (Pl. 52a) and Motto glasses (Pl. 51d) belong. These last are rare. The best portrait glasses are those showing the Prince in profile. His full-face portraits with the label 'Audentior Ibo' are relatively common, often crude, and they need examining with care. There are also reproductions which should not deceive.

Not a few Jacobite clubs sprang up, among them the 'Hunt' Clubs, such as the Caerwys, the Tarporley, and the Friendly, which hid their rather vaporous Jacobitism behind a *façade* of dining and drinking. Their history is obscure, but they have bequeathed us a glass or two. More important was the Oak Society, to which there seems reason to attribute a few glasses with the word 'Redeat' (Pl. 51c). In Scotland, there were Rose glasses inscribed 'Success to the Society', which meant the Society of Jesus. Such glasses are both later and rarer.

But what could not be achieved after Fontenoy could certainly not be accomplished after Aix-la-Chapelle. The government knew well enough that the bark of all these clubs and coteries was much worse than their bite. It permitted them to play at being traitor until monotony begat indifference. A third forgetful generation soon grew up.

Something must now be said about the other emblems commonly employed. Of these the most important is the Thistle, which was the Scottish counterpart of the Rose. It represented the Scottish crown, and may be provided either with one or two buds, but it has no set form. Examples are considerably scarcer than the Rose glasses. It may appear on a glass which has also a Rose and bud, and in one stable type is shown rising from the same stem as the Rose, which is then multi-petalled and in profile, with but the single sinister bud. Accordingly, such glasses date after the Old Pretender's death in 1766.

The Star is found on a number of mid-century and later glasses (Pl. 51c), some of which carry the 'Fiat'. It signifies the aim, the object, the guiding principle of Jacobitism, and so expresses loyalty and perseverance.

The Oak Leaf is at least as often seen as the Star. There is something very English about the oak and, as its leaf was then used on no recognizably Scottish glass that I know of, it may have come to mean Restoration to the English throne, a train of thought derived from the Boscobel Oak of Charles II and the oak twigs he wore on his return to London in 1660. Usually the leaf is single and isolated on the reverse of a Rose glass, but twin leaves are known, as on the foot of a 'Redi' glass (Pl. 51d), and there are a very few exceptional uses of oak leaves on what are known as 'disguised Jacobites'. The Stricken Oak is in rather a different category. It stands for the unlucky House of Stuart, and may show a young sapling beneath, as in the 'Revirescit' glasses, or two sprouting leaves; less often it is flanked by two saplings, representing the recognized heirs. Finally, there is the Boscobel Oak itself, shown in full leaf and occasionally with the head of Charles II showing through. At best it is a memorial, and it may represent nothing more factious than the local 'Royal Oak'. Horridge regards both the Star and the Oak Leaf as referring to Charles personally. It is a view which merits attention, but I prefer the idea of 'Restoration.'

Another rare emblem is the Compass, apparently a special club device and generally taken to be that of the Cycle Club or some affiliated body. Then there is the Forget-me-not, used conversely to suggest mourning for James Francis Edward, an emblem whose importance has escaped recognition (Pl. 61b, c). In all but one of the examples of which I have a record it replaces the half-open dexter bud and may therefore be dated to 1766–7.

Less decisive is the Daffodil, but I now think it must be regarded as an emblem of mourning, comparable to the Forget-me-not. It occurs on a few disguised glasses, provided with oak leaves rising from a common stem, with a grub or grubs on stalk or leaf, and with one or two really life-like hovering butterflies. There are also a few Rose glasses showing the same grub on the stem, and the same butterflies. One of them, a most significant specimen, has the Forget-me-not in place of the larger dexter bud, and to me it is proof that the larger bud represented James. In another example the smaller bud is actually severed from the Rose; an allied glass has the Rose and buds, a caterpillar (not a grub) on the stalk, a cobweb between the Rose and the larger bud, and a fly hovering over.

In such glasses as these (Pl. 61a) I have wondered whether the grubs, caterpillar, and cobweb might not represent Jacobite intrigue, and the life-like butterflies Charles and James restored to power. But the Forget-me-not-*cum*-Rose glass referred to above has *two* butterflies, so that the theory fails in part, and otherwise is unconvincing. The same glass also dispels the thought that these 'grub glasses' were possibly a derisive Hanoverian gesture. The clue has not yet been found, and all that can safely be said is that they do *not*, as Grant Francis postulates, signify the decay of the Jacobite movement because no Jacobite would want to proclaim the failure of his own cause.

There is a large group of otherwise simple Rose glasses which, whether with one bud or two, have on the reverse an indeterminate insect which can be called butterfly or moth at will, and which is very different from the life-like insects on the disguised glasses. Much has been made of the 'hope' and 'despair' motifs supposedly to be inferred, but, apart from the difficulty of saying whether this stereotyped conventional insect is butterfly or moth, there is still the point that Jacobites were not at all likely to advertise 'the decay of the movement'. In point of fact (Pl. 61e), on later glasses, this ugly insect becomes quite a presentable bee. In lieu of any insect there may be found a conventional sprig, or a bird of unknown species, sometimes dubbed pheasant, and recently re-christened 'jay' for James, with curious abandon. I would rather believe that all these dubious insects, quaint birds, and conventional sprigs are purely decorative, the sort of thing the engraver could put on with his eyes shut, for all of them constantly appear on glasses devoid of any Jacobite emblem whatsoever. It should, however, be mentioned that Horridge regards the butterfly-moth as the symbol of the individual Jacobite owner-user, but only when it is on a Rose glass. The suggestion is intriguing, but not wholly convincing.

Other flowers, too, have had a certain Jacobite significance attached to them. Mostly I think they are decorative, but there is a saucer-topped bowl on an air twist stem which took a band of engraving very well, and there certainly is a set form of floral work not infrequently found on it, which shows the Rose and bud, the Carnation (or Pink if preferred) and Honeysuckle. A theory has been put forward that the Carnation stood for Carolus and the Honeysuckle for Henricus. But we have already seen that Henry did not come into Jacobite calculations at all, and he had been a cardinal for years before these glasses were made so that even on the old theory he ought not to be represented. If then the decorative idea is unacceptable, some other theory must be sought. There are other ingenuities, too, such as translating the Passion-flower (if and when it is such a flower) as Princeps. The Sunflower has also been given unexplained distinction, unless it can be claimed as the emblem for Louis XV, which seems highly improbable.

It does remain true that certain combinations of flowers do appear with surprising stability on many different kinds of glasses. Besides the design referred to above, a combination of the lily of the valley, the honeysuckle, and a large rosebud is frequent. The lily appears alone, and so quite often does the rosebud. I would not like to assert that these emblems do not carry some significance, but it does not have to be Jacobite.

Strangely enough, one entirely reputable type of Jacobite glass has been—rather illogically in any case—rejected by collectors because it is assumed to be of Dutch, or at least of continental origin. It appears to have been accepted that there was a party in the Low Countries which held Jacobite leanings, exactly why is nowhere explained. There is no evidence that James had any following or popularity in France where he was Louis' honoured guest, and any idea that the Protestant Dutch upheld his pretensions to a throne their own William of Orange had mounted seems outside all reason. The real reason why these glasses are labelled foreign is that they are made of soda metal (Pl. 55c) and English collectors have somehow become persuaded that because the Continent used soda metal, therefore soda metal glasses are continental.

Actually, these despised Jacobites were made on Tyneside, engraved on Tyneside, and no doubt sold there too. They tally in form and twist exactly with recognized English lead glasses, and the engraving tallies too, in every detail. The soda glasses are a cheaper, and usually (but not necessarily) an inferior production, but they are indubitable English Jacobite glasses for all that, and it is only fair that proper recognition should be accorded them.

A few words must be added about late Jacobite glasses and glasses in the Jacobite tradition. One finds the style of the Rose and single bud engraved in a descending scale, from a well-executed design down to a crude form in which the bud is hardly distinguishable from a leaf (Pl. 61f), or else is entirely non-existent. Cut and polished work is often incorporated, especially on the facet-stemmed series of glasses, and with it comes the bee. The best of these are quite definitely true Jacobite glasses (Pl. 61e). Just how far some others are late Jacobites, how far some are simply inexpensive Jacobites for those who could not pay for better work, and how far some are in fact purely decorative but decadent examples in the older Jacobite tradition, must be a matter of personal opinion. No rule can be laid down, but I am inclined to think that any Rose and bud engraved in the stylized form, however crudely, has at least some claim to inclusion in the Jacobite family. It must be admitted, however, that some are very poor relations indeed.

With a new appreciation of the significance of the Rose as emblematic of the Crown of England, all the inconsequences of the old theory vanish, and that holds whatever interpretation is given of the minor emblems. Collectors will realize that problems still remain for solution, in particular the precise meaning of the 'grub glasses', but whether solved or not, these and all other Jacobite glasses will never lack their devotees, if only on account of their sentimental and historical appeal.

FOR FURTHER READING

Francis, Grant R. *Old English Drinking Glasses.* 1926.
Hartshorne, A. *Old English Glasses.*

CHAPTER XI

Commemorative Glass

At the very beginning of this book the debt which civilization owes to glass was strongly emphasized and, as if in acknowledgment, civilization has continuously made use of its glasses to commemorate its people, their sentiments, conventions, hopes and deeds.

Naturally, the record we inherit is an imperfect one, but during those periods when glass was abundant it is sufficiently ample, and even continuous, to suggest that it perpetuated most important events and people. If human nature has changed at all during the past thirty-five centuries, it has not modified man's urge to transmit his name to posterity by one means or another. The schoolboy who carves his name on desk or panel has the desire in common with any would-be world conqueror to leave his name behind, perhaps knowing subconsciously how fleeting must be his importance.

History in glass began appropriately enough with our very earliest specimens, when Thotmes III had his name recorded on three glasses, fifteen centuries before the birth of Christ. There was much greater scope after the invention of glass-blowing, and we find Roman cups displaying chariot races or gladiatorial combats, generally with the names of the contestants, as in the Colchester-found 'Crescens Ave—Hierax Vale' specimen. Strangely, half the known glasses of this kind were found in England, which suggests that our enthusiasm for competitive sports is of very ancient standing. Comparable glasses ('Take the Victory') were given as prizes. By the 4th century there were also glasses inscribed with such legends as 'Bibe Vivas Multis Annis', a little more explicit than the English 'Success to', the German 'Vivat', and the Dutch 'Het Welvaaren', but the underlying idea was the same. There was the gilt glass of the cemeteries, not all of a religious nature, and above all there was—destroyed at Strasbourg in 1870—the cage cup with the name of the Emperor Maximianus, who was assassinated in 310.

Later, the names and titles of various Mamluk and other potentates were recorded on the finely-enamelled Islamic glass of the 13th century, and very occasionally (taking advantage of the opportunity) the name of the humble artificer as well. Of the later Middle Ages, it has been mentioned that few glasses now exist, but just enough commemorative specimens remain, such as the 15th century Berovieri marriage cups, to make it quite certain that more were made.

During the 16th century examples became commoner, particularly armorial glasses from Italy, the Low Countries, and Germany. By the end of the century these must have been very popular, if not universal, among those whose birth was lofty or whose wealth was great; to judge by the glasses which have survived, their good taste, or that of the artist, avoided undue ostentation. There were also social glasses of the period, including marriage and betrothal glasses from France (Pl. 12a), and England, these last being of course the Verzelini glasses.

Commemorative glasses became increasingly frequent during the 17th century, and actual historical events were first recorded, including events of English history. But England was decidedly behind the Continent in this respect, and it was not until the final years of the century that she could, thanks to the Ravenscroft revolution, challenge the lead of the Low Countries and Germany. Then, however, she made amends in full and, throughout the 18th century, historical, political, and social happenings of all kinds were recorded on her glass, ranging from events of world-wide importance to social matters now hardly understood, and to personal records never intended to interest the world at large. Their name is legion, and in their execution they varied from the simple and straightforward to the obscurely allegorical and sentimental.

Most commemorative glass was wheel-engraved, and it came chiefly from Holland, Germany, and England, the countries in which wheel-engraving particularly flourished. The designs could of course be traced by other methods. 'Diamond-point' engraving, stippling, enamelling, cold painting, and gilding were alternative devices. Glasses could be blown into a prepared mould, in the old Roman and Venetian fashion, and in the 19th century they could be press-moulded. A few glasses, such as coin glasses and casts of notable men, required no subsequent decoration at all.

Taking a bird's-eye view of this commemorative glass as a whole, it can be divided into certain well-defined categories, although there are glasses which might fall into more than one class, and a few whose true import is not now clear. There are so many glasses of historic or social interest, covering such a wide range of human thought and effort, that a perfect analysis is impossible, and no particular importance need be attached to the classification given here. It should be understood that not every inscribed glass is contemporary with the event. Most are, or very nearly so, but some may be much later, such as centenary glasses. The table does not go behind the 16th century, and many of the examples mentioned will be found illustrated in our standard textbooks. The schedule includes many foreign glasses. Some continental records often appear on English glasses; the reverse is seldom the case.

A. CLASSIFICATION OF COMMEMORATIVE GLASS

I. *Records of Public Congratulation or Appreciation*

A. SPECIFIC ROYALTIES, ON ACCESSION, MARRIAGE, JUBILEE, OR DEATH

All English sovereigns from Charles II. The Emperors Leopold I, Joseph I, Francis I: Maria Theresa: Elizabeth Petrovna, Catherine the Great, Alexander I, of Russia. Augustus II and III, Kings of Poland. Frederick William I and Frederick the Great, of Prussia, Ferdinand IV,

King of Naples and Sicily. Cosmo III, Grand Duke of Tuscany. Very many minor rulers, such as electors, landgraves, princes, bishops, and counts.

B. PARTICULAR COUNTRIES OR RULING HOUSES

The United Netherlands, the Seven Provinces, the Province of Utrecht. The Cape of Good Hope. The Houses of Hanover, Nassau. *Reichsadlerhumpen.*

C. ESTABLISHED AUTHORITIES OR INSTITUTIONS

'George & Liberty' and other glasses of our Hanoverian dynasty. 'King and Constitution.' 'Success to the British Fleet.' 'Salus Patriae' glasses. *Kurfürstengläser.*

D. SPECIFIC SAILORS, SOLDIERS, STATESMEN, AND PUBLIC CHARACTERS, ON THEIR ACHIEVEMENTS OR DEATH

Admiral van Tromp. George Walker of Derry. 'Amen' glasses and portrait glasses of the Young Pretender. The Duke of Cumberland. The King of Prussia. Dean Swift. George Washington. Admiral Keppel. Hendrik Hooft. Lord Nelson. The Duke of Wellington. Napoleon III. Disraeli. Jenny Lind. Lord Roberts.

E. BATTLES ON SEA OR LAND

Siege of Landau. Capture of Gibraltar. Quiberon Bay. Dogger Bank. Trafalgar. Peninsular battles and Waterloo. The 'Endymion' and the 'President'.

F. TREATIES OF PEACE

Ryswick. Utrecht. Aix-la-Chapelle. Treaty of Paris (Britannia glasses). Amiens. Second Treaty of Paris.

G. HISTORICAL EVENTS

The Restoration. 'Union' (of 1801) glasses. Repeal of Test Act. Reform Bill.

II. *Similar Records of a more Restricted or Semi-Private Nature*

A. PUBLIC WORKS

Hereford Cathedral. Sunderland Bridge. The Great Exhibition of 1851. Very many German and Bohemian churches, town halls, and institutions.

B. Specific Men of War

'*'t Welvaaren Van de Leepelaer.*' 'Success to the Renown.' 'Prince George—Admiral Digby.' Privateer glasses.

C. Specific Regiments

Londonderry Fusiliers. First Regiment. Loyal Colchester Volunteers. Argyllshire Militia. Many Irish Volunteer units.

D. Cities, Towns, and Villages

Norwich. Newcastle. Utrecht. Dresden. Nuremberg. Scenic representations: Rialto, Baden, Wiesbaden. Map beakers.

E. City Companies and Guilds

Turners. Goldsmiths. Stationers. Weavers. Dutch East India Company. Various German trade guilds.

F. Clubs and Associations

Masonic Lodges. The 'Gore Inn' Club. The 'Sober' Club. The 'Black Face o't'.

III. *Records of Political or Controversial Import*

A. Party or Faction

Jacobite and Williamite glasses. 'Orange' glasses. Queen Caroline—'God and My Right.' 'The King and the Friends of His Majesty's American Loyalists.' Carlos III. 'Liberty and American Independence.'

B. Movements and Agitations

Jacobite Club glasses. Admiral Byng glasses. The Dundee Martyrs. 'No Excise.' 'Rights of Man.' 'Liberty and Wilkes.'

C. Parliamentary Elections

'Liberty and Clavering For Ever.' 'Sir I. Pole For Ever.' 'Success to Sir Francis Knollys.'

D. Of Derision

Napoleonic cartoons and St. Helena 'silhouette' glasses. 'Bute' glasses (?).

IV. *Records of Social and Private Interest*

A. Individual Ownership

(a) Personal Armorial glasses of many persons from Royalty downwards.

(b) Cipher, Crest, and Monogram glasses of the same.

(c) College wine bottles with impressed seals.

B. Friendship

(a) Allegorical. '*Concordia*' and billing doves. David and Jonathan. '*Amicitia*' and clasped hands. Conversation scenes.

(b) Gift Glasses.
'Brid[t] Alderson to Ann Brooks.'
'Elizabeth Lumby, the gift of her Mother 1806.'
'A Present from Ramsgate.'
Souvenir rolling-pins, mugs, and tankards.

(c) Formal Presentation Glasses.
'Arch[d] Govan, Clerk to the Lord Drumore, 1754.'

(d) Portrait glasses.
Silhouette and medallion portrait glasses.

C. Family Occasions

(a) Births and Christenings.
'Charlotte Hayward Born March the 9, 1774.'

(b) Coming of Age.
'Prosperity to the House of Downing made . . . to commemorate the coming of age of David Pennant Esqr. . . .'

(c) Betrothal.
'*Aux Bonnes Etrennes.*' '*Ik Bemin Maar Een.*'
Allegorical and sentimental scenes.

(d) Marriage.
The 'Dier' glass. ''*T Goed Success Van 't Huywelyk.*' '*Floreat die Ruhr fahrt*' and respective Arms. 'S.I. to Mr. Hutchinson. Stony Gill 1764' and a verse. Allegories.

(e) Anniversaries.
'*Zilver Bruiloss Feest. . . .*'

(f) Death.
Hearts and initials on a sarcophagus (plague glass).
Memorial portraits.

D. RECREATION

(a) Sport.

Cock-fighting. Stag, Fox, Bear and Chamois hunting. Coursing. Steeple-chasing. Fishing. Skating. Yachting. Shooting.

(b) Games of Chance.

Cards. Dice beakers. Gambling scenes.

(c) Travel.

Coach and Four. Riding. Ballooning.

E. PROPERTY AND POSSESSIONS

(a) Real Estate.

Farms. Homesteads. Vineyards. Windmills. Alnwick Castle.

(b) Animals.

Racehorses. Prize bulls. Foxhounds.

(c) Ships.

Success of Boston. *William & Mary*.

F. COMMERCE AND BUSINESS

(a) Good Luck glasses.

'*Vivat Negosiae*.' 'Success to Irish Navigation and Trade.' 'Speed the Plough.'

(b) Specific Trades or Firms.

Whaling. Agriculture. Inns. The Linen Trade. The Coal Trade. 'Success to the Swordmakers.' 'Cowan & Co.', with the Leith and Scottish Arms.

(c) Memorials of Trade or Work.

Launch of the *Nelson*. 'Up to Sowerby Bridge' (canal). Lock gates. Mills. The York Coach.

G. SENTIMENT AND CONVIVIALITY

(a) Extolling liquor.

Bacchus glasses. 'Take a Dram Old Boy.'

(b) Toasts.

'Families, Friends, & Favourites.' 'No Grumbling.' '*Au Premier Plaisir*.' '*Le Vin Guérit la Tristesse*.'

(c) Religious or Philosophical.

Apostelgläser. Madonna and Child. St. Christopher. St. Hubert. Samson and the Lion. Ten Ages glasses. The Twelve Months. The Four Continents. The Four Seasons.

(d) Cryptic and Double Entendre.

'*Maat Houd Staat*' with Daedalus and Icarus. 'I elevate what I consume.'

(e) Comic.
'Hansie in de Kelder' glasses. Strolling Players. Crude love and drinking scenes.

(f) Allegorical.
'Aurea Libertas' with escaping bird. Conversation scenes.

(g) Repeats of drawings.
Æsop's Fables.

A great many of these commemorative glasses are recognizable at sight and offer no problem. Others, however, require to be 'read' before they have any meaning for collectors of the 20th century. Here, for instance, is the description of an English mid-18th century glass, engraved in Holland. Behind a rounded hill the sun is rising. On either side, in the foreground, stand a drummer and a trumpeter. Above the hill is a pair of crossed naked swords, and round the rim runs an inscription in Dutch. At first sight it looks rather like some elaborately sentimental picture of a dawn or sunset. But that leaves no obvious reason for the crossed swords, and no particular reason for drummer or trumpeter. Taken as an allegory, however, it is apparent that the engraving represented some important change in fortune. A translation of the inscription *'Den Goeden Oorlogh'* (The Fortunate War) confirms this, and reference to history makes it possible to say that the glass (Pl. 47d) is a Dutch commemorative of the Peace of Aix-la-Chapelle in 1748.

In another case, an elaborately engraved Zechlin glass bears a representation of an army parade at Busau, together with armorials and the inscriptions *'Séjour Agréable'* and *'Vive l'Armée Prussienne'*. That appears odd, because Franco-Prussian relations have not been conspicuous for their cordiality. Again, history comes to the rescue. For a short while during the War of the Austrian Succession, France and Prussia were allied against Maria Theresa, and of course England, whose attitude was automatically anti-French. Some rather complicated manœuvres culminated in the battle of Czaslau in May, 1742. The '*Séjour Agréable*' at Busau or Brusau, which places lay on the line of march, a few miles from Zwittau on the Bohemian-Moravian border, must have occurred between January and May, 1742. The armorials are those of Von Oppen, of Silesia, Saxony, and Anhalt, and the glass (Pl. 26a) was doubtless a present from a French officer to his temporary host and ally.

Now, no particular intelligence is required to read glasses like this. A little imagination is necessary, and quite often some book of reference. The point is that old glasses were not decorated with unexpected designs without reason. Outside purely formal or decorative engraving the design had a definite meaning. It is a part of glass-knowledge to realize on sight when there is a meaning, and an omniscient connoisseur would know what is its purport.

That, however, needs a degree of knowledge which nobody has yet reached, or is soon likely to reach. It would entail an impeccable memory and scholarship in a score of the sciences. To mention but a few, one would need acquaintance with languages, especially Latin, Dutch, and German, and with their contemporary usages and script, together with a capacity to make allowances for the artists' errors in transcription. Mythology is another requirement. History, especially of the 17th and 18th centuries, is essential, and this means not only facts and names and dates, but also an appreciation of 17th and 18th century thought, manners, and customs. Topography and continental geography, as it used to be, is needful. We speak learnedly enough to-day of 'Netherlandish' glasses without troubling to consider whether we cannot be more precise. Frontier changes and political supremacies have continually to be kept in mind. Heraldry is constantly in question, in respect both of coats arms and their identification, and of orders and insignia. Various emblems carry a meaning, or may have a meaning entrusted to them in a particular case. Allusions which were no doubt clear enough in the past now require interpretation. As an instance, there is the Bate rummer engraved with a cat playing the bagpipes, with the legend 'Honour and Friendship'. Nobody has discovered its meaning, and the two lines of approach I have found leave it still in doubt. The design bears a strong likeness to a French copper-plate engraving illustrating Æsop's fable of the wolf and the kid. Judging by another glass which is similarly but more lengthily inscribed and which mentions the Dee, the legend seems to be adapted, or perhaps wrongly rendered, from a song printed in Hogg's *Jacobite Relics*, in which the refrain is:

Let Honour and Friendship Unite
And Flourish on Both Sides the Tweed.

In another case, we have a goblet with the Jacobite Rose and two buds on one side, and the inscription 'Lyster And The Honest Freeholders' on the reverse. Perhaps one should have known, but much inquiry failed to elicit the significance of the 'Honest Freeholders' and only a chance reading of Macaulay showed that the phrase meant 'honest and sincere electors'. Lyster himself was the feudal-minded and feudal-living Shropshire squire of Rowton Castle, a Tory and a Jacobite, who sat almost continuously in the House for forty years. That suggests the very antithesis of democracy, yet he kept open house once a week for his country supporters, and his London tradesmen thought enough of him to meet his coach and six, and to escort him from Hampstead to his London house at Bow. When he died, in 1765, somebody neatly epitomized him and his loyal and friendly electors in this glass.

In case all this may tend to discourage any enthusiast for commemorative glass, he may find consolation in the fact that access to a good reference library will smooth out most of the difficulties. The interpretation is almost always perfectly simple, once the clue is discovered, and a little experience and a certain imagination will carry him a long way. Where highly specialized knowledge is called for, as for instance in the reading of Kufic epigraphy, early German script, or obscure continental heraldry, there are those who will gladly assist and take great pains and interest in so doing. It is hardly necessary to add that one should not expect such help to be gratuitous.

There is no end to the whimsicalities and indeed the extravagancies of History in Glass, and it will be found an absorbing subject, with not a few prizes for an imaginative collector. Purists, who regard any sort of extrinsic decoration on a glass with regret, will not be interested, and there is something to be said for that point of view. Collectors who are concerned only with glass forms will not need to be interested. But those whose imagination is touched by the human interest of specimens which speak of men and deeds and customs, now enshrined in or even forgotten by history, will find a field of never-ending interest in commemorative glass.

FOR FURTHER READING

Bate, P. *English Table Glass.*

Bles, J. *Rare English Glasses of 17th and 18th centuries.* 1926.

Churchill, Arthur, Ltd. *History in Glass.* 1937.

PART 2

ENGLISH GLASSES OF THE 18TH CENTURY

English Glasses of the 18th Century

NOMENCLATURE AND CLASSIFICATION

With the closing years of the 17th century, a state of affairs is found only matched in the heyday of Roman production. Every manufacturing country was making as much glass as it could, with Britain, thanks to Ravenscroft's discovery, coming very rapidly to the fore, and providing an article which in some respects was superior to all alternatives.

I am inclined to rank the combination of strength and clarity in front of all else. Strength meant durability, and durability meant economy, as anyone knows who has bought cheap modern glass. Clarity, however, was still a relative term. It did not mean the hard crystal-like brilliance of the glass of to-day. It meant even translucency, an absence of heightened tints where the metal was thicker. Our English lead glass for the better part of a century was not at all crystal-like. It might have a faint greenish, or, more often, a blackish tone, but these were uniform throughout the glass, and are now regarded as a merit, not a demerit. Any sort of a yellowish or amethystine cast is, on the other hand, looked on with disfavour by collectors, because such tints were accidental and unstable.

The lead metal had a softness of look which was very pleasing, and a further intrinsic softness which some continental engravers found very convenient. It had, as well, a quite new and lustrous quality, a power to diffuse light. As time went on, manufacturers eliminated the earlier greenish and blackish tints, but the metal retained its soft appearance, whilst its light-diffusing quality was exploited by suitable cutting. Only after 1760, when minium (dioxide of lead)

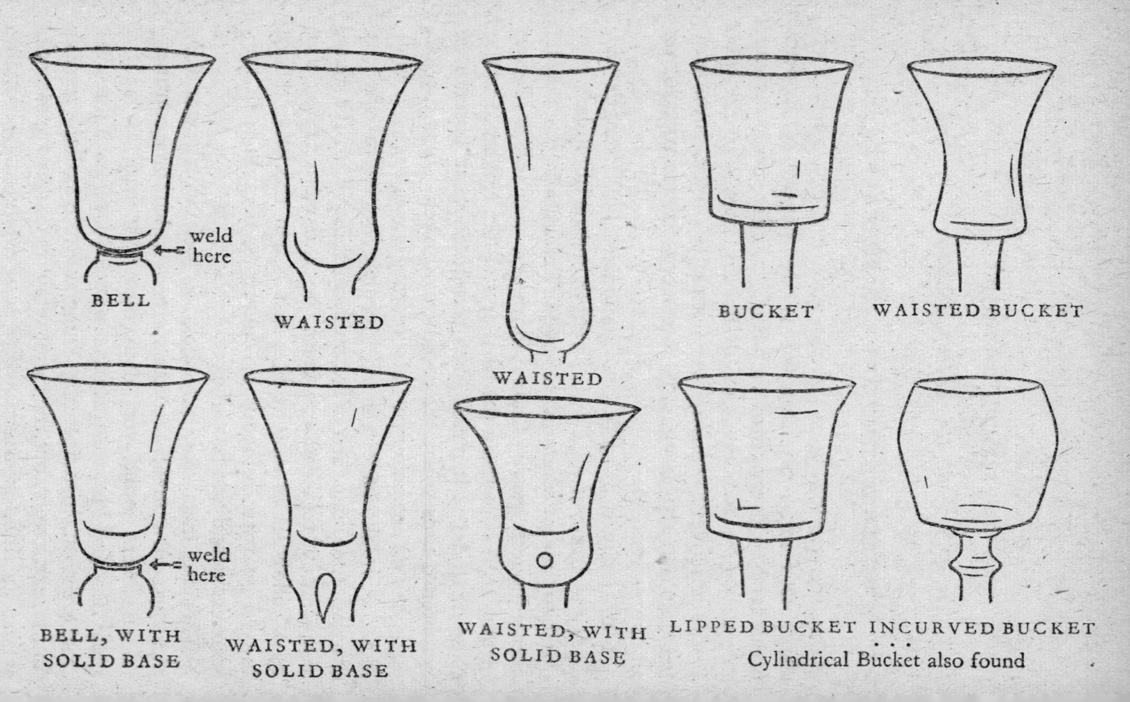
weld here
BELL
WAISTED
WAISTED
BUCKET
WAISTED BUCKET
weld here
BELL, WITH SOLID BASE
WAISTED, WITH SOLID BASE
WAISTED, WITH SOLID BASE
LIPPED BUCKET
INCURVED BUCKET
...
Cylindrical Bucket also found

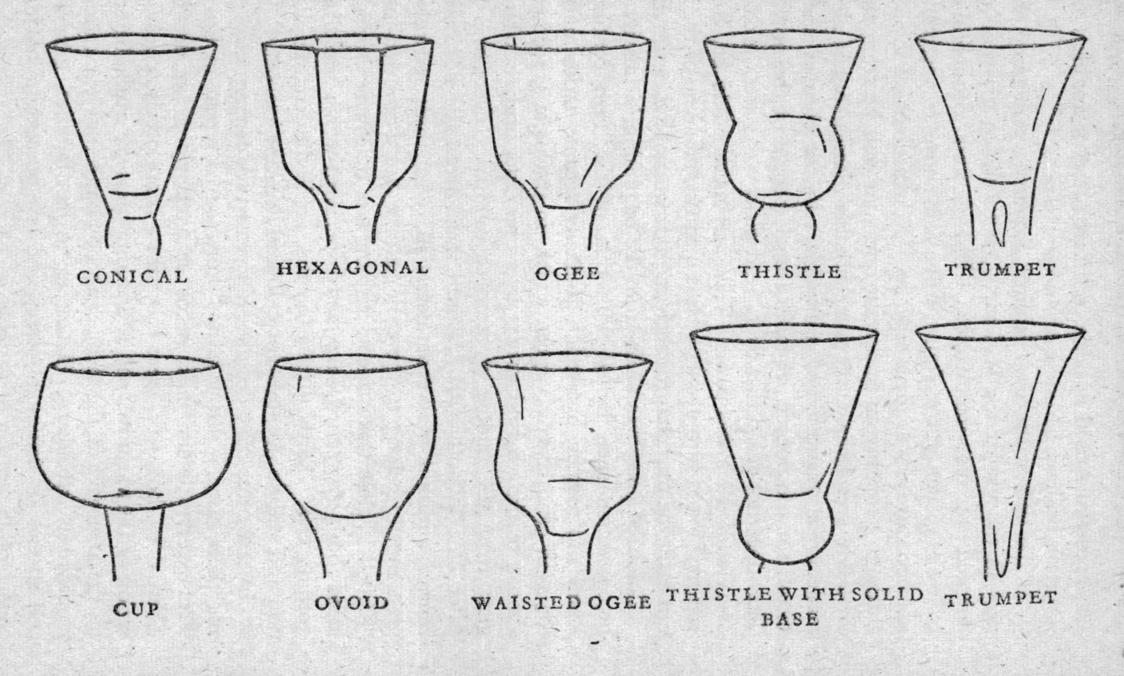
CONICAL
HEXAGONAL
OGEE
THISTLE
TRUMPET
CUP
OVOID
WAISTED OGEE
THISTLE WITH SOLID BASE
TRUMPET

was sometimes used in place of litharge (the protoxide), did a certain brilliant hardness of look eventuate.

At the end of the 17th century, London was leading the way in the use of the lead metal, with eleven glasshouses devoted to its manufacture. Bristol and Stourbridge followed distantly, with four and five such houses respectively, not necessarily of as great capacity. Newcastle had but one, although probably an important one. As will be seen, the Tyneside area turned out some notable glasses, but it also made great quantities of utility glass in the cheaper soda metal, for the poorer, or more frugal, people of the north. That does not mean that every lead glass was good, or that every soda glass was poor. The latter metal could be, and was, fashioned into glasses of fine quality, and some of them can easily be mistaken for their more frequent lead brethren.

Coloured glass was made from the beginning, primarily a green which then tallied with that of the 17th century Rhineland roemer, but which gradually became darker until the 19th century saw a green which, in thick glass, seemed almost black. Bristol made dark blue and opaque white glass from the middle of the 18th century. There was a paler blue in both soda and lead metal from the northern centres, and milk-glass from nearly all. Amethyst and ruby glass mostly belong to the 19th century, but a true red-ink 'Kunckel' glass was made at Birmingham by Mayer Oppenheim about 1755, for I have seen a specimen which could be nothing else. With all this, on the whole the English did not, and still do not, care for coloured drinking glasses.

Other writers have dealt so fully with 18th century glasses and their history that it is not proposed to repeat in brief what every student must needs read elsewhere in detail. There does, however, seem room for a more precise classification of the various types of drinking glass we made, based on the structure of the stem, with bowl and foot variations regarded as subsidiary. There are in fact families, genera, and species of drinking glasses, the last possessing no inconsiderable number of varieties.

There is also a crying need for a uniform terminology. Authors have used the same word to describe different things, and different words to describe the same thing, and they have not even been faithful to their own phraseology. It should be easy to visualize a glass from a description, and then to sketch it, but how seldom that is possible at present will be learned by referring to lists and catalogues which appear in print. It matters very little what terminology is employed, provided it is generally accepted and steadfastly observed.

The following, then, is a list of the types of 18th century (1690–1830) drinking glasses. The stem is presumed to be of normal length and thickness unless otherwise stated. The figures of capacity are in liquid measure and represent normal expectation. The basis of comparison is the normal wine bowl of the mid-18th century.

Ale: capacity 3 to 4 oz.; with long and relatively narrow bowl.

Short Ale: the same, but stem shortened.

Dwarf Ale: the same, but stem very short, rudimentary, or absent.

Giant Ale: over 12 ins. in height with appropriate capacity.

Georgian Ale: 4 to 5 oz. ; a Georgian wine (*q.v.*) with long bowl.

Champagne: 6 oz.; a wine or small goblet; bowl width equal to or greater than its depth.

Low Champagne: 4 oz.; the same, but stem shortened.

Cordial: 1 oz.; a small bowl on a rather tall and extra-stout stem.

Short Cordial: 1 oz. to 1½ oz.; the same, but stem shortened to normal length.

Semi-Cordial: the same, but stem of normal length and thickness.

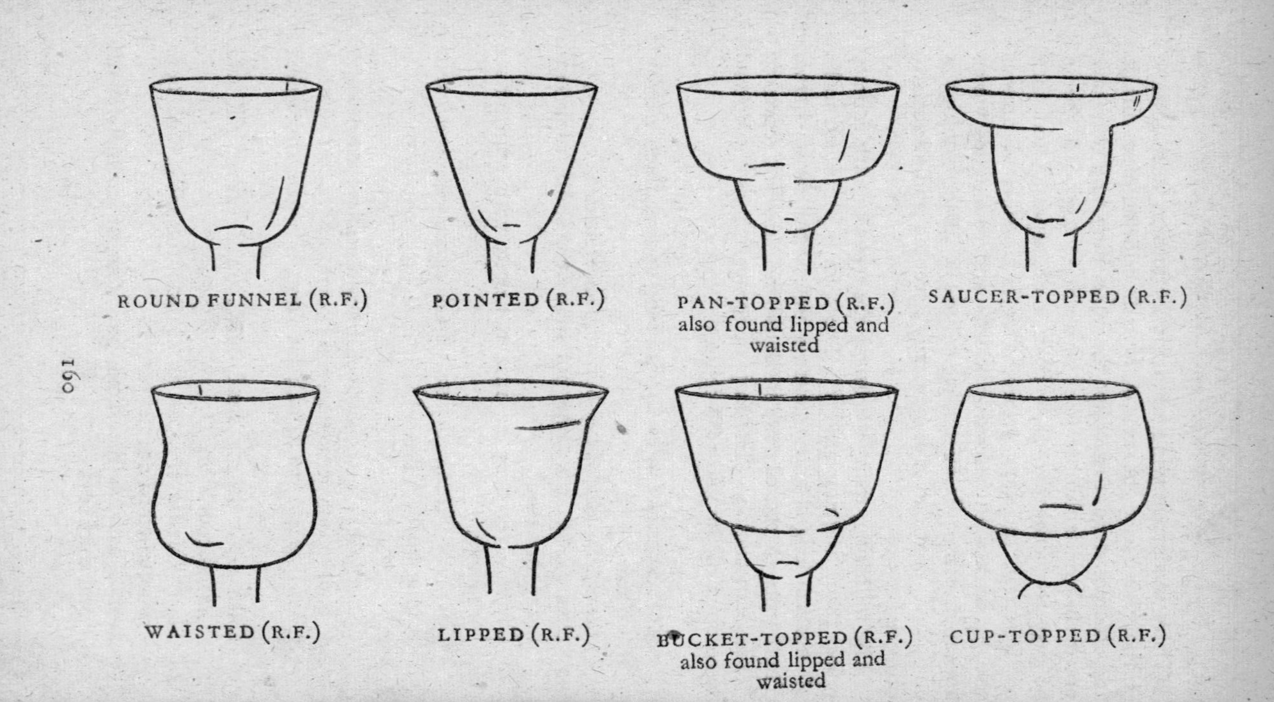
ROUND FUNNEL (R.F.)
POINTED (R.F.)
PAN-TOPPED (R.F.) also found lipped and waisted
SAUCER-TOPPED (R.F.)
WAISTED (R.F.)
LIPPED (R.F.)
BUCKET-TOPPED (R.F.) also found lipped and waisted
CUP-TOPPED (R.F.)

FOOT FORMS

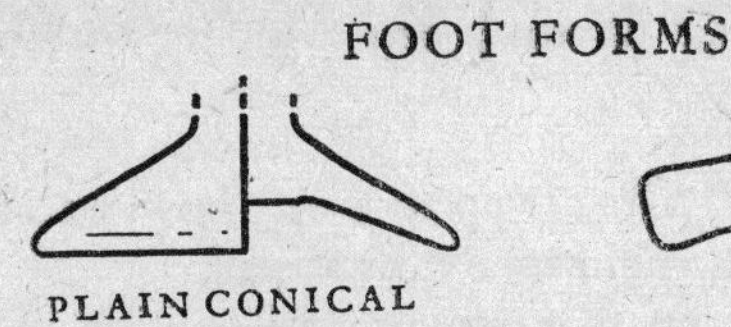

PLAIN CONICAL

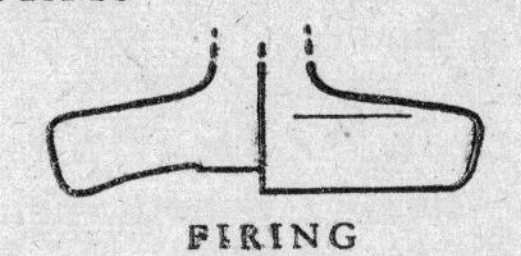

FIRING

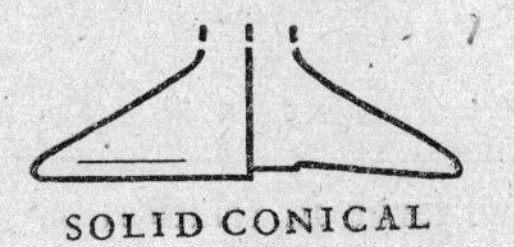

SOLID CONICAL

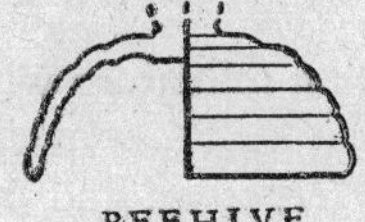

BEEHIVE

FOLDED

PEDESTAL

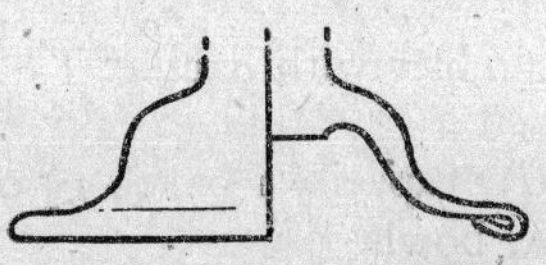

DOMED AND FOLDED

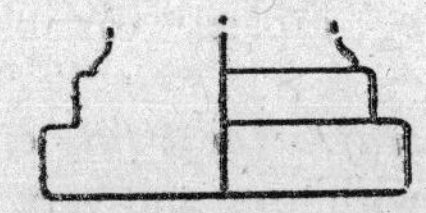

STEPPED SQUARE FOOT

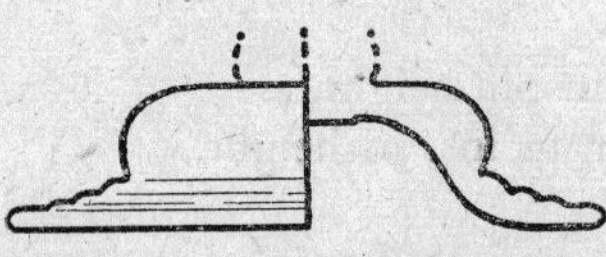

DOMED AND TERRACED

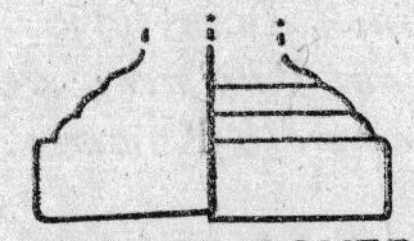

TERRACE-DOMED SOLID SQUARE FOOT

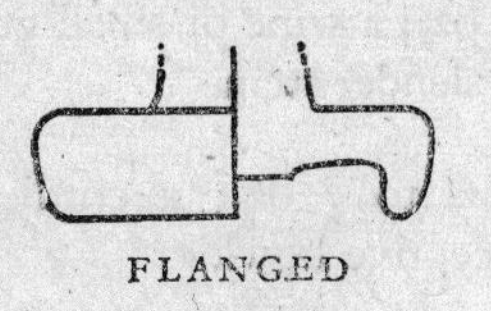

FLANGED

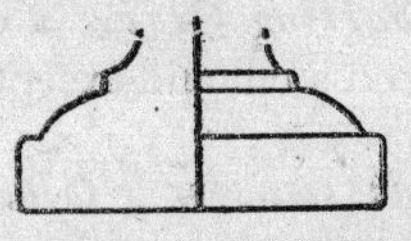

DOMED SQUARE FOOT

Cup (and Saucer): up to 3 oz.; with or without a handle.

Dram (or Spirit) Glass: up to 3 oz.; bowl variable; stem very short, rudimentary, or absent.
Georgian Dram: up to 2 oz.; a small edition of the Georgian wine (*q.v.*).

Gin: a miniature wine-glass.

Goblet: 4 oz. and over; bowl large in relation to stem height.
Giant Goblet: over 10 ins. in height.
Mammoth Goblet: over 12 ins. in height.

Mead Glass: a goblet with stem rudimentary or absent; not after *c.* 1760.

Mug: capacity variable; a tumbler with handle.

Ratafia (or Flute Cordial): capacity 1 oz. to 1½ oz.; with long and very narrow bowl.

Rummer: 4 oz. and over; a goblet with short stem; only after *c.* 1770.
Giant Rummer: over 10 ins. in height.
Mammoth Rummer: over 12 ins. in height.

Tankard: capacity variable; a footed mug.

Toasting Glass: 2 oz. to 4 oz.; a wine or small goblet on a tall and exceptionally slender stem.

Toastmaster's Glass: ½ oz. to ¾ oz.; a cordial or dram glass with highly deceptive bowl.

Tumbler: capacity variable; a more or less cylindrical vessel on a flat base.

Giant Tumbler: over 10 ins. in height.
Mammoth Tumbler: over 12 ins. in height.

Wine: 2 oz. to 3 oz.
Georgian Wine: 3 oz. to 4 oz.; with shortened stem; related to the Rummer as the Wine is to the Goblet; only after *c.* 1770.

Besides the foregoing, which are purely drinking glasses, certain other types of table glass are found.

Candlesticks and Tapersticks.

Jelly Glasses: a parallel to the dwarf ales, but may have a handle or handles, when they may be termed Posset glasses. Many were no doubt intended, or at least used, for drinking purposes.

Sweetmeat Glasses: a parallel to the champagnes. No sure distinction has been formulated. Broadly speaking, it is possible to drink conveniently from champagnes, but not from sweetmeats. The terms are used with small discrimination.

Less often collected, unless for their decorative or intrinsic usefulness, are the following:

Baskets: for dessert, e.g. fruit.

Bottles: especially wine, tea, toilet, and water bottles (carafes).
A bottle is a hollow vessel with narrow neck and mouth; no foot or handle.

Bowls and Basins: especially caddy, cream and milk, sugar, punch, and finger bowls.
A bowl is a vessel with concave sides with or without a foot or foot-rim.
A basin has sloping sides, the width greater than the height, with or without foot-rim.

STEM FORMATIONS

(*simple*)

THE KNOP PROPER

FLATTENED KNOP

ANNULAR KNOP

BALL KNOP

BAND KNOP

SWELLING KNOP

ANGULAR KNOP

BLADED KNOP

COLLAR

(*specialised*)

TRUE BALUSTER

INVERTED BALUSTER

STEM FORMATIONS
(*specialised contd*)

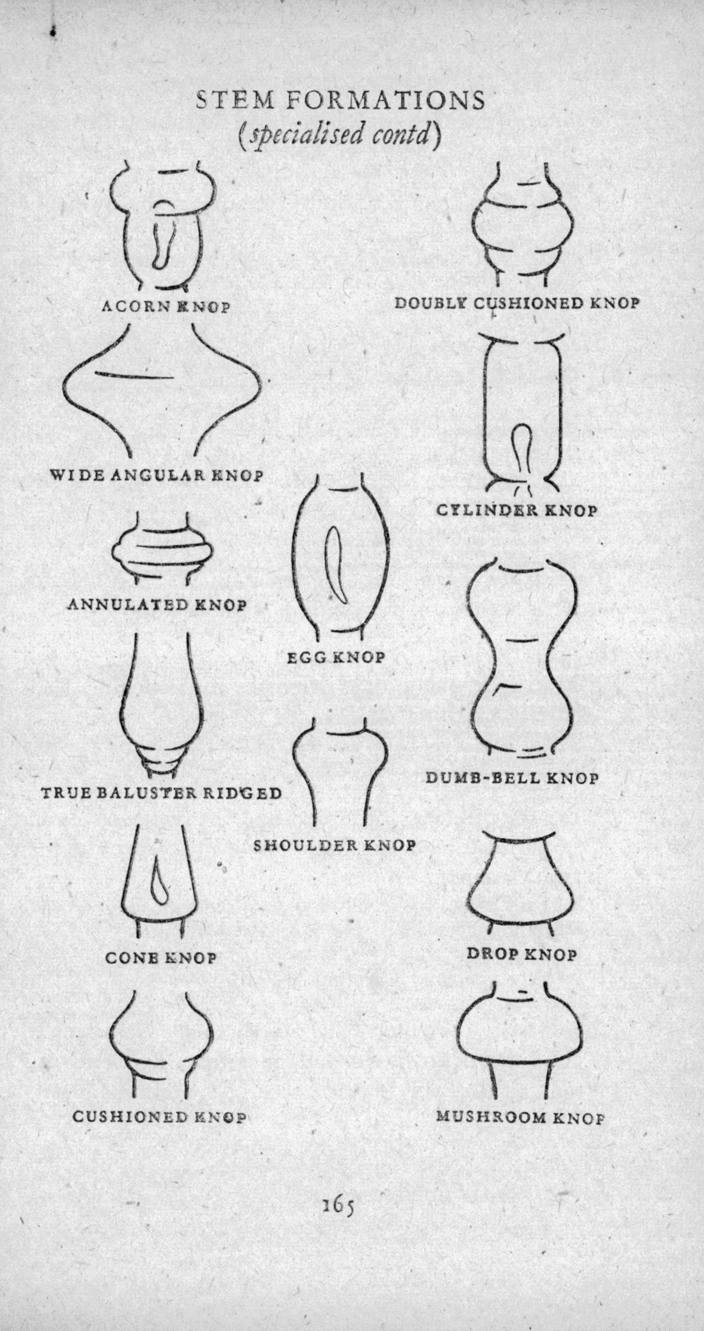

Standing Bowls: especially boat, harvest and kettle-drum bowls; with foot and a pronounced stem.

Chandeliers: pendant, or for the table, walls, or mantel.

Cruets and Condiments: bottles with stoppers or caps, some with feet.

Decanters, and Spirits (Bottles): for polite use at the table.

Dishes: including epergne dishes.

A dish is a shallow, concave vessel without foot or foot-rim; with or without a cover, and often with a *Stand*, which is either a tray or a solid or hollow plinth shaped to receive the dish and give it stability.

Ewers and Jugs: the former with wide, the latter with narrow mouth; with or without a foot.

A claret jug is stoppered.

Flasks: flat, oval bottles originally for travelling needs, latterly mainly decorative, or for infantile use.

Saddle bottles are larger and less flat, with longer neck. Scent flasks are small and of any shape.

Jars: for preserves or honey, and then with cover and stand. Storage jars were used for herbs, liquors, and household supplies.

A jar is a deep, wide-mouthed vessel without lip, foot or handle. When provided with an 'ear' it becomes a piggin.

Lamps: especially Lacemaker's lamps.

Monteiths (or Bonnet Glasses): small glasses with cup-topped bowl, etc. and no stem. Reputedly for salt but probably punch or cheap sweetmeat glasses.

Monteith Bowls: specialized punch bowls.

Patchstands: miniature tazze.

Plates: to be distinguished from stands; see dishes.

Pots: for tea and coffee, and then with a single handle and spout; for possets, and then with a pair of handles; for oil, with long spout; and for ink.

Salts: of many forms, e.g. hollow blown, trencher, and boat-shaped; with and without feet.

Salvers: i.e. Trays.

Tazze: shallow saucer-shaped dishes on foot, with or without stem; or flat-topped, with or without a rim.

Toddy Lifters: a decanter-bodied pipette used to transfer liquor from bowl to glass.

Toys; Implements; Apparatus; Insignia: in great variety.

Urns: which properly include comports; anciently an oviform vase on foot, especially a pedestal or plinth, but a cinerary urn might dispense with a foot; with cover.

Vases: especially celery, flower, and ornamental vases.
A vase is a vessel, especially an ornamental one, of greater height than width, with or without a foot.

A variety of meanings has been attached to some of the foregoing terms. For instance, the tazza as above is often called a stand, a salver, and a waiter, so that a reader has to guess what is really meant. Other terms have come into use which appear to me redundant, even erroneous, such as 'butter cooler', 'butter boat', and 'brandy saucepan'. The lists do not include quite every article made of English glass, while some articles which might have been expected do not exist, or at least I have not seen them. I cannot remember, for instance, a sauce boat.

A TWO PIECE GLASS WITH NORMAL STEM – (2 NS)

A THREE PIECE GLASS WITH NORMAL STEM – (3 NS)

A THREE PIECE GLASS WITH WELDED STEM – (3 WS)

A FOUR PIECE GLASS WITH WELDED STEM – (4 WS)

A very wide variety of terms is in use to describe stem, bowl and foot features, and they have inevitably been inconsistently employed. The line drawings given show all the main forms and shapes a collector is likely to meet with, and the captions will assist understanding of, at least, the analysis and classification which follows. Without some such guide, it would have little value.

In so far as drinking glasses and some few other types of vessel are concerned, a classification based on stem formation is wholly satisfactory until the last quarter of the 18th century is reached, when stem forms tend to become subsidiary to the bowl, and we find rummers, dwarf ales, jelly glasses, and Georgian wines and ales becoming preponderant. However, all these later types of glass have one point in common, and they can fairly and conveniently be classified under the heading of 'Other Glasses with Short or Rudimentary Stems', the word 'Other' being important because the earlier groups include varieties in which the stem is insignificant or, indeed, entirely absent.

Most glasses fall clearly within one or other of the following groups, although a certain number of specimens may lie between two of them. There are, for instance, glasses intermediate between Groups I and III, and others referable either to Group VI or XIII. In such cases they should be allotted to the less important category. Some arbitrary distinctions have had to be made in respect of Groups III, IV, and V, in the interests of simplicity. Practised collectors will recognize the difficulties. There are a few freak glasses which fit in nowhere, and some out-of-period glasses which are here neglected. The groupings to be recorded, then, are as under, the datings representing the effective currency of the group.

GROUP	I.	BALUSTER STEMS	1685–1725
	II.	MOULDED PEDESTAL STEMS	1715–1765
	III.	BALUSTROID STEMS	1725–1755

IV.	Light (Newcastle) Balusters	1735–1765
V.	Composite Stems	1740–1770
VI.	Plain Straight Stems	1740–1770
VII.	Air Twist Stems	1740–1770
VIII.	Hollow Stems	1750–1760
IX.	Incised Twist Stems	1750–1765
X.	Opaque Twist Stems	1750–1780
XI.	Mixed and Colour Twist Stems	1755–1775
XII.	Faceted Stems	1760–1800
XIII.	Other Glasses with Short or Rudimentary Stems: Dwarf Ales; Jelly Glasses; Rummers; Georgian Ales, Wines, and Drams;	18th–19th cent.

Most of these groups can be sub-divided into sections and sub-sections according to the more precise formation of the stem, and each section will contain a certain number of bowl and foot forms. The line drawings show and name these forms and illustrations show the types of moulded decoration adopted by the manufacturer. The drawings showing the ways in which a glass can be built up may be found useful when considering Groups III to V.

The sub-division of the above groups can now be tabulated. Throughout this classification it is the more familiar variations of stem, bowl, foot, and decoration which are generally noted, though some others of special interest are recorded.

Certain abbreviations have been used, to economize space.

bal.	for baluster.	c.t.	for cup-topped.
bkt.	for bucket.	p.t.	for pan-topped.
inv.	for inverted.	s.t.	for saucer-topped.

r.f.	for round funnel.	*t.*	for top.
tpt.	for trumpet.	*c.*	for centre.
wstd.	for waisted.	*b.*	for base.

FOR FURTHER READING

The most useful books on English 18th century glass have been mentioned. The various works by Percy Bate, Francis Buckley, Grant R. Francis, Albert Hartshorne, H. J. Powell, W. A. Thorpe and M. S. Dudley Westropp may all be studied with advantage.

Group I

GLASSES WITH BALUSTER STEMS

(1685–1725)

A PRIMARY sub-division is into Single Flint and Double Flint glasses. The former, now rare, are not known to be any earlier in date, but they are so in form, being closely related to Greene's designs. They have deep conical or round funnel bowls on a short inverted baluster or wide angular knop, and they probably dropped out of production about 1690, although I have seen one or two with longer stems which must date well after 1700. The double flint glasses are much more numerous, and from their weight and, on occasion, great size, are often termed 'heavy' balusters. They were simple enough at first, with conical or round funnel bowls over a stout inverted baluster. Features suggestive of a particularly early date are a very heavy base to the bowl, even to half its height, and a light and inadequate folded foot. About 1690 this foot was strengthened by a dome, the stems grew taller and more complicated, and a waisted bowl was added to the repertoire. About 1700–1710 the stem was all-dominant. A wide and heavy angular knop is often seen, less frequently a drop-knop, single or double, and certainly rare specialized formations. The annulated knop followed and then the true baluster, perhaps about 1715.

Coincidently with these last comes a bucket bowl and a neatly-made trumpet, and at any time after 1700 simple knopping might occur, particularly on those glasses with a small bowl, such as cordials. From a peak point in the first decade of the century, there was a tendency towards smaller size and lighter weight, until the series merges into the Balustroid group which follows.

I regard a Baluster glass as requiring either a solid base

to the bowl or a stem with pronounced emphasis or complication of knopping wherein one feature dominates. Its size is immaterial. A Balustroid glass, on the other hand, lacks the solid bowl base (except to some extent in the waisted bowl) or the stem is without any knopping of particular emphasis. In practice, the distinction is not often difficult. It should be added that baluster glasses are almost always of the simple drawn stem build-up (2 NS) and much more often than not the stem has a substantial tear. Few champagnes occur and engraving is uncommon. Good specimens in soda metal are known.

SUB-GROUP A: *Single Flint Glasses*

These are early glasses, lightly made of thin metal. They will chiefly be found as described in Sec. 1 (a) and (b) and Sec. 2 (a) of Sub-group B. From 1682.

SUB-GROUP B: *Double Flint Glasses*

SECTION 1. Glasses in which an Inverted Baluster is the stem feature.

There are at least fifteen variations of stem, the commonest being those listed below.

(a) Inverted Baluster only.
Bowl, at first conical or r.f., later wstd. Foot, folded, then domed and folded. Giant goblets are found. From 1685.

(b) Inverted Baluster with Knop at *b*.
Bowl, conical or r.f., later wstd. or bkt. Foot, folded or domed and folded, later plain. Giant goblets are included. From 1690.

(c) Knop over an Inverted Baluster.
Bowl, wstd. Foot, folded, domed, or plain. About 1720.

(d) Knop over an Inverted Baluster with Knop at *b*.
As for (c).

(e) Knop and Flat Knop over an Inverted Baluster, with Knop at *b*.
Bowl, wstd. Foot, folded or domed and folded. About 1720.

SECTION 2. Glasses in which a Wide Angular Knop is the stem feature.

Five variations have been noted, the commonest being those with:

(a) Wide Angular Knop at *t.* and Knop at *b.*

Bowl, conical or r.f. Foot, folded or domed and folded. Includes giant goblets and the great majority of the glasses of the Section. From 1690.

(b) Wide Angular Knop at *c.* and Knop at *b.*

Bowl, r.f. Foot, folded. About 1700.

(c) Knop at *t.*, Wide Angular Knop at *c.* and Knop at *b.*

Bowl, r.f., or thistle. Foot, folded. After 1700.

SECTION 3. Glasses in which a Drop knop is the stem feature.

At least ten variations, the commonest being listed. In most cases (b) and (c) are not very different from the rarer variety with two drop knops, also with waisted bowl and domed and folded foot. A good variety of the drop knop occurs in the form of an inverted cone.

(a) Drop knop at *t.* and Knop at *b.*

Bowl, variable. Foot, domed and folded. From 1700.

(b) Drop knop over a True Baluster.

Bowl, wstd. Foot, domed and folded. About 1710.

(c) The same, with Knop at *t.* and *b.*

Bowl, wstd. Foot, domed and folded. About 1710.

SECTION 4. Glasses in which an Annulated Knop is the stem feature.

There are at least twelve variations of stem. The annulated knop usually has three rings, but may consist of five, seven, or nine. The following are the commonest stem forms.

(a) Annulated Knop at *t.* and Knop at *b.*

Bowl, bkt, r.f., or wstd. Foot, folded or domed and folded. From 1710.

(b) Annulated Knop at *t.*, Angular or Swelling Knop at *c.* and Knop at *b.*

Bowl, wstd. Foot, folded, domed and folded, and later plain. From 1715.

(c) Annulated Knop over Inverted Baluster.

Bowl, wstd. Foot, folded, domed and folded, and later plain. From 1715.

(d) Annulated Knop over Inverted Baluster with Knop at *b.* As (c).

(e) Annulated Knop at *c.* and Knop at *b.*

Bowl, r.f., or wstd. Foot, folded or domed and folded. From 1710.

Section 5. Glasses in which a Cushioned Knop is the stem feature.

There are at least four variations of stem.

Cushioned Knop at *t.* and Knop at *b.*

Bowl, r.f. Foot, folded, domed, or domed and folded. Includes nearly all the glasses of the Section. From 1705.

Section 6. Glasses in which a True Baluster is the stem feature.

There are at least sixteen stem variations, most importantly:

(a) and (b) True Baluster, with or without Knop at *b.*
Bowl, wstd., or tpt. Foot, folded. About 1715.

(c) Knop over a True Baluster.
Bowl, tpt. Foot, domed, or domed and folded. About 1715.

(d) The same, with Knop at *b.*
Bowl, tpt., or wstd. Foot, folded or plain. From 1715.

(e) Angular Knop over a True Baluster.
Bowl, r.f., or wstd. Foot, folded, domed and folded, or plain. About 1715.

(f) Two True Balusters.
Bowl, wstd. Foot, folded or domed and folded. About 1710.

Section 7 to 10. Glasses in which a particular Specialized Knop is the stem feature.

These are rare and comprise the Acorn, Cylinder, Egg, and Mushroom Knops. They all date around 1710.

Section 11. Glasses with Simple Knopping, alone or in combination.

There are nine variations or more, chiefly:

(a) Knop at *t.*
Bowl, conical or r.f. Foot, folded. Mostly dram glasses. From 1700.

(b) and (c) Angular or Swelling Knop at *c.*, with or without Knop at *b.*
Bowl, r.f., lipped r.f., tpt., or wstd. Foot, folded, domed, or later plain. Cordials occur and collaring may appear under the bowl. From 1715.

(d) Knops at *t.*, *c.* and *b.*
Bowl, r.f., or wstd. Foot, folded, domed, or plain. About 1720.

SECTION 12. Glasses without Stem.

There are at least three variations and there are out-of-period specimens. All are dram glasses.

(a) Foot and stem replaced by an Inverted Bowl.

These are the 'double glasses'. Bowls usually r.f. About 1700.

(b) The stem replaced by a heavy Knop.

Bowl, conical or r.f. Foot, plain. After 1700.

Group II

GLASSES WITH MOULDED PEDESTAL STEMS
(1715–1765)

THE Baluster glasses had passed their best when George I came to his English throne, and with him came a type of stem utterly different from anything else we ever made. It was in fact a moulded pedestal, nearly always semi-hollow or with a long tear, and, strictly speaking, always inverted: one very early specimen, apart from being solid, had every appearance of being hand-fashioned. Glasses of this group are widely known as 'Silesian stemmed,' without any justification as far as I can see. The comparable German glasses came from Thuringia at a later date.

Classification is relatively simple, but as many champagnes and sweetmeats are included, differences in detail are numerous. Probably no glasses have been so mis-dated as these. The four-sided pedestal was early and short-lived. The six-sided variety can hardly have been made more than a little later, or more than a little longer. Then, at a more uncertain interval, there followed the eight-sided form, some examples of which belong to the decade 1725–35. Most, however, will be found to have collaring at the base of the stem, and these are all much later, about and around 1750. It does not follow that all without this collaring are early. The build-up of the glasses is 3 NS, 3 WS, or 4 WS.

It is noticeable that the four-sided pedestal is never collared at the base, and I have no record that it was used to support a champagne or sweetmeat bowl. The six-sided form is rarely collared; still less frequently is it used for anything but wines and goblets. The eight-sided stem, however, is much more often collared than not, and common, while champagnes and sweetmeats greatly outnumber other types of vessel. The conclusion is inescapable, that champagnes and sweetmeats are, with few exceptions, late, and not early. In the same category are some rather leggy six-sided and eight-sided stems hailing from Newcastle. They are contemporary with Light Balusters and with some Composite Stems which will later be described, and they are distinguishable quite easily by their metal, and sometimes also by their foreign engraving. The group dies out with some not too common debased forms of stem which are hardly more than rib-twisted, a great contrast to the clean taper lines of the original four-sided pedestal, a grand form which deserved a better fate.

SECTION 1. Glasses in which the stem is a Four-sided Pedestal.

There are at least three variations, none common.

(a) Shoulders Rounded.

Bowl, conical, r.f., or tpt. Foot, folded. From 1715 for a few years only. A notable variety is impressed with the words *God Save King George* on the four sides, with or without crowns on the shoulders. Presumably 1715.

(b) Shoulders Rounded, and with letters *GR*, small crowns, or sceptres moulded in relief thereon.

As (a)

(c) Shoulders Diamond-topped.

Bowl, foot, and date as (a).

SECTION 2. Glasses in which the stem consists of a Knop over a Four-sided Pedestal.

Two variations have been noted, both scarce.

(a) Shoulders Rounded.

Bowl, foot, and date as 1 (a). Some Coronation glasses.

(b) Shoulders Diamond-topped.

Bowl, r.f. Foot, folded. About 1715.

SECTION 3. Glasses in which the stem is a Six-sided Pedestal.

There are at least four variations, all scarce.

(a) Shoulders Rounded.

Bowl, conical or r.f. Foot, folded. About 1720.

(b) Shoulders Rounded, stem collared at base.
Bowl, conical, or in champagne-sweetmeat styles. Foot, domed, or domed and folded. Mid-18th century.

(c) Shoulders Diamond-topped.
Bowl, r.f., or wstd. Foot, folded, domed or plain. Some specimens early; others, including examples with panel-moulded feet, are of Newcastle origin and late.

(d) as (c) but with five small stars in relief also on shoulders.
Bowl, conical or r.f. Foot, folded. 1715–20.

SECTION 4. Glasses in which the stem consists of a Knop over a Six-sided Pedestal.

Three variations, all scarce.

(a) Shoulders Diamond-topped.
Bowl, r.f. Foot, folded. 1720-25.

(b) as (a) but stem collared at base.
Bowl, r.f. Foot, folded, or domed and folded. Includes Newcastle glasses. Mid-18th century.

SECTION 5. Glasses in which the stem consists of Two Knops (one may be Angular) over a Six-sided Pedestal.

With Shoulders Diamond-topped.
Bowl, r.f. Foot, domed and folded. Examples, which are rare, are of Newcastle origin, build-up 3 WS. With or without basal collaring, they are mid-18th century.

SECTION 6. Glasses in which the stem consists of an Annulated Knop over a Six-sided Pedestal.

Shoulders Diamond-topped, stem collared at base.
Bowl, bell (or wstd.). Foot, domed. Newcastle glasses, rare, build-up 3 WS or 4 WS. Mid-18th century.

SECTION 7. Glasses in which the stem is an Eight-sided Pedestal.

Five variations noted, only those with collaring at base or stem being common. In these later glasses, moulded decoration to bowl or foot, or to both, is frequent, ribbing, panel-moulding, and wide flutes being the favourite themes. Sweetmeats and champagnes are common and nearly all are collared just below the bowl.

(a) Rounded Shoulders.
Bowl, conical or r.f. Foot, folded. Wines are relatively early.

There are also champagnes and sweetmeats, especially low ones, with pan type bowls and various feet. These are late, or rather late, perhaps 1740-50.

(b) The same, but stem collared at base.

Examples are common and almost exclusively champagnes and sweetmeats. Bowl, variable but usually with everted rim. Duplex forms (pan-topped and saucer-topped) are frequent. The foot is folded, domed, or domed and folded; rarely plain. There is much decorative moulding, diamond and honeycomb patterns being the most desirable. Collaring under bowl is almost universal. A few tall sweetmeats with denticulated bowl rims ('fringed sweetmeats') occur. I attribute them to Tyneside, as well as the few wines and goblets which also belong to this sub-section. All are about 1750.

(c) Shoulders Diamond-topped.

Bowl, conical, r.f., or thistle. Foot, folded. Wines and goblets are uncommon, but may claim early dating. Low champagnes are found as in (a) but rather less frequently.

(d) The same, but stem collared at base.

Specimens are only slightly less common than in (b) and precisely the same remarks apply.

SECTION 8. Glasses in which the stem consists of a Knop over an Eight-sided Pedestal.

Two variations have been noted. Examples are rare, only a few goblets and wines having been noticed.

(a) Shoulders Diamond-topped.

Bowl, r.f. Foot, folded, or domed. A giant goblet is clearly of the Baluster period but the normal date is about 1725-35.

(b) The same, but stem collared at base.

Bowl, r.f. Foot, domed and folded. Only Newcastle wines, build-up 3 WS, have been noted. The lack of champagnes and sweetmeats is surprising. Around 1750.

SECTION 9. Glasses in which the stem consists of a Knop (with tears) over an Eight-sided Pedestal.

Two variations, both with the late basal collaring. Examples are rather scarce, especially in (a). All are collared beneath the bowl.

(a) Shoulders Rounded, stem collared at base.

Bowl, variable. Foot, domed. Champagnes only. Around 1750.

(b) Shoulders Diamond-topped, stem collared at base.

As (a) but includes some veritable sweetmeats. Around 1750.

SECTION 10. Glasses in which the stem consists of an Annulated Knop over an Eight-sided Pedestal.

Two varieties only noted. Rare.

Shoulders Diamond-topped, the stem collared at base.

Bowl, r.f. Foot, domed. Newcastle wines, including some moulded motifs. Build-up 3 WS or 4 WS. Mid-18th century.

SECTION 11. Glasses in which the stem is a moulded Pedestal of Debased form.

Three or more variations, only (c) being fairly common.

(a) Four-sided, hollow, and strongly tapered: with Rounded Shoulders.
Bowl, r.f. or wstd. ogee. Foot, folded or plain. A few cordials, but they are rare. About 1760.

(b) The same, but tear in stem and lightly tapered.
As for (a).

(c) Vertically Ribbed, slightly twisted, and collared at base.
Bowl, variable, always collared. Foot, domed, or domed and folded. Some decorative moulding, chiefly ribbing. Champagnes and sweetmeats only. 1760-65.

Group III

GLASSES WITH BALUSTROID STEMS

(1725–1755)

AFTER 1715 the Baluster glasses became gradually lighter and smaller. Because of overlap, no particular date can be given for its beginning but out of that first group, the third—the Balustroid—was born. Its earliest glasses are very near relations indeed. Their metal shares the same blackish tint, later becoming greyish, and it is sufficiently thick. They are built on the same lines, but less well, and a good many were, and for that matter still are, quite inexpensive glasses. The bowl, except sometimes the waisted bowl, has lost the solidity, and the stem has lost the emphasis, of the Baluster glass. The group finishes with numerous very simply knopped glasses.

Most specimens of the group are of the 2 NS build-up. A few only have been given separately-made moulded bowls and are 3 NS. But I have included some 3 WS forms in a section of their own, more because they fit still less well into either Group IV or V than because they are perfectly accommodated here. They are few in number but wide in range, and some may be Group IV glasses before its metal became distinctive or its forms aristocratic. Practised collectors will recognize the difficulties of allocation. Some glasses have claim for inclusion in more than one group, hence some stem formations will be found again in Group IV, but the metal is then so distinct, and the proportions often so different, that separation is easy.

It is in the simpler glasses of this group that moulded bowls appear, but they are uncommon. Even faint fluting at the base of the bowl is quite scarce, and, in the instances noted, it comes on 2 NS glasses, as it does often enough in Group VI. Stems may be semi-hollow, with a tear, or solid, and it seems that it was the simpler stems which were solid. Engraving of the 'flowered' kind is to be found on the later specimens, but it is not yet common.

All types of drinking glass are represented in the group, with the possible exception of ratafias. Goblets and ales are infrequent, and out-size specimens rare. There is a fair number of champagnes and I have come to believe that most such glasses with knopped stems belong to this group. Gin glasses are fairly common.

SECTION 1. Glasses in which an Inverted Baluster is the stem feature.

The Baluster is not necessarily prominent or decisive, and it tends towards a shoulder knop. There are at least eleven stem formations, some of which are also to be found in Group IV. Those generally seen have the

(a) Inverted Baluster only.
Bowl, r.f., tpt., wstd., and various champagne types. Foot, folded or plain; various in champagnes, including a radially grooved foot to a low sweetmeat with denticulated rim. About 1725-55.

(b) Inverted Baluster with tears.
Bowl, wstd. Foot, folded or plain. Scarce. About 1735-45.

(c) Inverted Baluster with knop at *b*. The commonest form.
Gin glasses are not rare, and there are champagnes and low denticulated sweetmeats. Bowl, various, but generally wstd., or of pan formation. Foot, various. 1730-55.

(d) Knop over an Inverted Baluster with Knop at *b*. Details as in (c) but examples are considerably scarcer. 1735-45.

(e) Angular (or flattened) Knop over an Inverted Baluster, with Knop at *b*.
Bowl, wstd. Foot, folded. Scarce except for gins. 1740-45.

SECTION 2. Glasses (called 'Kit-Kat' glasses) in which an Inverted Baluster usually appears.

These are all normal two-piece glasses. Hardly anything but a wine appears. The straight portion of the stem may contain a tear but is more usually solid. A few similar glasses will be found in Section 9, with a 3 WS build-up. Some Group IV glasses may also be compared. There are nine stem formations, those with a base knop being rare. All date about 1740-50.

(a) Short Plain Section over a Long Inverted Baluster.
Bowl, tpt. Foot, folded or plain. Scarce.
(b) Medium Plain Section over a Medium Inverted Baluster.
Bowl, tpt., or wstd. Foot, folded, domed or plain. Frequent.
(c) Long Plain Section over a Short Inverted Baluster.
Bowl, and foot as in (b). Frequent.

SECTION 3. Glasses in which a True Baluster is the stem feature.

These most nearly approach glasses in Group I. There is hardly anything but wines. At least ten stem formation soccur and none is common. All date about 1725-35.
(a) True Baluster with Knop at *b*.
Bowl, r.f., tpt., or wstd. Foot, folded, or domed and folded.
(b) True Baluster, ridged beneath with Knop at *b*.
Bowl, tpt. Foot, domed. Rare.
(c) Knop at top over a True Baluster.
Bowl, tpt., or wstd. Foot, folded.
(d) As last but with Knop at *b*.
Bowl, tpt., or wstd. Foot, folded, or plain.

SECTION 4. Glasses whose stem contains an Annulated Knop.

Certain glasses of similar formations will be found in Group IV. The Annulated Knop has normally three ridges, but is known with five or seven. It is mostly wines which are found, but there are some champagnes with cup or pan type bowls. There are at least twelve stem formations, only two being at all frequent.
(a) Annulated Knop at *t*. and Knop at *b*.
Bowl, r.f., wstd., or pan type. Foot, folded, or domed and folded. Includes a few champagnes. About 1725-35.
(b) Annulated Knop at *t*. over an Inverted Baluster with Knop at *b*.
Bowl, wstd., or pan type. Foot as for (a) but a domed and terraced foot is to be found.
About 1730-40.

SECTIONS 5, 6, 7 AND 8. Glasses in which a particular Specialized Knop is the stem feature.

These Knops, the Cushioned, the Cylinder, the Acorn, and the Dumb-bell, are rare. Four stem variations of the first are available, one only of the second, and two of the others. In one or two cases, inclusion in this

Group is provisional. The most important stem form is the following, which, like all the others, dates about 1730-40. Its bowl is generally engraved with the early Jacobite rose and single bud.

Knop and Cushioned Knop (with tears) over a Swelling (or Angular) Knop with Knop at *b*.

Bowl, wstd. Foot, domed and folded. Scarce.

SECTION 9. Glasses with Welded Stems.

This includes specimens in which the stem is composed of two sections welded together, the bowl being integral with the upper section (build-up 3 WS). Forms similar at sight will be found in Sections 2 and 3. Some formations are inserted on the evidence of the metal, but may prove to be early glasses in the Group IV series. There are at least fifteen stem variations, most of them very scarce. Representative types are as under.

(a) Knop over a True Baluster with Knop at *b*.
Bowl, tpt. Foot, folded. See Section 3. Rare. About 1725

(b) Short Plain Section set over or into a Long Tapered Section.
Bowl, conical or tpt. Foot, folded, domed, or plain. This is one of the less infrequent formations. Wines only have been noted. About 1740-45.

(c) Short Plain Section set over or into a Short Wide Section (or deep collar).
Bowl, tpt. Foot, plain. Drams only. About 1745-50.

(d) Short Plain Section set over a Long Inverted Baluster (with tears) with Knop at *b*.
Bowl, tpt., or wstd. Foot, domed, or plain. Scarce. About 1740.

(e) Short Plain Section set over a long Section having Shoulder (or Angular) Knop (with tears) at *t*. and Angular Knop at *c*.
Bowl, tpt. Foot, plain. A distinctive type but scarce. About 1735.

(f) Medium Plain Section set over a Medium Inverted Baluster (with tears).
Bowl, tpt. Foot, plain. Rare. About 1740.

(g) Long Plain Section set over a Short Inverted Baluster.
Bowl, tpt. Foot, domed. See Section 2. Rare. About 1740.

(h) Long Plain Section set over an Acorn Knop (with tears) with Knop at *b*.
Bowl, tpt. Foot, domed. Rare. About 1735-40.

(j) Long Plain Section having a central Swelling Knop set over or into a Flattened Knop (with tears). A goblet has been seen.
Bowl, wstd. Foot, domed. Rare. About 1735.

SECTION 10. Glasses in which the stems have Simple Knopping.

This section includes at least half the glasses of the group. Generally speaking, they are of wine glass size, ales and goblets being uncommon. There are some champagnes and low sweetmeats, and mead glasses occasionally occur. Most forms of bowl appear in one section or another, moulded or engraved decoration being infrequent. Two-piece glasses greatly predominate. There are at least three dozen stem variations, some very scarce. The commonest or most notable are as under.

(*The following have a Single Knop.*)

(a) Knop (or Flattened or Shoulder Knop) at *t*.
Bowl, various, chiefly r.f. Foot, folded. Frequent. About 1745-55.

(b) Band Knop at *t*. and (c) with Bladed Knop at *t*.
Bowl, wstd. Foot, plain. Both rare. About 1735-40.

(d) Knop at centre.
Bowl, various, the ogee predominating. Foot, folded, or plain; in a few champagnes, domed, or domed and folded. Frequent. About 1745-55.

(e) Swelling Knop at centre.
Except that champagnes are rare, and specimens generally scarcer, the remarks as for (d) apply.

(f) Knop near the base.
Bowl, wstd. Foot, folded or domed, seldom plain. Rather scarce. About 1735-45.

(g) Knop at base.
Bowl, various, the wstd. form predominating. Foot, folded, domed, domed and folded, or plain, all in conjunction with the wstd. bowl; otherwise plain. The base knop is not as a rule prominent. 1745-55.

(*The following have Two Knops.*)

(h) Knop (or Flattened or Shoulder Knop) at *t*. and Knop at *c*.
Includes a few champagnes with pan type bowls, and domed, or domed and folded feet. Wines are not uncommon with r.f. bowl, otherwise examples are scarce. Foot, folded, or plain. 1740-50.

(j) Knop (or Flattened or Shoulder Knop) at *t*. and Knop at *b*.
Bowl, r.f., or wstd. Foot, folded. Includes champagnes as in (h) and a number of gin glasses. Frequent. 1745-55.

(k) Knop (or Angular Knop) at *c*. and Knop at *b*.
Bowl, various. Foot, folded. Not very common. 1745-55.

(l) The stem Trisected by Two Knops.
Bowl, r.f. or tpt. Foot, folded. Scarce. 1745-50.

(*The following have Three Knops.*)

(m) Knop (or Flattened or Shoulder Knop) at *t.*, Knop (or Flattened Knop) at *c.* and Knop at *b.*
Bowl, r.f., or wstd. Foot, folded. Fairly frequent. 1740-50.

(n) Stem semi-hollow with Knop (or Flattened or Shoulder Knop) at *t.*, Bladed Knop at *c.* and Knop at *b.*
Bowl, r.f. Foot, folded. A not very common but distinctive form. About 1745.

(o) With Knop and Collar at *t.* Knop at *c.* and Knop at *b.*
Bowl, wstd. Foot, folded. Scarce. 1745-50.

Group IV

THE LIGHT NEWCASTLE BALUSTER GLASSES

(1735–1765)

THE term Light Baluster was coined to describe certain rather tall glasses with slender stems having a series of knops of different kinds, none of which was especially dominant. Such glasses are now known to have been made on Tyneside, as well as others with more simple knopping. Very many are found with Dutch engraving, and apparently for that reason various authors have regarded them as possibly, or actually, continental. They are still poorly represented in the majority of collections.

They are distinguishable by their elegant form, careful manufacture, and also by their metal. This is thinner than in Balusters and Balustroids. It is clearer, often approaches brilliancy, and, once in mind, is quite distinctive. Striations in the bowl are inconsiderable. The feet also have slighter striation than before, and tend to be flatter, often without a fold, and they are consequently liable to be chipped. Small capacity bowls do not occur, though large ones are frequent. Much use is made of multiple tears in the knopping.

Not all glasses made in the Newcastle factory or factories concerned have elaborate knopping. A certain number are of simple stem formation and correspond exactly in description with glasses in Groups I and III, though very different to look at. Those with plain straight stems will be found in Group VI; those with moulded pedestals in Group II, and others, possessing a composite stem, are dealt with in Group V.

The build-up varies. The simpler forms are 2 NS, but there are some 3 NS as well. Of the elaborately knopped Light Balusters, some are 2 NS, and these, I believe, are generally earlier than those with 3 WS and 4 WS formations;

there was a considerable degree of overlap. The dating is not satisfactorily settled, and there are almost certainly a few late-made Balusters in the Newcastle metal. But I question whether any Light Balusters were made before the 1730's, notwithstanding some quite famous specimens with an engraved signature and earlier date. For most specimens a mid-18th century date is all that caution will permit, the heavier stems as usual preceding the lighter. Complicated knopping does not necessarily indicate heaviness, though it may indicate height.

Analysis of the more complicated stem formations does present difficulties, partly because a slender knop is not always decisive, partly because the stem can be 'read' in more than one way. Some familiarity with actual specimens, and a study of the illustrations provided will help to elucidate the manner in which these elaborate stems have been analysed. In the following classification the date is mid-18th century, unless otherwise stated.

SECTION 1. Glasses in which the Knopping is based on the Inverted Baluster.

There are at least thirty stem variations, many very scarce. The following have been selected for notice, and their usual build-up is given. There is sometimes an unmentioned alternative build-up.

(a) Cigar-shaped Baluster. 3 NS.
Bowl, conical or tpt. Foot, folded. Scarce. Before 1750.

(b) and (c) Inverted Baluster with, or without, a Knop at *b*. 2 NS.
Bowl, r.f. Foot, folded, or domed and folded. Both scarce.

(d) and (e) Knop over an Inverted Baluster, with, or without, a Knop (or Knops) at *b*. 3 WS.
Bowl, r.f. Foot, plain. Both rare.

(f) and (g) Knop over an Inverted Baluster (with tears), with, or without, a Knop at *b*. 3 WS.
Bowl, wstd., or tpt. Foot, plain. Both rare.

(h) and (j) Knop (with tears) over an Inverted Baluster, with, or without, Knop at *b*. 3 NS or 4 WS.
Bowl, r.f., and wstd. Foot, plain. Both very uncommon.

(k) Three Knops, the centre one with tears, over an Inverted Baluster, with Knop (with tears) at *b*. 4 WS.
Bowl, r.f. Foot, plain. Very rare. After 1750.

(l) Short Section with central Angular (or Flat) Knop over an Inverted Baluster (with tears) and Knop at *b*. 2 NS or 3 WS.
Bowl r.f. Foot, plain. The weld, when present, is above the baluster. Fairly common. After 1750.

(m) Short Section with Angular (or Flat) Knop and Knop over an Inverted Baluster (with tears) and Knop at *b*. 3 WS.
Bowl, r.f., sometimes wstd. Foot, plain. The weld is above the baluster. This is the commonest form of stem and very large glasses exist. The same stem, with the baluster lacking the tears, is quite scarce. Both after 1750.

(n) and (o) Angular (or Flat) Knop and Knop (with tears) over an Inverted Baluster with, or without, Knop at *b*. 3 WS.
Bowl, r.f., wstd. r.f., or more often wstd. Foot, plain. Both stems are scarce. Both after 1750.

(p) Two Angular Knops (or Short True Balusters), over an Inverted Baluster with Knop (or Knops) at *b*. 2 NS.
Bowl, r.f., or wstd. Foot, domed, or plain. Fairly frequent. Before 1750.

SECTION 2. Glasses in whose stems an Annulated Knop appears.

The annulated knop was not made great use of, but still at least nine stem variations exist. All are scarce. It was also used in a few Newcastle glasses of Group II. In nearly every instance a three-ring knop is employed, but a five-ring knop is known. As in Section 1, the build-up varies. The following comprise the more notable stem forms:

(a) Annulated Knop at *t*. 3 NS.
Bowl, tpt. Foot, plain. The Knop is quite small.

(b) Annulated Knop at *t*. over an Inverted Baluster, with Knop at *b*. 2 NS.
Bowl, r.f., or wstd. Foot, plain, folded, or domed and folded. This is the most frequent form. The stem without the base Knop is much scarcer.

(c) and (d) Annulated Knop at *t*. over an Inverted Baluster (with tears), with, or without, a Knop at *b*. 2 NS or 3 WS.
Bowl, r.f. Foot, plain. Both forms are scarce. After 1750.

(e) Medium Section having an Angular Knop over an Annulated Knop, set on a Medium Section with Angular Knop over an Inverted Baluster. 3 WS.
Bowl, bell. Foot, plain. Rare. About 1755.

(f) True Baluster above, Annulated Knop at *c*. and Inverted Baluster below. 3 WS.
Bowl, r.f. Foot, domed and folded. The weld is above the annulated knop. Rare. About 1755.

SECTION 3. Glasses in which the Knopping is based on a True Baluster.

These are rather infrequent glasses, and no form is common. Eight stem variations have been noted, among them the following:

(a) Two Short True Balusters over a Knop and a True Baluster. 2 NS or 3 WS.
Bowl, r.f. Foot, domed.

(b) Knop and Swelling Knop over a True Baluster. 2 NS.
Bowl, r.f. Foot, folded. About 1745.

(c) Swelling Knop at *t.* Knop (or Angular Knop) at *c.* over a True Baluster. 3 WS.
Bowl, r.f., or wstd. Foot, plain.

(d) Inverted Baluster above, Knop at *c.* and True Baluster below. 2 NS.
Bowl, r.f. Foot, domed, or domed and folded. This is one of the more stoutly stemmed glasses. From 1735.

SECTION 4. Glasses in which a Cushioned Knop is the stem feature.

Half a dozen stems are to be found, in all of which the Cushioned Knop is at the head of, or high up in, the stem. All are scarce or rare. Among them are these:

(a) Knop with Cushioned Knop (with tears) over an Inverted Baluster with Knop at *b.* 4 WS.
Bowl, tpt. Foot, plain. About 1735.

(b) Doubly Cushioned Knop (with tears) set over a section with Angular (or Shoulder) Knop (with tears) at *t.* and Knop at *b.* 3 WS.
Bowl, r.f., or wstd. Foot, plain.

(c) Doubly Cushioned Knop (with tears) over an Inverted Baluster (with tears). 3 WS.
Bowl, wstd. Foot, plain.

SECTION 5. Glasses in which a Mushroom Knop is the stem feature.

Only one stem formation has been noted and it is very rare.

Knop and Mushroom Knop (with tears) over an Inverted Baluster. 3 WS.
Bowl, tpt. Foot, plain. About 1740.

SECTION 6. Glasses in which the stem has a Dumb-bell formation.

Five stem formations have been noted, all scarce, and about 1760 date.

(a) Dumb-bell at *t.* over an Inverted Baluster (or Shoulder Knop). 4 WS.
Bowl, r.f. Foot, plain. Two such glasses break the almost universal rule of this group in having a moulded bowl.

(b) As (a) but with Bladed Knop near the base. 3 WS.
Bowl, r.f. Foot, folded. Rare.

(c) Dumb-bell (with tears) over an Inverted Baluster (or Shoulder Knop) with Knop at *b.* 4 WS.
Bowl, r.f. Foot, plain. This appears to be the most frequent form.

Section 7. Glasses in which the Knops are of Simple Form.

This section includes a good many glasses, some of which have quite imposing height and knopping. There are at least nineteen stem variations, few being at all common, and quite half being very scarce. Among the types:

(The following have a Single Knop Formation.)

(a) Knop (or Angular Knop) at *c.* 2 NS.
Bowl, tpt. Foot, plain. Scarce.

(b) Swelling Knop at *c.* 2 NS.
Bowl, r.f. Foot, plain. Uncommon.

(The following has Two Knop Formations.)

(c) Knop (with tears) at *t.* and Angular Knop at *c.* 3 WS.
Bowl, r.f. Foot, plain. Rare.

(The following have Three Knop Formations.)

(d) Knop, Angular (or Annular) Knop, and Knop, all at *c.* 2 NS.
Bowl, tpt. Foot, plain. Uncommon.

(e) Knop at *t.*, Swelling Knop at *c.* and Knop at *b.* 2 NS.
Bowl, r.f. Foot, folded. Very scarce. About 1745.

(f) Knop (with tears) and Knop at *t.* and Knop at *b.* 3 WS.
Bowl, r.f. Foot, plain. Rare.

(g) Two Swelling Knops and Knop at *b.* 2 NS.
Bowl, r.f., or wstd. Foot, plain or domed. Infrequent. About 1745.

(h) Three Swelling (or Angular) Knops. 2 NS.
Bowl, r.f. Foot, plain or domed. Scarce. About 1740.

(The following have Four or more Knop Formations.)

(j) Upper Section having an Angular Knop and Knop set over a Longer Section with Angular Knop at *t.* and Knop at *b.* 3 WS.
Bowl, r.f. Foot, plain. Scarce.

(k) Medium upper Section having a Knop, Angular (or Flattened) Knop and Knop, over a Medium Section with Angular (or Swelling) Knop at *c.* and Knop at *b.* 3 WS.
Bowl, r.f. Foot, plain, folded, domed, or domed and folded. Fairly common.

(l) Three Bobbin Knops over a centre Ball Knop (with tears) and three Bobbin Knops below. 3 WS. (Pl. 47d.)
Bowl, r.f. Foot, plain. Rare. About 1745-50.

SECTION 8. Glasses in which the stem is replaced by Knopping.

Very few glasses will be found to qualify for inclusion here, and only one example can be given.

The Stem replaced by a Knop and a larger Knop (with tears).
Bowl, tpt. Foot, plain. A gin glass. About 1750-60.

Group V

GLASSES WITH COMPOSITE STEMS

(1740–1770)

THIS group has been raised to cover glasses which have two or more different types of stem welded together, the build-up being therefore 3 WS, 4 WS, or even 5 WS. A considerable number of these glasses derive from the same house or houses which were responsible for Group IV. Some others are closely related to the 'Kit-Kat' glasses of Group III.

A good many stem formations have been noted, and others are no doubt to be found. Few are common, and many very rare. Their dating is much in line with that of Group IV, with, probably, a later commencement. Throughout the analysis their date may be taken as mid-18th century, unless otherwise stated. They are well made and handsome specimens, ill-represented in most collections. Some good decorative and commemorative engraving is to be found on their bowls. Moulded motifs appear to be absent, except in a few champagnes, and any fold to the foot is quite exceptional.

SECTION 1. Glasses with stem consisting of a Plain Section over an Air Twist Section.

At least eleven stem formations are to be found, only one of which appears with any frequency. The following types are representative. The abbreviation MSAT for Multiple Spiral Air Twist is used where appropriate.

(a) Medium Plain Section over a Medium Inverted Baluster with MSAT.
Bowl, tpt. Foot, plain. Scarce.

(b) Short Plain Section over a Long Inverted Baluster with MSAT.
Bowl, tpt., or wstd. Foot, plain, less often domed. Includes goblets, and ales, and is the most usual glass of the Section.

(c) Knop at *t.* over a Long MSAT Section with Knop (or Shoulder Knop) at *t.* and Knop (or Swelling Knop) at *c.*
Bowl, wstd. Foot, plain. Rare.

(d) Knop (with tears) at *t.* over a Long Section with Spiral Gauze.
Bowl, r.f., or bell. Foot plain. A Newcastle model of 4 WS build-up. Rare. About 1760.

(e) Knop (with tears) at *t.* over a Long MSAT Inverted Baluster, with Knop at *b.*
Bowl, bell. Foot, plain. Another Newcastle pattern. Rare. About 1760.

(f) Heavy Knop (with tears) and Two Flattened Knops over a MSAT Section.
Bowl, r.f. slightly wstd. Foot, domed. Very rare. About 1760.

SECTION 2. Glasses with stem consisting of an Air Twist Section over a Plain Section.

There are at least eighteen stem formations. Only one is really common, but most varieties are rather more frequent than those of Section 1. Some are very attractive types. The following stem formations are representative.

(a) Long MSAT Section set into a Knop (with tears) at *b.* of stem.
Bowl, tpt., or wstd. Foot, plain, domed, or domed and folded. Very scarce. About 1740-5.

(b), (c) and (d) As (a) but respectively with Bladed Knop, Annulated Knop, or Collar and Knop at *b.* of stem.
Bowl, wstd. Foot, domed. This applies in each case. Examples are rare. About 1740-5.

(e) Long MSAT Section with triple (or quadruple) Collars at *b.*, set into a Knop (with tears) at *b.* of stem.
Bowl, tpt., or wstd. Foot, domed. Goblets are known. Scarce. About 1745-55.

(f) Long MSAT Section over a squat Inverted Baluster.
Bowl, ogee, r.f., or wstd. Foot, domed; rarely plain. Scarce.

(g) Long MSAT Section over a squat Inverted Baluster (with tears).
Bowl, r.f., tpt., or wstd. Foot, plain, less often domed. Other types of bowl occur, and ales, cordials and goblets are known. Frequent.

(h) Medium MSAT Section over a Medium Inverted Baluster (with tears) with Knop at *b.*
Bowl, tpt., or wstd. Foot, plain or domed. The same stem formation without the base knop is rare. Scarce.

(j) Short MSAT Section over a Long Inverted Baluster (with tears).
Bowl, tpt. Foot, plain. Rare.

(k) Long Shoulder Knopped MSAT Section set into a Flat Knop (with tears).
Bowl, pan type. Foot, plain, or domed and folded. Only champagnes have been noted. Very scarce. About 1745.

(l) Short MSAT Section with central Angular Knop, set on a Longer Inverted Baluster (or Shouldered Section) with tears, with Knop at *b*.
Bowl, r.f. Foot, plain. A 4 WS Newcastle glass, and rare. About 1755.

(m) Medium MSAT Dumb-bell Section set on a Medium Inverted Baluster (or Shouldered Section) with tears, with Knop at *b*.
Bowl, r.f. Foot, plain. The air twist may be squeezed out of the shank of the dumb-bell. Newcastle glasses. About 1760-70.

SECTION 3. Glasses with stem consisting of Two Air Twist Sections.

Examples are rare, and only three stem formations have been noted. For convenience these glasses are placed here rather than in Group VII.

(a) Short MSAT Section over a Long MSAT Inverted Baluster.
Bowl, tpt. Foot, plain. About 1755. 3 WS.

(b) True Baluster above an Annulated Knop at *c.* and an Inverted Baluster below; the whole with MSAT. 4 WS.
Bowl, bell. Foot, plain. The weld is in the annulated Knop. A very rare Newcastle glass. About 1760.

SECTION 4. Glasses with stem consisting of a Plain Section over an Opaque Twist Section.

Again, examples are very scarce. Five stem formations have been noted, and all are believed to be of Newcastle origin. Both single and double series twists occur.

(a) Knop (with tears) at *t.* over a long Opaque Twist Section. Both single and double series twists occur.
Bowl, bell or r.f. Foot, plain, or domed. About 1760.

(b) Angular Knop and Knop over a Shouldered Opaque Twist Section.
Bowl, bell. Foot, domed. Single series twist. About 1760.

(c) Annulated Knop at *t.* over a Shouldered Opaque Twist Section with Knop at *b*.
Bowl, r.f. Foot, plain. Double series twist. About 1760.

(d) Dumb-bell Section over a Shouldered Opaque Twist Section with Knop at *b*.
Bowl, r.f. Foot, plain. Double series twist. About 1765.

SECTION 5. Glasses with stem consisting of an Air Twist, a Plain, and an Opaque Twist Section.

Extremely rare. Only one form of stem can be given.

MSAT Knop at *t.* and a Plain Annulated Knop over an Opaque Twist Section Knopped at *t.* and *b.* 5 WS.

Bowl, r.f. Foot, plain. Double series twist. About 1765.

SECTION 6. Glasses with stem consisting of a Mixed Twist and a Plain Section.

Very rare. Only one stem formation can be given. These glasses may be of Scottish origin.

A Long Section containing a single series Mixed Twist (spiral air gauze and an opaque white corkscrew) set into a Knop or short Inverted Baluster.

Bowl, wstd. r.f. Foot, domed. Goblets.

Group VI

GLASSES WITH PLAIN STRAIGHT STEMS

(1740–1770)

THEIR simplicity and consequent cheapness naturally made these the glasses of the people and of the inns and taverns of the country. None the less, beauty could be combined with utility if the proportions of the glass were right. Variation in the stem could not go beyond differences in length and diameter and the use of the tear, ranging from a pointed air-bead to a long misshapen cavity. There was a slightly non-cylindrical stem of almost 'sausage' form, but it is rare.

All types of bowl are to be found, though duplex forms are uncommon and elaborate champagne types are either very rare or absent. The bowl forms commenced with the trumpet and the waisted, the former of which never died out. Ogee and r.f. bowls were used before 1750, and are very common in small wines. Towards the end of the series there were a good many ovoid bowls which have little grace.

Some foot forms are found additional to those mentioned in earlier groups, a solid conical foot in wines, a flanged, oversewn, and overstrung foot in dram glasses, and a firing foot in both. Domed, and domed and folded feet are scarce.

The great majority of specimens are of two-piece formation. Only about three per cent are of 3 NS form, and these have separately made moulded bowls displaying faint or wide fluting. There are a few rarer motifs, but they are scarce. Two-piece glasses with faint flutes are fairly common in ogee, ovoid, and r.f. wines. The metal is generally in line with that of the Balustroid glasses, but towards the end a coldly brilliant minium metal made its appearance, though by no means universally, and this may have been used well beyond the 1770 date.

Plain stemmed glasses have been given a very early date, even back to the end of the 17th century, but for all practical purposes the series starts about 1740 and lasts until 1770 when the trumpet bowl, for instance, merges into a smaller type here called 'Georgian'. It is not possible to say where the glasses were made. Probably they were nearly universal, but it is possible to assert that only a small proportion came from Tyneside. These have taller and more slender stems, almost always with trumpet bowls, in distinctive metal, and some with good engraved work of a baroque character. There are soda metal examples, including, I believe, some of the trumpet bowl toasting glasses commonly attributed to the Low Countries at the end of the 17th century. The classification is necessarily based on bowl form, of which there are at least eighteen. It must suffice to mention those most frequently seen.

(a) Bucket Bowl.

Foot, plain, as often folded, occasionally domed and folded. Mainly wines and a few goblets, but examples are not common, and moulded forms rare or absent. From about 1750.

(b) Cup Bowl.

Foot, plain or folded; rarely otherwise. As for (a) but rather scarcer. A late dram with flanged foot occurs. From about 1750.

(c) Ogee Bowl.

Foot, plain or folded, but in wines much more often folded than otherwise. A terraced foot is not too scarce in drams. Apart from wines, which greatly predominate, there are drams, goblets, and a few short ales. Among wines are a few 3 NS glasses and an occasional specimen with a deceptive bowl. Many wines have 'flowered' engraving. Very common. From 1745.

(d) Ovoid Bowl.

Foot, plain or folded, and also (in drams) of firing, flanged, over-sewn, overstrung, and terraced type. The glasses to be found are as for (c), but wines are much less common, and drams and short ales are more frequent. A good many glasses are in minium metal. There is not much decorative engraving. Common. From about 1760.

(e) R.F. Bowl.

Foot, plain or folded, sometimes domed, rarely domed and folded. The firing foot is also scarce, and a terraced foot very scarce. The oversewn and overstrung types have not been noted with this bowl, but they may exist. Wines are less common than in (c) but otherwise the range is wider. There are more ales, and a few cordials and ratafias. The deceptive bowl gains ground in drams of the tavern class, and a Lynn bowl appears. Among rather more 3 NS glasses, honeycomb moulding is found, and a goblet with 'sausage' stem. A few drawn semi-hollow stems appear. Decorative engraving is common. Common. From about 1745.

(f) Trumpet Bowl.

Foot, plain, more often folded. The tear is considerably commoner with the folded foot. The domed, and the domed and folded foot is scarce, even rare, comparatively speaking. Drams may have a firing foot and still more often a flanged foot. Wines may have a solid conical foot. Most types of glass are found, including a toastmaster's glass, but not champagnes. There are some wines and goblets from Newcastle. Toasting glasses in lead metal and cordials are uncommon; semi-cordials are less so. Three-piece glasses are naturally rare. Engraving is infrequent except on ale glasses. Very common. Mainly from about 1740.

(g) Waisted Bowl.

Foot, plain, more often folded in wines; domed, and domed and folded feet occur as in (f). The types of glass include little but ales, goblets, wines, and a very few drams with firing feet. Three-piece glasses are rare and only panel moulded specimens have been noted. Engraving is the exception. Very common. Mainly from about 1740.

Group VII

GLASSES WITH AIR TWIST STEMS

(1740–1770)

THE glasses of this group may claim a more exclusively English origin than any others. For the opaque white and coloured interior twists there were continental precedents, but it fell to us to adopt the economical method of using spirals of imprisoned air as a decorative device. Mere tears, of course, were international, and it is generally assumed that the air spiral was developed, almost accidentally, from a series of elongated tears. I can find no evidence to support that theory; the existence of a few imperfect twists proves nothing, except the incompetence of their maker.

All classes of drinking vessel and all types of bowl occur, though their incidence varies greatly in the six sections into which the group easily divides. There is very little specialization in foot forms, and not much use is made of moulded decoration. There is a certain amount of wheel-engraving, but as a whole I think that the makers realized they had something new and something good, and that their lily needed no gilding. None the less, glasses can be found with traces of gilding over their engraved work, and a few others with decorative or inscriptional gilding, or with white enamelling.

There are a number of differing types of twist. The multiple spiral type was the first to appear and it was never seriously challenged, though very rare in combination. A note on twist formations is given under Group X. One kind of twist is so brilliant that it has been called a 'mercury' twist. Needless to say, mercury is not in question, the exceptional brilliance being due to the relatively wide cross section of the air spiral or spirals, and to its close turns.

The group contains 2 NS and 3 NS glasses only, and the twist must be continuous throughout the stem. Where there is a plain neck, it is integral with the bowl and not over a quarter of an inch or so in length. Other glasses with partial air twist stem, or with more than one air twist section, will be found in Group V.

SECTION 1. Knopped Two-piece glasses with Single Series Twist.

Most of the glasses here are very scarce, and taken all together they do not comprise more than about four per cent of the whole group. All will have the multiple spiral air twist, and there are half a dozen stem formations, among them the following:

(a) Inverted Baluster (or Shoulder Knop).

Bowl, wstd. Foot, plain, less often folded. Wines and a few goblets occur. These glasses comprise at least three-quarters of the glasses in the section, and must be distinguished from very similar ones of 3 NS. build. In some cases the spirals appear in the bowl base, and these may travel through the neck and so on down the stem, but more often the twist is squeezed out of the neck. If the bowl-base spirals are equal in number to, and as regular as, the stem spirals, the glass will certainly be of 2 NS build and belong here. More frequently the twist ceases at, or in, the neck, and only the absence of a weld mark distinguishes these from similar 3 NS glasses. About 1740-50.

(b) Swelling (or Angular) Knop at *c*.

Bowl, wstd., or tpt. Foot, plain, or folded. Rare. About 1745-50.

(c) The Stem Trisected by Two Knops.

Bowl, tpt., or s.t. tpt. Foot, plain. Rare. About 1745-50.

(d) The Stem with Four Knops.

Bowl, wstd. Foot, plain. The third knop from the top is more like a small Inverted Baluster. Very rare. About 1745.

SECTION 2. Unknopped Two-piece glasses with Single Series Twist.

Nearly one in every three air twist glasses will belong to this section because of the frequency of wines with drawn trumpet and drawn waisted bowls. Most types of vessel occur, but not ratafias or toastmaster's glasses. The plain foot predominates; the folded foot is fairly common, perhaps on one specimen in five; the domed foot is scarce, being found once in twenty glasses, and anything else is rare. Decorative moulding has not been noted, and little engraving other than commemorative. There are three types of twist.

(a) Pair of Corkscrews.

Bowl, tpt. Foot, plain. Includes a few ales, cordials and goblets, but examples are uncommon. The twist is one of the brilliant ones. Not infrequent. From about 1745.

(b) Four Corkscrews.

As for (a) but rather scarcer. A domed foot occurs, but no ales have been noted. From about 1745.

(c) Multiple Spirals.

Bowl, tpt., or wstd., any other form is rare. Foot, usually plain, or folded, occasionally domed. At least ninety per cent of the glasses in this section have this twist. Most types of vessel appear, including giant goblets, though wines greatly predominate. Round the centre of the stem there may be found a double or triple ring or collar, or a bladed or vermicular collar. This last is nearly always on a plain-footed wine with waisted bowl, and is a good deal less scarce than the other types of collar. Common. From about 1745.

SECTION 3. Unknopped Two-piece glasses with Double Series Twist.

Extremely and unaccountably rare. Only one type of stem can be given.

Vertical Column/Four Spiral Threads.

Bowl, tpt. Foot, plain. A very few cordials.

SECTION 4. Knopped Three-piece glasses with Single Series Twist.

Glasses coming under this heading are only a little less common than those of Section 2, the proportion being 13-15. The range of vessels is rather more limited; besides wines, only ales and goblets are ordinarily seen. A few champagnes appear. The folded foot becomes scarce, and a domed foot rare. On the other hand, most of the bowl forms may be found, headed by the r.f., the bell (or wstd.), and rather surprisingly, the duplex s.t. r.f. form, in that order. Decorative moulding begins to appear, but is still scarce; faint fluting and honeycomb moulding are the most frequently seen devices. One glass in a dozen, perhaps, will be provided with a collar beneath the bowl. Almost every glass of this section will have the multiple spiral twist, and there are at least eighteen kinds of knopping, of which the most frequent are given below. A mid-18th century date will usually be accurate enough.

(a) Inverted Baluster (or Shoulder Knop).
Bowl, bell (or wstd.), or r.f. Foot, plain; rarely folded or domed. Ales and goblets occur. To distinguish specimens from Section 1 (a) glasses, the weld mark should be looked for, especially in those very infrequent cases where there are tears in the bowl base. These will not be nearly so regular as in the 2 NS glasses, and will seldom be equal in number to the spirals in the stem. Some decorative moulding is found, faint fluting, honeycomb moulding, and ribbing. Collaring occasionally occurs beneath the bowl. Fairly common.

(b) Swelling Knop at *c*.
Bowl, s.t. r.f.; other forms occur, but not commonly. Foot, plain; rarely otherwise. Types of glass are as for (a) but a gin has been noted. Decorative moulding is much less frequent. Fairly common. After 1750.

(c) Knop (or Shoulder Knop) at *t*. and Knop (or Angular Knop) at *c*.
Bowl, bell (or wstd.) and r.f.; other forms are rare, save the bkt. Foot, as for (a). Goblets and especially ales are relatively frequent. A cordial appears, but not often. Honeycomb moulding only has been noted, and the collar to the bowl is not very scarce.

(d) Knop (or Shoulder Knop) at *t*. and Knop at *b*.
Bowl, bell (or wstd.), bkt., or r.f. Foot, plain; rarely folded; domed in a very few champagnes with p.t. bowls. Scarce. After 1750. A sweetmeat with a Pair of Corkscrews exists.

(e), (f), (g) and (h) With Four Knops; Five Knops; Trisected by Two Knops; Acorn Knop at *t*. and Angular Knop at *c*.
These are among the rarer formations and examples will seldom be seen.

Section 5. Unknopped Three-piece glasses with Single Series Twist.

While the glasses of this section as a whole are as numerous as those in Section 4, there is a variety of twists and no individual glass is especially common. The range of vessel is as for Section 4, though cordials are more frequent, and a very few ratafias and toastmaster's glasses occur. The folded foot is rather commoner, and the domed foot distinctly commoner, though that is not to say that either is at all frequent. Each will occur once in about fifteen specimens. The bowl forms also are much as in Section 4, with the r.f. four times as common as any other, and the ogee and wstd. bkt. displacing the s.t. r.f. and the bell. The fall from grace of these two is quite striking. Moulded decoration is three times as frequent, faint fluting and honeycomb moulding sharing a still indifferent popularity. Collaring under the bowl almost disappears. Classification is based on the twist. Eleven kinds have been recorded, among them the following, the dating throughout being 1750-1765.

(a) A Pair, and (b) Four Spiral Threads.
Bowl, r.f. Foot, plain. Both are rare.

(c) Multiple Spirals.
Bowl, mainly r.f. with some bkt. and a few p.t. forms. Foot, plain; much less often folded or domed. Includes nearly half the glasses of the section. One rare variety has the stem trisected by two vermicular collars.

(d) Spiral Gauze.
Bowl, chiefly r.f. with some eight other forms, none popular. Foot, as for (c). Frequent.

(e) Pair of Spiral Gauzes.
Bowl, r.f., with four other forms. Foot, only very occasionally folded. Rather scarce.

(f) Pair of Corkscrews.
Bowl, r.f. or ogee, with half a dozen less used forms. Foot, rarely otherwise than plain. More cordials occur, some with faint fluting. Not uncommon.

SECTION 6. Unknopped Three-piece glasses with Double Series Twist.

This section is numerically small, including only about twelve per cent of all the air twist glasses. Wines are less preponderant though still three times as frequent as goblets, and four times as frequent as ales and cordials, which latter have gained considerable ground. The plain foot is almost universal, only one glass in twenty having any other type. The bowl forms are mainly the r.f., with the ogee only a little less frequent. Of the others, the least unpopular are the bucket and waisted bucket. Moulded decoration is almost confined to faint fluting and honeycomb moulding, but is relatively more frequent than in Section 5. The range of vessel types is much as before. Most of the toastmaster's glasses seen will have a double series twist. The classification is again on twist type, of which fifteen varieties have been noticed, all of approximately 1760-70 date. The corkscrew types have the 'mercurial' touch. The following may be mentioned:

(a) Gauze/Pr. Spiral Threads.
Bowl, ogee and r.f. Foot, plain. Wines, goblets and a few ales. Fairly frequent.

(b) Gauze/Pr. Corkscrews.
Bowl, ogee and r.f. Foot, plain. A good proportion of moulded forms is included. Rather scarce.

(c) Pr. Spiral Threads/Pr. 4, 5, or 6 ply Spiral Bands.
Bowl, r.f. Foot, plain. Cordials predominate. Scarce.

(d) Vertical Column/Four Spiral Threads.
Bowl, r.f. or ogee, and four much scarcer forms. Foot, occasionally domed. Cordials and toastmaster's glasses occur, and there is some moulding. Fairly frequent.

(e) Corkscrew (or Spiral Column)/Single 6-12 ply Spiral Band.
Bowl, ogee, with some scarcer forms. Foot, rarely domed. It is mainly wines and cordials which are included here. Scarce.

Group VIII

GLASSES WITH HOLLOW STEMS

(1750–1760)

THIS is a very small group, the stems being fashioned from a precise hollow tube. Usually it remains a cylinder, but it can be manipulated to show protuberances which, for convenience, may still be termed knops. The hollow stem saved weight, and may have been an attempted counter to the Excise Act of 1745–46. It might have had a better chance had the foot been more often folded; generally speaking, specimens are fragile and the feet liable to chipping. All must be of 3 NS formation.

SECTION 1. Glasses in which the Stem is Knopped.

Examples are rare and all seen have been of the champagne-sweetmeat order. Stem variation is very limited.

(a) Swelling Knop at *c*.
Bowl, ogee. Foot, plain or domed and folded. The rim of the bowl may be denticulated.

(b) Swelling Knop at *c*. and Collaring at *b*.
Bowl, lipped r.f. Foot, plain.

(c) Angular Knop at *c*.
Bowl, wstd.r.f./bell. Foot, flanged. The examples noted had honeycomb moulding to both bowl and foot.

SECTION 2. Glasses in which the Stem is Unknopped.

Specimens are uncommon and most of them have a trumpet bowl. Engraving is the exception. The following four bowl forms have been noted:

(a) Ogee Bowl.
Foot, folded. A wine.

(b) Ovoid Bowl.
Foot, plain. Wines only.

(c) R.F. Bowl.

Foot, plain, less often folded and rarely domed. Wines and goblets. Faint fluting occurs.

(d) Trumpet Bowl.

Foot, plain. Mainly wines, but an ale has also been seen.

Group IX

GLASSES WITH INCISED TWIST STEMS

(1750–1765)

THESE form another small group, though rather more than twice as numerous as glasses in Group VIII; none the less they are esteemed twice as highly by collectors. The classification is very much the same as for the last group and the dating little different. Most, but not all, examples are of 3 NS form. There are 2 NS specimens in soda metal. The foot is almost always plain and a folded one has not come my way. The glasses are presumed to have a north country origin.

SECTION 1. Glasses in which the Stem is Knopped.

The specimens examined have had a medium to coarse incised twist, and there are at least three forms of stem. They date around 1750.

(a) Half-knop at *t*.

Bowl, r.f., set directly on the half-knop without any neck to the stem. Foot, plain. Wines and a few goblets. The former may be moulded with faint flutes rising into honeycomb moulding. Scarce.

(b) Angular Knop at *c*.

Bowl, p.t. Foot, domed. A champagne has been noted, the bowl and foot being ribbed. Very rare.

SECTION 2. Glasses in which the Stem is Unknopped.

There are two types of twist, otherwise the classification is on bowl form. The coarser twist is the commoner and earlier, examples belonging to the mid-18th century.

A. With Coarse Incised Twist.

(a) R.F. Bowl.

Foot, plain, rarely domed. Goblets and wines, the latter with honeycomb moulding more often than not. Faint fluting also occurs. Fairly frequent.

(b) Trumpet Bowl.

Foot, plain, rarely domed. Wines with diamond or honeycomb moulding, and a plain cordial. Uncommon.

(c) Waisted Bowl.

Foot, plain. Honeycomb moulded wines. Rare.

B. With Fine Incised Twist.

(a) Ogee Bowl.

Foot, plain. One exceptional example noted with toasting stem of normal length, perhaps made for the Netherlandish market. About 1760.

(b) R.F. Bowl.

Foot, plain. Wines, mainly faint fluted. The bowl is large and the stem rather short, giving an unbalanced effect. The form can be exactly matched in an air twist and a hollow-stemmed glass. Rather uncommon. 1760-5.

Group X

GLASSES WITH OPAQUE TWIST STEMS (1750–1780)

In view of the many combinations of twist, this group contains a greater variety of glasses than any other. All types of vessel occur, as do all types of bowl, the r.f. and ogee forms being much the commonest. Most types of foot may be found, though variation here would be inconsiderable were it not for dram glasses and, in lesser degree, for champagnes and sweetmeats. Tall glasses of these types are rare; low ones are less so, as they include a good many with the denticulated rim.

The twist may consist of one formation by itself or of two reciprocal spiral formations; these are here termed 'single series twists'. More commonly, the twist is composed of two formations, the one inside the other, and these are called 'double series twists'. Very rarely, there may be a triple series twist. The twists are made by placing rods of white (or of colour) upright in a circular mould; the clear metal is poured in, and the resulting mass is drawn out, until of the required stem diameter, and twisted with regularity at the same time. The different twists result from different placings of the rods. In the case of air twist glasses, bubbles of air are used, and the regularity of those twists suggests surprising accuracy on the part of the workman, or some mechanical contrivance for placing the bubbles precisely.

The terminology applied to the twist formations has indeed been various. The illustrations selected will suffice to show all the varieties I have found, and all are named according to the terminology here chosen. Some single and many double series twists are surprisingly rare.

The range of decoration, mainly of moulded motifs, is

wide, but still confined to one glass in five. The Lynn bowl is commonest on an opaque twist stem. Engraved decoration is not uncommon on the smaller wines; gilding and white enamelling is scarce. Every opaque stemmed glass is of 3 NS build; a very few appear to be 2NS but in fact have the bowl 'side-welded', not horizontally welded, to the stem.

The third quarter of the 18th century is the period during which these glasses flourished. Few can be earlier than 1750; some of the double series twists may date later than 1780. There are examples belonging to the first half of the 19th century, though not many, and quite a number of modern specimens, generally discernible by a certain inaccuracy in the twist and by their appearance in sets. There are specimens of the requisite age in soda metal.

SECTION 1. Knopped Glasses with a Single Series Twist.

Fully a third of this section, which still only accounts for six per cent of all the Opaque Twists, is made up of champagnes and sweetmeats, and these again are mainly low sweetmeats with denticulated rims to their pan-topped bowls. Of other glasses, wines will be found five times as often as any other sort; gin glasses, ratafias, and toastmaster's glasses have not been noted. They come early, from 1750, and practically all have the Multiple Spiral Twist. A plain foot is to be presumed; some exceptions are noted. Decoration of any sort, except in low sweetmeats, is unusual. At least four types of knopping are found.

(a) With Knop (or Shoulder Knop) at top.

There are three types of twist.

i. Four Spiral Threads.

Bowl, bell. Wines only. Very rare.

ii. Eight Spiral Threads.

Bowl, s.t. r.f. Wines only. Very rare.

iii. Multiple Spirals.

Bowl, bell, r.f., or tpt. A few wines and still fewer cordials and goblets. One particular variety has the twist rising into the base of the bell bowl. Very scarce.

Bowl, p.t., collared at base, with flanged, denticulated, or looped rim. Foot, domed, or domed and folded. Sweetmeats. Rare.

Bowl, p.t., the rim usually denticulated. Foot,

pressed radial grooves. Decoration, wide or faint fluting. Low sweetmeats. Fairly frequent.

(b) With Knop at centre.

i. Multiple Spirals.

Bowl, chiefly ogee or r.f. Foot, rarely folded. Decoration, almost confined to faint fluting. Mainly wines, but ales, drams and goblets occasionally occur. Fairly frequent.

ii. Gauze.

Bowl, bell or ogee. Wines only. Rare.

SECTION 2. Knopped Glasses with a Double Series Twist.

These seem to be scarcer than they formerly were. The tally shows them to be rather less numerous than glasses in Section 1; however, as champagnes and sweetmeats are considerably rarer, the usual drinking glasses are commoner. Many are certainly of Newcastle manufacture. Except in the few low sweetmeats, the foot is invariably plain; otherwise only wines and ales have been recorded. Decoration is rare and almost confined to faint fluting. There are at least six forms of knopping.

(a) With Knop (or Shoulder Knop) at *t*.

Four types of twist will be found.

i. Gauze/Pr. 6-10 ply Spiral Bands.

Bowl, bell. Wines. Scarce.

ii. Lace Twist/Pr. Spiral Threads or Tapes.

As for (i).

iii. Pr. Spiral Threads or Tapes/Pr. close Multi-ply Spiral Bands.

Bowl, bell. Ales. Rare.

(b) With Knop at *c*.

There are six types of twist.

i. Gauze/Pr. Spiral Threads or Tapes.

Bowl, lipped ogee. Wines. Scarce.

ii. Gauze/Pr. 2-4 ply Spiral Bands.

Bowl, ogee. Ales and wines. Scarce.

iii. Lace Twist/Pr. Spiral Threads or Tapes.

Bowl, ogee. Wines. Scarce.

iv. Pr. Spiral Threads or Tapes/Pr. Corkscrews.

Bowl, lipped ogee and others. Wines. Fairly frequent.

(c) With Knops at *t*. and *c*.

There are three types of twist.

i. Gauze/Four 2-4 ply Spiral Bands.

Bowl, r.f. or bell. Ales and wines. Fairly frequent.

ii. Lace Twist/Pr. Spiral Threads or Tapes.
Bowl, bell or tpt. Wines. Fairly frequent.

(d) With Knop (or Shoulder Knop) at *t.* and Knop at *b.*
There are four types of twist.

i. Gauze/Pr. Spiral Threads or Tapes.
Bowl, r.f. Wines. Scarce.
Bowl, p.t., flanged. Foot, radially grooved. Low sweetmeats. Scarce.

ii. Gauze/Four Spiral Threads or Tapes.
Bowl, p.t., denticulated. Foot, radially grooved. Low sweetmeats. Scarce.

iii. Multi-ply Corkscrew/Pr. Spiral Threads or Tapes.
Bowl, bell. Wines. Rare.
Bowl, p.t., denticulated. Decoration, sometimes wide fluting. Foot radially grooved.
Low sweetmeats. Scarce.

(e) With Knops at *t.*, *c.* and *b.*
There are five types of twist, among them:

i. Gauze/Pr. Spiral Threads or Tapes.
Bowl, bell. Ales. Fairly frequent.

ii. Gauze/Four Spiral Threads or Tapes.
Bowl, bell. Wines. Scarce.

iii. Gauze/Four 2-4 ply Spiral Bands.
Bowl, bell. Wines. The most frequent glass of the section.

(f) With Four Knops.
Again there are four types of twist, including:

i. Gauze/Pr. Spiral Threads or Tapes.
Bowl, bell. Wines. Rather scarce.

ii. Gauze/Four Spiral Threads or Tapes.
Bowl, bell. Wines. Scarce.

iii. Gauze/Four 2-4 ply Spiral Bands.
Bowl, bell. Wines. Fairly frequent.

SECTION 3. Unknopped Glasses with a Single Series Twist.

This section includes a further seventeen per cent of all the Opaque Twists. Probably all types of normal drinking glass are to be found, though giant goblets have not been actually noted. Champagnes and sweetmeats of normal height begin to outnumber the low sweetmeats, only one of which occurs in every hundred glasses of the section. Wines are six times as numerous as ales, and nine times as numerous as goblets. There are just a few cordials; drams, ratafias, and toastmaster's glasses are rare. The r.f. bowl is slightly more common than the ogee; it is five and six times as frequent as the bell and the bucket respectively. Most other forms occur. Less than three glasses in a hundred will have a folded foot, the few champagnes and sweetmeats providing almost all the other variations, save a firing foot on an occasional dram glass. Decoration gains ground, one in seven glasses having faint fluting; other motifs are scarce or rare. Engraving is not very infrequent, but still the exception. Thirty types of twist have been seen, of which eighteen must be accounted rare, while some others are scarce. The following are the most frequent ones.

(a) Spiral Gauze.
Bowl, r.f. and a few other forms. Foot, rarely folded. Wines, a few goblets and fewer low sweetmeats. There is a little faint fluting and honeycomb moulding. Fairly frequent.

(b) Spiral Gauze and a Single 2-ply Spiral Band.
As for (a) but the range of vessels may be a little wider. Fairly frequent.

(c) Spiral Gauze and a Corkscrew.
As for (b) but there are no champagnes recorded.

(d) Pr. Spiral Gauzes.
Bowl, r.f. and others. Foot, occasionally folded, and known domed in a toastmaster's glass. Includes most vessel types. There is honeycomb moulding, and one of the rare 'side-welded' glasses occurs, with a tpt. bowl. Fairly common.

(e) Four Spiral Gauzes.
Bowl, r.f. or ogee, with a few others. Wines and ales. There is ribbing and faint and wide fluting. Fairly frequent.

(f) Lace Twist Outlined.
Bowl, r.f. or bell, with others. Mainly wines; a ratafia occurs. There is some faint fluting. Rather common.

(g) Multiple Spiral Twist.
Bowl, ogee, rarely otherwise. Foot, sometimes folded. Wines. A Lynn bowl appears. Infrequent.

(h) Multi-ply Corkscrew.
Bowl, r.f. and others. Chiefly wines and ales, with a few goblets and cordials. There is faint fluting, ribbing, and wide fluting. A glass has been seen with an opalescent stem. Common.

(j) Pr. Spiral Cables.
Bowl, r.f. or ogee. Foot, known domed in cordials. A few wines, ales and cordials. There are some sweetmeats with denticulated p.t. bowl, collared beneath; the stem is also collared at its base; the foot domed and folded. These are rare.

Section 4. Unknopped Glasses with a Double Series Twist.

This is very much the largest section, accounting for seventy-three per cent of all Opaque Twists. All types of vessel are found, seven out of ten specimens being wines. These are five times as common as ales, twelve times as common as goblets, and more than sixteen times as common as either drams or cordials. Champagnes and sweetmeats, whether normal or low, are rare. Every type of bowl form is to be found, the ogee predominating and rather commoner than the r.f. The trumpet and ovoid forms are each found once in every ten glasses; the bell hardly once in twenty-five; the others are scarcer still. The folded foot is more frequent than before, but not relatively so. The firing foot however is actually so, occurring three times in a hundred glasses, almost always on drams; the terraced foot is another, but scarcer, feature of the drams here. Other foot forms are really rare. About one glass in every five will have some decoration, faint fluting being ten times as frequent as ribbing or honeycomb moulding; there are at least ten moulded motifs and two of cut form. Engraving is still much the exception. There are at least seventy different forms of twist, disregarding minor variations, but only eleven of them are common, and many are very rare.

(a) Gauze/Pr. Spiral Threads or Tapes.
Bowl, ogee, r.f., or tpt., with a good many others. Foot, rarely other than plain. Includes all vessel types except perhaps champagnes and sweetmeats. Very common.

(b) Gauze/Four Spiral Threads or Tapes.
As for (a) but the range a little less wide and examples rather scarcer. The ovoid bowl is commoner. Some firing feet occur. Common.

(c) Lace Twist/Pr. Spiral Threads or Tapes.
As for (b) but the tpt. bowl easily predominates. Common.

(d) Lace Twist/Pr. 2-5 ply Spiral Bands.
Bowl, ogee and r.f., with others. Foot, sometimes folded. A Lynn bowl occurs. Not scarce.

(e) Lace Twist/Pr. 6-10 ply Spiral Bands.
Bowl, mainly ogee. Foot, occasionally terraced in drams. Wines, goblets, ales, and drams. Fairly frequent.

(f) Lace Twist/Pr. Corkscrews.
Bowl, mainly r.f. Foot, relatively often folded. Wines, goblets, ales and drams. Lynn bowls appear. Fairly frequent.

(g) Pr. Spiral Threads or Tapes/Single 10-20 ply Spiral Band.
Bowl, mainly ogee and r.f., with at least seven other forms, including a hexagonal bowl. Foot, very rarely other than

plain. Includes all vessel types. Moulded forms appear to be commoner than usual. Common.

(h) Pr. Spiral Threads or Tapes/Pr. Corkscrews or Multi-ply Corkscrews.
Bowl, ogee or r.f. With the possible exception of champagnes and sweetmeats, all vessel types exist; ratafias are relatively often seen. Fairly frequent.

(j) Four Spiral Threads or Tapes/Single 10-20 ply Spiral Band.
Bowl, r.f. Foot, nearly always plain. Mainly wines and ales. Fairly frequent.

(k) Corkscrew/Pr. Corkscrews or Multi-ply Corkscrews.
Bowl, chiefly ogee. Foot, not noted otherwise than plain. Includes most vessel types. Fairly frequent.

(l) Vertical Column/Pr. Spiral Threads or Tapes.
Bowl, r.f. or cup. Foot always plain. Mainly wines. A late type of twist, with very little decoration. Fairly frequent.

SECTION 5. Unknopped Glasses with a Triple Series Twist.

These are extremely rare and the only specimens seen have been wines with r.f. or ogee bowls, with plain feet. Except that they are likely to be contemporary with glasses of Section 4 (l), there is no more to be said about them.

Group XI

GLASSES WITH MIXED AND COLOUR TWIST STEMS (1755–1775)

IN collector's parlance a Mixed Twist is one partly of air and partly of opaque white spirals, and a Colour Twist is one which contains a coloured component. But, as a Colour Twist is generally found together with opaque white, sometimes with air, and sometimes with both those spirals, there seem to be no grounds for giving Colour Twists a separate grouping in this classification.

Within the whole group there is no single glass which is common, and most varieties are rare; there is, indeed, much less difference in rarity between a conventional Mixed Twist and a Colour Twist than is generally supposed. One exceptional specimen has a composite stem, and will therefore be found listed in Group V.

There must be a considerable number of further varieties still to be recorded, particularly in Colour Twists. In these, no individual type is anything but scarce, and most varieties are represented in the schedule by less than half a dozen specimens; some are listed on the strength of a single specimen.

The colours most desired by collectors are canary, emerald green, and a royal purple, but all intense colours are welcome. Some greens, blues, and ruby tints are translucent and sometimes ill-defined, as a result of the use of coloured glass rods instead of enamel ones. These are rather less satisfactory, but they can be good, as in Section 4, B. A rubber red occurs and is attractive when used with discretion. A good pink is found, and there is also a pale pink of which no notice has been taken because it is not far removed from opaque white and is popularly regarded as an accident. I think this is not the case, because the pale pink and the dead opaque white may appear in the same glass.

Goblets and cordials occur, but not often; there are drams, and wines with semi-toasting stems, both with colour in the twist. Bowl forms are very much as for the other three-piece interior twists; the bell, however, is relatively rather more frequent, and it is looked upon with some disfavour by collectors, partly because it is often ill-proportioned, and partly because of a misty legend that colour twists with this bowl might be Netherlandish in origin. There is nothing to show that colour twists are any earlier, or any later, than the others, and there are insufficient data to justify precise dating within the group. An early 19th century Colour Twist has been seen.

SECTION 1. Glasses with a combined Air and Opaque White Twist.

A. Glasses with Unknopped Stems and Single Series Twist.

There are four differing twists and together they comprise only one fifth of the section. Cordials rarely occur, but when found they are likely to be of high quality, with domed feet.

(i) Spiral Air Gauze and a Single Opaque White Spiral Thread.
Bowl, bell, wstd. bkt. or s.t. bkt. Foot, plain; domed in cordials. Wines and cordials. Somewhat scarce.

(ii) Spiral Air Gauze and a Single thick Opaque White Spiral.
Bowl, bell, bkt. forms, and r.f. Foot, plain. Wines. Scarce.

(iii) Spiral Air Gauze and an Opaque White Corkscrew.
As for (a). Rare.

B. Glasses with Unknopped Stems and a Double Series Twist.

(a) In the following, the inner component is an Air Twist.
The glasses here comprise forty per cent of the section. There are at least seven different twists, only those mentioned being at all frequent. The bell and the r.f. bowls are equal favourites, and are found in two glasses out of every three; the wstd. bkt., wstd. r.f. and tpt. forms also occur. The foot is almost always plain, and wines only have been noted.

i. Air Gauze/Pr. Opaque White Spiral Threads.
Bowl, usually r.f. Foot, plain. Wines. Rather scarce.

ii. Air Gauze/Four Opaque White Spiral Threads.
Bowl, usually bell. Foot, plain. Wines. Rather scarce.

(b) In the following the inner component is an Opaque White Twist. These comprise the remaining forty per cent of the section. Four different twists have been noted, one being the commonest Mixed Twist to be found. A few wines have faint fluting. The tpt. bowl easily predominates; there are also ogee, r.f., and s.t. r.f. bowls. The foot is plain.

i. Opaque White Gauze/Pr. of Spiral Air Threads.
Bowl, tpt. Foot, plain. Wines of the flute type or ales. A stem of semi-toasting type is found. Fairly common.

ii. Opaque White Corkscrew/Multiple Spiral Air Twist.
Bowl, s.t. r.f. Foot, plain. Wines. Very rare.

Section 2. Glasses with a Colour Twist alone.

These are rare, and though seen, no individual examples have been recorded. A vertical charcoal-coloured column is recalled, and a very slender single ruby spiral, neither of much attraction; there should be finer examples.

Section 3. Glasses with a combined Air and Colour Twist.

These also are rare. Three combinations have been noted, all with a single series twist, a spiral air gauze combining with a green spiral, a blue spiral, or with a two-ply spiral band in red and blue.

Bowl, bell or r.f. Foot, plain.

Section 4. Glasses with a combined Opaque White and Colour Twist.

This divides into five parts. Sub-sections A and E are represented by very few glasses. B is composed of finely made, brilliant glasses of Newcastle origin. C and D comprise the usual colour twists found in collections. Some are very fine glasses indeed; others enjoy a reflected glory.

Glasses with bell bowls are sometimes of clumsy build; others, with a certain solidity to the bowl base, are good. A few which are attached to the stem in quite ugly fashion contain a heavy green twist, and I have never been able to assure myself of their authenticity. There are many patent reproductions which should never deceive.

A. Knopped Glasses with a Single Series Twist.
Two types of Knopping, both rare.

(a) With Shoulder Knop at *t*.
An Opaque White Corkscrew edged in purple. Bowl, bell. Foot, plain. A wine.

(b) With Knop at *c*.

An Opaque White Spiral Gauze and an Opaque White Corkscrew edged in green and ruby.

Bowl, r.f. Foot, plain. Wines.

B. Knopped Glasses with a Double Series Twist.

These glasses come with at least two types of knopping.

(a) With Knop (or Shoulder Knop) at *t*. and Knop at *c*.

Opaque White Gauze/Three Spiral Threads, in blue, green, and red backed in white (or alternatively ruby).

Bowl, bell. Foot, plain. Wines. Very scarce.

(b) With Knops at *t*., *c*. and *b*.

Opaque White Gauze/Four Spiral Threads, in blue, green, ruby, and opaque white.

Bowl, bell. Foot, plain. The similarity with the Twist in (a) will be noticed. Wines. Scarce.

C. Unknopped Glasses with a Single Series Twist.

Sixteen twist combinations have been noted, chiefly (i) a single opaque white spiral gauze with a further coloured formation, and (ii) an opaque white multi-ply corkscrew with edges and/or the centre plies in colour. The bowl is more often ogee than r.f., bell or tpt. Perhaps the least uncommon is the following: An Opaque White Spiral Gauze and an Opaque White Corkscrew edged in green and ruby.

Bowl, ogee, r.f. Foot, plain. Wines. Scarce.

D. Unknopped Glasses with a Double Series Twist.

(a) The Inner Component of the Twist in Opaque White only.

Twelve different twists are scheduled, all being very scarce. The bowl is a bell, ogee, r.f. or tpt. Dram glasses exist with a firing foot, and faint fluting may occur. The least infrequent twist is probably the following:

An Opaque White Gauze/Pr. Sapphire Spirals.

Bowl, r.f. Foot, plain. Wines.

(b) The Inner Component of the Twist in Opaque White and Colour.

Here, there are at least eighteen different twists. A cordial is known incorporating a striking sapphire spiral column, on a domed foot. There are a few tpt. bowl wines on semi-toasting stems; goblets also exist. The bell bowl greatly predominates; anything else is rare. The commonest twist is the following:

An Opaque White Multi-ply Corkscrew edged green and rubber red/Pr. White Opaque Spiral Threads.

Bowl, bell. Foot, plain. Wines.

(c) The Inner Component of the Twist in Colour only.

Nine combinations of twist have been noted, all rare. They include sapphire gauzes and canary spirals. The bowl is usually r.f., with an occasional bell or bucket form. One of the least uncommon twists is the following:

A Pair of Blue Spirals/Pr. of 4 or 5 ply Opaque White Spiral Bands.

Bowl, ogee or r.f. Foot, plain. Wines with faint fluting or honeycomb moulding.

E. Unknopped Glasses with a Triple Series Twist.

Only one conclusive example has been noted, a fine cordial with faint fluted r.f. bowl. The twist was an Opaque White Gauze/Pr. of Blue Spirals/Pr. Opaque White Spiral Gauzes.

Section 5. Glasses with a combined Air, Colour and Opaque White Twist.

These again are of very great rarity, and only two twist combinations have been recorded. A wine with ogee bowl, faint fluted, the stem with an opaque white vertical thread/spiral air gauze and a single blue spiral, is the type most likely to be seen.

Group XII

GLASSES WITH FACETED STEMS

(1760–1800)

THIS group includes only such glasses as were cut by the manufacturer before being placed on the market. After-cut glasses are excluded as also are cut sweetmeats and champagnes, partly because of the difficulty of deciding when they were cut, and partly because the intricacy of their cutting and shape makes a written record almost impossible of understanding, but all this should not be taken to mean that they are not highly desirable glasses, exhibiting some of the finest work that English glass-makers ever produced.

Of the ordinary kinds of drinking glasses, throughout the whole group, wines are ten times as common as either goblets or ales, and twenty times as common as cordials; drams and ratafias are very rare. Bowl forms vary in incidence in the different sections, but as a whole the ovoid and r.f. forms greatly outnumber anything else. Because of the cutting, it is often a moot point whether the bowl is an ogee, ovoid, or r.f. Doubtful specimens are best regarded as ovoid. There are some lipped ogee and lipped r.f. bowls, otherwise there is little to find.

Moulded decorations hardly ever occur, and if found on a three-piece glass I regard it as axiomatic that the faceting was done later, except perhaps on some quite late glasses of the group. The normal bowl decoration is provided by one or more rows of scale-cutting at its base; these scales may be replaced by small circles, and varied, or supplemented, by a row of sprigs or arches. All these appear in rather widely differing forms, and there are a number of less common motifs such as relief diamonds. The great majority of bowls will be 'bridge-fluted', that is, the faceting will bridge the junction of the bowl and stem.

The foot is frequently cut in the more elaborate and expensive glasses; the rim is often scalloped or petal cut, and an arch and point outline is a still more attractive feature now rarely found perfect; the surface of the foot may have radial fluting, or slice-cutting, or a shallow sprig circuit. It is seldom bridge-fluted. There are a few quite heavy feet of firing type, sometimes, rather surprisingly, on ale glasses, but they are relatively rare. Folded feet occur, but in such cases the glass may be a plain-stemmed one cut later; on a three-piece glass that is almost certainly the case.

Engraving is common, and much of it is like shallow cut work, afterwards polished. A popular rim decoration is a circuit of little engraved stars and polished circles, or ovals, alternately. The fruiting vine has a pleasant effect when the grapes are polished.

Facet stems came into vogue about 1760 and were at their best between then and 1780. Thereafter, they follow the trend of all other English drinking glasses of the time, and deteriorate both in size and style, and lack individuality, but they continued to be made well into the 19th century. Early cut stems of the second quarter of the 18th century are credibly recorded, but I find it very hard to believe that these are other than experimental or apocryphal. There is certainly no recognizable series of them to be found.

The group divides into seven sections, only three of which are at all frequent.

Section 1. Knopped Glasses with Faceted Stems.

Here are found most of the finest specimens and the section comprises about 18 per cent of the whole group. Wines are ten times as common as either goblets, ales, or cordials, these last rather indistinguishable from wines with small bowls since their stems are not of notable thickness. The r.f. bowl is a little commoner than the ogee; both of these may be found lipped, and there is an ovoid bowl as well. Only two forms of knopping are found, both simple and chosen to emphasize the cutting without embarrassing the cutter.

A. The Stem with Shoulder Knop.

There are at least five types of cutting. Wines and goblets only have been noted and all have had a bridge-fluted r.f. bowl with some or other cutting at the base, usually scales.

(a) The Stem and Knop cut Vertical Flutes, staggered beneath the Knop.
Bowl, bridge-fluted r.f. Foot, cut wide radial flutes. Wines and goblets. Infrequent. About 1780.

(b) The Stem cut Diamond Facets, the Knop cut Vertical Flutes.
Details as (a) but the foot uncut. Scarce. About 1775.

B. The Stem with Knop at *c*.

This knopping is preferred in four glasses out of five, and not less than a dozen varieties of cutting may be collected. Four of these have true faceting and may be regarded as preceding the rest which are given some form of vertical fluting. Goblets, ales, and cordials are not unduly rare. There are six bowl forms, the r.f. a little commoner than the ogee, which is here more decisive than elsewhere in the group; both are three times as frequent as either the ovoid or the lipped r.f., and other types are little seen. Up to four rows of scales may be found on the bowl. The foot is less often cut than in A.

(a) The Stem and Knop Diamond Faceted.
The conventional term is retained although the knop is really cut with vertical flutes, sometimes of considerable length; when short, as is more usual, these flutes diminish to triangular or half-diamond shape.
Bowl, usually a marked ogee, but the ovoid and r.f. also occur. Scale or sprig cutting to the *b.* is usual, though little is done to the foot. There are a few ales, cordials, and goblets. Frequent, from 1765.

(b) The Stem and Knop cut Spade Diamonds.
Bowl, various, normally with cut decoration. Most of the feet are scalloped in one way or another. Wines and cordials. Scarce. About 1780.

(c) The Stem cut Vertical Flutes, the Knop with Relief Diamonds.
Bowl, lipped r.f. Foot, with arch and point outline, sometimes described as 'rose-cut'. Perhaps the most attractive of the flute-cut stems. Cordials and wines occur. Scarce. About 1775.

(d) The Stem and Knop cut Vertical Flutes, the alternate angles notched.
Bowl, ovoid. Foot, petal cut and sliced radial flutes. Wines. Very scarce. About 1780.

SECTION 2. The Stems Unknopped and Diamond Faceted.

These account for nearly forty per cent of all the glasses in the group.

Wines are nine times as common as ales, twelve times as common as goblets, and there are a few drams and fewer cordials. Diamond faceting came in early, and on stout-stemmed glasses with r.f. bowls it remained popular for many years. Further classification is on bowl form, the ovoid predominating in virtue of its claims to include the latter and commoner indecisive bowls, and it accounts for one in every two glasses. The r.f. provides barely one in three, and the ogee one in eight. A few tpts., and still fewer s.t. r.f. bowls make up the tally. More than two rows of scales is unusual, and no moulded decoration has been noted.

(a) Ogee Bowl.

Foot, rarely bridge-fluted and normally uncut. There are a few goblets, and nearly every bowl has some decoration. Fairly frequent. From 1760.

(b) Ovoid Bowl.

Foot, as (a), with a few of firing type. All vessel types as already noted, but small wines are the feature, only two in three having bowl decoration. Common. Mostly about 1780 and on.

(c) R.F. Bowl.

Foot, as (b), very rarely domed, the firing foot being usually scalloped or otherwise cut. Ales are relatively frequent, but not goblets. Few wines escape decoration, which has a considerable range. Frequent. About 1760-1775.

Section 3. The Stems Unknopped and Hexagonally Faceted.

These are a near parallel to the glasses in Section 2, and equal them in numbers. The range of vessels is wider, ratafias and short ales being found, the former rarely. Wines are eight times as common as goblets and thirteen times as common as ales. The firing foot is a good deal scarcer, but the folded foot more likely here than in the other sections. A very little diamond moulding and faint fluting may exist. The r.f. and ovoid bowls are equally common, and together account for nine out of every ten glasses; a distinct ogee bowl is found eight times in a hundred glasses; lipped r.f., tpt., and wstd. bowls make up the exiguous balance. Scale-cutting does not often exceed two rows.

(a) Ovoid Bowl.

Foot, rarely folded or firing. There are very few goblets or cordials and no ales. Only one wine in three will have bowl decoration. Common. From 1770.

(b) R.F. Bowl.

Foot, as (a) and known domed. The range of vessel is wider and ales occur. Bowl-cutting again is the exception. Common. From 1765.

SECTION 4. The Stems Unknopped, with Vertical Flute cutting.

These are few, and late. Ales occur as frequently as anything else. From 1790.

SECTIONS 5, 6 AND 7. The Glasses Unknopped with Vertical Flute cutting (i) Sliced horizontally; (ii) grooved horizontally; and (iii) with the alternate angles notched.

All are scarce and some examples may be as late as, or later than, those in Section 4. Only wines have been noted.

Group XIII

OTHER GLASSES WITH SHORT OR RUDIMENTARY STEMS (18TH–19TH CENTURY)

THIS final group is a large one, and it includes four main types of table glass: dwarf ales; Georgian ales, wines, and drams; jelly glasses; and rummers. They can be divided into their several kinds, if too hard and fast a line be not drawn, but their stems are so duplicated that this is unnecessary in a formal analysis.

There may be differences of opinion as to the date of certain dwarf ales and jelly glasses. Here, if there is error, it is on the conservative side. Without any doubt, most specimens will belong to the years 1775–1825: some are still later, and a few stretch into the Victorian era. There may be a few early dwarf ales; those with flammiform gadrooning are conventionally given a late 17th century date, but I would put most of those listed below a century later. There are also just a few jelly glasses, in metal thin and distinctive enough to suggest, if not to warrant, a late 17th century date. Logically, there should be, and I think there are, others not so very much later, but unless they are undecorated and the metal quite definite, a much later date is more than probable. In small glasses it is easy to misread heavy 1800 metal. Mr. Francis Buckley is the safest guide on datings, and it will do no harm to be still more cautious.

Rummers and the Georgian glasses present little difficulty. In these, and to a much less extent in dwarf ales and jellies, there is one feature which, generally speaking, divides the earlier from the later. This is the provision of what I have called an 'upper reinforcement' at the junction of bowl and stem. On conical, ovoid/ogee, and trumpet bowls it appears as a collar or series of collars. On bucket and r.f. bowls it becomes a disc or discs on the bowl base. The purpose is the same, and although not a perfect guide (because the non-reinforced type may never have entirely disappeared) it is a good rule-of-thumb that non-reinforced stems are pre-1800 and reinforced ones post-1800.

Particularly in the smaller glasses, decorative moulding, such as faint or wide flutes, wrything, and corrugation, is very apt to be continued down the stem where it appears as fine twisted ribbing; this, of course, can only appear on two-piece glasses. Engraving on the small glasses is perfunctory; on rummers, however, it may be of high quality and often of a commemorative nature. Soda metal specimens are to be found of all four types of vessel.

SECTION 1. Glasses in which the Stem and Foot are replaced by a Bowl.

This is a very small series, a reproduction of the Double Glasses of Group I. Examples can be distinguished by the metal which tends to be thick and of an indeterminate greyish tone, lacking the brilliance of the early glasses. Light Victorian pieces are not uncommon.

SECTION 2. Glasses in which the Bowl is set directly on the Foot.

This is a fairly numerous section, almost entirely composed of dwarf ales and jelly glasses. Variation is provided by foot forms, by the different moulded motifs, and by the bowl, on which the classification must be based. Specimens generally belong to the late 18th and early 19th centuries, with a few possibly earlier, but not 17th century. There are at least seven bowl forms.

(a) Conical Bowl.

Dwarf ales. Foot, sometimes folded. All with some form of moulded decoration, sunken and flammiform gadrooning being fairly frequent. Some of these are short enough to be called drams. Frequent.

Jelly glasses. Foot, plain, or a milled thistle foot. The bowl rim is always flanged and generally folded also, either upwards or downwards. There is a little ribbing. Frequent.

Drams. Foot, a thistle, or a domed square foot. Not noted with decoration. Scarce.

(b) Hexagonal Bowl.

Foot, domed. Jelly glasses only. Scarce.

(c) Lipped R.F. Bowl.

Foot, as often domed as plain. Jelly glasses only, with bowl and foot honeycomb or panel moulded. Uncommon.

(d) Waisted (or Bell) Bowl.

Foot, sometimes domed, rarely thistle or domed and folded. Jelly glasses only, sometimes with single or double handles. The decoration included wrything, ribbing, and panel moulding; this last may sometimes be applied also to the foot. Common.

SECTION 3. Glasses with Knopping in lieu of Stem.

There are at least a dozen different forms of 'stem', but it is unnecessary to give details of more than three. The rest are seldom seen, and some are clearly 19th century forms, such as a Wide Flattened Knop and another with tears; a Knop only; or Twin Knops. Others, of earlier date, include an Angular Knop; an Annulated Knop; and a Collar (or reinforcement) and Annulated Knop. These last three forms seem to be represented by jelly glasses only, and all are rare. The classification of the usual types follows.

A. Glasses with a Flattened, Half-knop, or Rudimentary Knop in lieu of stem.

This sub-section is almost entirely composed of jelly glasses. There are at least seven bowl types, not all very precise. Nearly half the glasses will have some form of moulded decoration to bowl, knop, or foot. The most frequent bowl forms are:

(a) Hexagonal Bowl.

Foot, nearly always domed. Plain examples are fairly common. Handled specimens are scarce and those with moulded decoration are rare. Later 18th century. Frequent.

(b) Lipped R.F. Bowl.

Foot, plain. Handled glasses are infrequent; others are common. The rims may be flanged. Moulded decoration is often applied to the bowl and knop, and there should be examples of foot decoration. Ribbing predominates; also used are panel moulding, wide flutes, wrythen and closely wrythen decoration. This bowl form merges into (d). Late 18th to early 19th century. Common.

(c) Saucer Topped R.F. Bowl.

Foot, plain or domed; less frequently domed and folded. Jelly glasses of a pleasing form. Handled examples are seen as often as in (a) and (b). Ribbing is the commonest decoration, sometimes combined with panel moulding to the foot. From mid-18th century. Not infrequent.

(d) Waisted (or Bell) Bowl.

Foot, various but usually domed; a terraced firing foot has been noted. This type merges into (b). Most handled glasses have this bowl. Moulded decoration is as in (b) but honeycomb moulding may be added. A deceptive bowl is recorded (early 19th century), and a curious 'tight waisted' variety which may be rather early. Mostly late 18th and early 19th century. Frequent.

B. Glasses with a Collar in lieu of Stem.

Sometimes there is the shortest possible section of plain stem under the collar, unworthy of regard. Two bowl forms only have been noted, and neither is frequent. Only jelly glasses are found, and most of them appear to have ribbed bowls but these may in fact be panel moulded as are the accompanying feet. Their approximate date is the third quarter of the 18th century.

(a) Saucer Topped R.F. Bowl.

Foot, domed and folded, or domed. Infrequent.

(b) Waisted Bowl.

Foot, domed, or domed and folded. Scarce.

C. Glasses with a Flattened or Half-knop (with tears) in lieu of Stem.

There are some half-dozen bowl forms found, and the general run of the glasses, all of which are jellies, follows that in A, but specimens are less frequent.

(a) Saucer Topped R.F. Bowl.

Foot, more often domed than plain. The decoration includes ribbing and panel moulding. Later 18th century. Rather scarce.

(b) Waisted (or Bell) Bowl.

Foot, domed, occasionally domed and terraced. Some handled examples are found, and most specimens have both bowl and foot panel moulded. Later 18th century. Not uncommon.

D. Glasses with a Flattened or Half Knop, with Opaque White Twist, in lieu of Stem.

Jelly glasses only have been seen, with wstd. bowl and a domed foot. Very scarce. About 1760.

SECTION 4. Glasses with Short Knopped Stems.

This is a very large section, containing more than a score of stem forms, less than half of which are commonly seen. All glasses of the group occur. The classification is given in some detail, to show how the various classes of vessel prefer certain types of stem, and also to show the prevalence of the reinforced stem. The term of rummer has been used without qualification and includes a certain number of large and heavy glasses and also some of quite small capacity; these last are not goblets in the true sense although perfectly proportionate in make.

A. The Stem with Knop at *t.* and Knop (or cyst) at *b.*

There are at least half a dozen bowl forms, only the first mentioned being at all common.

(a) Conical/R.F. Bowl.

Dwarf ales only. Foot, plain or folded, in the proportion 3-1. The bowl is imprecise and might perhaps be more aptly described as a sharply pointed r.f. Moulded forms predominate, particularly when the foot is plain. The motifs, which are not extended to the foot are as under. Except possibly for the gadrooned glasses with folded foot which may go back to 1750-60, the normal date for all the above may be put at about 1800.

i. Part Wrything: not infrequent.
ii. Wrything throughout; common with plain foot, much less so with the folded foot.
iii. Swirled Ribbing: this merges into ii ; good examples are not infrequent with the plain foot: otherwise rare.
iv. Faint Flutes: rare.
v. Wide Flutes: fairly common, especially with a plain foot.
vi. Flammiform Gadrooning: rare with a plain foot but frequent with a folded foot.

(b) Cup Bowl.

A few Georgian wines and drams. Foot, folded or domed and folded. Examples are few, and plain.

(c) Lipped R.F. Bowl.

Jelly glasses. Foot, plain. Some have a flanged rim. Infrequent.

B. The Stem with Annular Knop at *t.* and Knop (or cyst) at *b.*

Only one bowl form has been noted and all specimens have been dwarf ales. They are not very uncommon and date around 1800.

R.F. Bowl.

Foot, plain or folded. Moulded bowls, which are less often seen than the plain form, may have swirled ribbing or wide fluting.

C. The Stem as last but with Upper Reinforcement.

Except for a rummer with incurved bucket bowl, belonging to the early Victorian period, no specimen has been seen.

D. The Stem with Winged Knop at *t.* and Knop at *b.*

The upper knop varies somewhat and may have five wings or four, the latter normal, or elongated, or rudimentary. Two bowl forms are available to collectors, but examples are scarce. They are all dwarf ales and are conventionally dated to the late 17th century, but this cannot be accepted unreservedly. All are decorated.

(a) Conical Bowl.

Foot, folded. There is a collar or reinforcement beneath the bowl, which may be wrythen, part wrythen, or given flammiform gadrooning. (?) Second half 18th century. Scarce.

(b) R.F. Bowl.

Foot, folded. No collar, and with rudimentary wings. With part wrythen decoration. Perhaps late 18th century. Apparently rare.

E. The Stem with Knop at *c.* and Knop (or cyst) at *b.*

At least eight bowl forms are available, and except for a few rummers, the specimens seen have been Georgian ales, wines, and drams. The great majority are of Irish origin.

(a) Bucket Bowl.

Foot, plain, or folded. There are about as many decorated glasses as there are plain; wide fluting is the favourite motif; faint flutes are scarce. Late 18th or early 19th century. Fairly common.

(b) Lipped Bucket Bowl.

As (a) but rather less common. Plain examples predominate.

(c) Conical/Trumpet Bowl.

Imprecise. Foot, plain or folded. Glasses with wide fluting predominate. Late 18th to early 19th century. Fairly common.

(d) Ovoid/Ogee Bowl.

Foot, plain or folded, the latter the commoner. This bowl has only been noted with wide fluting. Late 18th to early 19th century. Rather uncommon.

(e) R.F. Bowl.

Foot, plain or folded. As (d) but the plain foot is the commoner. Scarce.

(f) Lipped R.F. Bowl.

Foot, plain. Plain bowls predominate. Early 19th century. Fairly common.

F. The Stem as last but with Upper Reinforcement.

Glasses with this stem include a number of rummers in addition to Georgian ales, wines and drams. The bowl forms are rather fewer; an incurved bkt. makes its appearance. The general date of examples is early 19th century.

(a) Bucket Bowl.

Foot, plain. Chiefly rummers. There are Georgian ales, and a few Georgian drams with deceptive bowls. Not infrequent.

(b) Incurved Bucket Bowl.

Foot, plain; a wide firing foot has been noted. Rummers are again in the majority. Fairly common.

(c) R.F. Bowl.

Foot, plain. Rummers and Georgian ales, the latter sometimes with wide fluting. Rather uncommon.

(d) With Thistle Bowl.

Foot, plain. Georgian drams. Scarce.

G. The Stem with Annular Knop at *c.* and Knop (or cyst) at *b.* Exceptionally, the centre knop may be bladed. At least seven bowl forms exist. Rummers, Georgian ales, wines and drams only are found, some from Ireland. Their general date is from the late 18th to the early 19th century, but where the stem is longer than usual a mid-18th century date seems not impossible.

(a) Bucket Bowl.

Foot, plain, less often folded. Plain glasses predominate and wide fluting is the normal type of moulding. Fairly common.

(b) Lipped Bucket Bowl.

Foot, plain. Georgian wines and drams, in plain form only. Scarce.

(c) Incurved Bucket Bowl.

Foot, plain or folded. Few or no moulded specimens will be seen and not many rummers. Fairly common.

(d) Waisted Bucket Bowl.

Foot, plain. Mainly rummers. Rather infrequent.

(e) Cup Topped Bucket Bowl.

Foot, plain or folded. Georgian wines and drams. Some must belong to the third quarter of the 18th century. Scarce.

(f) Cup Bowl.

Foot, plain, less often folded. Rummers mainly. Scarce.

H. The Stem Reinforced, with Annular (or Bladed) Knop at *c.* and Knop (or cyst) at *b.*

This is in fact the same stem as G reinforced, but a bladed knop replaces the annular knop. Quite rarely, the earlier annular knop may survive, just as in G the bladed knop may be seen in advance of its time. Examples of this stem are very numerous. Eleven bowl forms have been noted, principally as in G. The folded foot becomes rare. The vessel types are as in G and all are early 19th century.

(a) Bucket Bowl.

Foot, plain, sometimes folded. Rummers and Georgian ales are especially common. A few may have wide fluting.

(b) Incurved Bucket Bowl.

Foot, plain. Rummers predominate. Frequent.

(c) Cup Topped Bucket Bowl.
Foot, plain. Rummers and Georgian wines and drams. Some of the rummers are quite late and of a variable and debased form. Not infrequent.

(d) Conical/Trumpet Bowl.
Foot nearly always plain. The Georgian types only. A glass with a deceptive bowl, commonly called an ice-cream glass such as has been made until recently, is often seen, and some at least must belong to the second quarter of the 19th century. There are wrythen and part wrythen bowls, and others with wide flutes. Common.

(e) Cup Bowl.
Foot, plain. Mainly rummers. Rather uncommon.

(f), (g) and (h) Ovoid/Ogee, R.F., and Thistle Bowls.
Foot, plain in each. Represented by a few specimens only.

J. The Stem with Annulated Knop at *c.* and Knop (or cyst) at *b.*
Examples are rarely found and are represented by Georgian bkt. wines. Late 18th century.

K. The Stem as last but with Upper Reinforcement.
Some rummers, and rather fewer Georgian wines, are found, but they are uncommon. The bowl is generally a bkt.; a cup also occurs, and the foot is plain. Early 19th century.

L. The Stem consisting of an Inverted Baluster.
These are dram glasses, not typically Georgian, and are rather scarce. A dwarf ale with r.f. bowl and flammiform gadrooning may be found on a plain foot. Later 18th century.

M. The Stem as last with Knop (or cyst) at *b.*
Occasionally seen. Later 18th century.

(a) R.F. Bowl.
Foot, plain, and probably also folded. Drams with wide flutes.

(b) Lipped R.F. Bowl.
Foot, folded. Drams, with wide flutes. This is the less infrequent form.

N. The Stem consisting of a True Baluster with Knop (or cyst) at *b.*
Rather rare. Drams with conical or lipped r.f. bowls. Foot, plain or folded. All the specimens noted have had wide fluting. Late 18th century.

O. The Stem as last but with Upper Reinforcement.
Drams with lipped r.f. bowl and plain foot. Rare. About 1800.

SECTION 5. The Glasses with Unknopped Stems.

These are again numerous; the classification is based on the presence or absence of the upper reinforcement.

A. The Stem short, with Knop (or cyst) at *b*.
Occasionally the basal cyst may be lacking. There are at least eleven bowl forms, some quite scarce. Hardly any jelly glasses are included and not many dwarf ales.

(a) Cup Topped Bucket Bowl.
Foot, plain. Rummers only, in thin metal. Late 18th century.

(b) Conical/Trumpet Bowl.
Foot, plain. Dwarf ales, plain, part wrythen, or with wide fluting. Fairly common. About 1800.

(c) Cup Bowl.
Foot, plain or folded, occasionally firing. Rummers with plain feet occur, otherwise Georgian wines and drams, including very obvious tavern glasses with thick-walled corrugated bowls. Moulded motifs include faint and wide flutes, and wrything. Common. Around 1800.

(d) Ovoid Bowl.
As for (c) but rummers seem not to occur, and the folded foot is a good deal rarer. Frequent.

(e) Ovoid/Ogee Bowl.
Foot, plain. Rummers only, though some are small. Two out of three will have wide fluting. Very common. Late 18th century and on.

(f) R.F. Bowl.
Foot, plain or folded. Includes all the vessel types but raggedly. Dwarf ales with sunk or plain gadrooning occur. Uncommon. Late 18th or early 19th century.

(g) Trumpet Bowl.
Foot, plain or folded. Georgian wines and drams only, mainly plain. Moulded forms occur as in (c).

B. The Stem as last but with Upper Reinforcement.
Nearly always it is rummers and dwarf ales which are found, the former being very numerous. The folded foot no longer occurs, but a square foot is not unusual, always with a dome or a terrace-dome above it. Decoration is practically confined to wide fluting. Nine bowl forms at least are found, some rare. An early 19th century date will normally be correct.

(a) Bucket Bowl.
Foot, plain; occasionally domed and square. No decoration has been noted, though cut forms become increasingly common. Mainly rummers. There are a few dwarf ales and Georgian drams. Common.

(b) Conical Bowl.

Foot, usually plain, or domed and square. There is an occasional deceptive bowl, and wide fluting is as often present as not. Dwarf ales only. Frequent.

(c) Conical/Trumpet Bowl.

Foot, plain. A few rummers only.

(d) Ovoid/Ogee Bowl.

Foot, four out of five are plain; the remainder domed or terrace-domed and square. These latter may be solid, or hollow under and impressed with radial fluting. There are a few semi-deceptive bowls, no doubt tavern glasses, and about one in five of the rest will have wide fluting. Rummers only. Very common.

(e) R.F. Bowl.

Dwarf ales. Foot, plain. Wide fluting is usual. Fairly frequent. Rummers. Foot, plain. Wide fluting is found on one in every five glasses. These are heavy, for tavern use; many are also large and not a few in soda metal. Frequent.

(f) S.T. Tpt. Bowl.

Foot, plain. Rummers only, nearly all plain. This bowl is a later development of the ovoid/ogee form, and again an occasional semi-deceptive bowl occurs. Frequent.

SECTION 6. Glasses with a Pedestal Stem.

These are not common but include glasses of the finest quality. Cutting is found applied to the pedestal, though such specimens are not included in the analysis. Rummers and dwarf ales occur, the latter infrequently. Bowl forms are few.

A. The Stem a reinforced 4-sided Spreading Pedestal.

With Ovoid/Ogee Bowl. Foot, square; solid, concave, or hollow under and then with or without impressed radial flutes. Quite rarely the foot may further be stepped. All these variations are uncommon. Rummers only, rarely with ribbing. Early 19th century.

B. The Stem a reinforced 6-sided Spreading Pedestal.

With R.F. Bowl. Foot, hexagonal, hollow under with impressed radial flutes. Dwarf ales, undecorated. Early 19th century. Rare.

POSTSCRIPT

The task of summarizing the story of glass over a period of 3,500 years has been rather like filling in the lost pages and, indeed, chapters of a manuscript written in a dozen different languages.

Nobody who chances to read the result can be more conscious than the author that if the account given could have been written ten years hence, it would have been a more accurate story. But if complete accuracy were the primary objective of every author, I believe few or no books would be written at all. The objective in this case has not been an unattainable standard, but a consecutive story wherein reasonable speculation has been permitted to replace unknown facts until further research condemns or approves. I have thought that most of those who would read about the glass of the eastern world would find continuity, even a speculative continuity, essential if their reading is not to be hazardous, their curiosity unassuaged, and their further study of the subject impeded. I have offered a working hypothesis to bridge the usual gaps in glass history, with the explicit warning that nothing ought to be accepted as wholly true until it is sufficiently supported by personal experience and study. At the same time, nothing should be condemned simply because it differs from the opinion of earlier authorities.

The analysis of English 18th century glass is something of a novelty and it will interest collectors more than it can interest the casual reader. Its compilation has been no small task, but with the wealth of material which I have fortunately had at hand, it has long seemed a feasible task, and the result will I hope assist inexperienced collectors to bring some sort of order out of chaos. They must indeed find it—as who has not?—extraordinarily difficult to know what to collect if, as hitherto, they have had no balanced summary of what there is to be collected, and but a small idea of comparative rarity and therefore of value.

It will be clear that this analysis does not do more than classify; space precludes actual mention of more than a part of the many stem types available, but whether mentioned or not there is a place for practically every drinking glass, and for many others such as lacemaker's lamps, tazze and patch-stands. I will repeat that the analysis is more or less confined to glasses of the 18th century and that it excludes coloured glasses and glasses in soda metal; these can be inserted in their proper place by anybody who studies the classification.

To any reader who may be induced to take up the study and collection of old glass I will offer a few words. Let him not be afraid of making mistakes; we all do that, and a cheap mistake to-day may be an important future economy. If, as an unknowing beginner, he will be bold enough to hazard a five pound note and go out and buy a score or more glasses of which none cost more than a few shillings, and if he does this entirely on his own judgment and without the slightest notice of what friend or foe may advise, he may then have his purchases safely attributed and dated. He is not likely to have bought any specimen of value, but something he needs more, that is to say, knowledge. To know what *not* to buy again is a considerable safeguard.

Let him read all he can find, and listen to all who can speak on the subject, but let him do both with a receptive, not an acceptive mind. Let him also see all the old glasses he can. There are museums, and there are collectors who will willingly exhibit their glasses to some one genuinely interested, even a total stranger. It is not wise to try and read too much or see too much all at once. Museum visits should be short and frequent, and concentration given to a few glasses or a group of glasses. The eye has to be trained to appreciate so many things, the colour and texture of metal, form and proportion, types of decoration and quality of workmanship, and the mind has to record the results. Both can have indigestion if too much is attempted, but persistence pays, and what was bewildering on first acquaintance will become clear and familiar after a few visits.

There is such a thing as 'beginner's luck", but any idea that there is a host of bargains to be found up and down the country may be discarded. Profitable collecting is a matter of experience and knowledge; the profit is long deferred and often more apparent than real, since the purchasing power of our currency at the times of buying and selling may be very different.

In general, careful collections made over a period of years are saleable at some appreciation, at least on paper, and perhaps in actuality. In any case they should not show a real loss. Meanwhile they will have been a great addition to the amenities of individual life and a source of pleasure which can in no way be measured in terms of pounds, shillings, and pence. To any reader, then, who may take up collecting old glass, I will wish 'good hunting'. It is still a comparatively neglected pursuit.

The illustrations to this volume have all been drawn from the albums of Messrs. Arthur Churchill, Ltd., and all but two or three of the glasses themselves are, or have been, in the collections of that firm. Their selection has not been an easy task, and rarity has intruded itself in a general effort to figure ordinary every-day glasses.

In conclusion, I have to make acknowledgments to all those earlier writers whose works are referred to in the text or in the bibliographical footnotes. To disagree with some of their views is not to depreciate the value of their researches. To Mr. Howard Phillips, the artist who has taken such immense pains with the line drawings, I offer my sincere thanks, and I am still further in his debt, not only for a number of most useful suggestions, but for invaluable help in the troublesome *minutiæ* of book-making.

THE END